Unchristian : What a New Generation Really Thin

Kinnaman, David and Gabe L

P9-AZV-515

0000 6136

un
christian

un
christian

**WHAT A NEW GENERATION REALLY
THINKS ABOUT CHRISTIANITY**

. . . AND WHY IT MATTERS

DAVID KINNAMAN
AND GABE LYONS

BakerBooks
Grand Rapids, Michigan

Published by Baker Books
a division of Baker Publishing Group
P.O. Box 6287, Grand Rapids, MI 49516-6287
www.bakerbooks.com

Printed in the United States of America

Library of Congress Cataloging-in-Publication Data
Kinnaman, David, 1973–
    Unchristian : what a new generation really thinks about Christianity . . . and why it matters / David Kinnaman and Gabe Lyons
        p. cm.
    Includes bibliographical references.
    ISBN 10: 0-8010-1300-3 (cloth)
    ISBN 978-0-8010-1300-3 (cloth)
    ISBN 10: 0-8010-7066-X (intl. pbk.)
    ISBN 978-0-8010-7066-2 (intl. pbk.)
    1. Generation Y—Religious Life. 2. Young adults—Religious life. 3. Youth—Religious life. 4. Church work with young adults. 5. Church work with youth. I. Lyons, Gabe, 1975– II. Title.
    BV4529.2.K545 2007
    277.3'083—dc22   2007022852

Published in association with Yates & Yates, LLP, Attorneys and Counselors, Orange, California.

The participation of contributors in this book does not imply their endorsement of research interpretations or statements made by the authors and other contributors.

CONTENTS

FOREWORD

About twelve years ago we had an intern from Biola University start working with us. I didn't think much about it. We'd had other interns, and they were usually nice kids seeking some college credit while doing as little as they could possibly get away with. If they learned something along the way, they seemed to perceive it as a bonus.

But there's always the exception to the rule. David Kinnaman was ours.

David was a tall, skinny, quiet kid who asked a lot of questions—good ones—and worked hard. He was clearly intelligent and a team player. He seemed genuinely interested in learning how marketing research was done and how such information could advance meaningful ministry. He was committed to making a viable contribution to our efforts.

By the time his graduation approached, we realized he could be a significant asset to our team, so we offered him a job. Since that time, he has done practically every function in the business, from grunt work to high-level presentations with major business and ministry clients. He has managed hundreds of national research studies, generated new business opportunities, created syndicated reports, interacted with the media to describe our research results, spoken at conferences, developed internal systems, hired and fired staff—you name it; he's done it all. He has worked his way up to become the president of The Barna Group. Yet despite having written hundreds of client reports and dozens of published articles, David had never felt led to write a book.

But there's always an exception to the rule. *UnChristian* is his.

This is his first book, but it is an important book—for you, for the church, and for our nation. I encourage you to do four things in response to reading this volume.

First, appreciate David Kinnaman as one of a handful of young adults who are emerging today who understand the church, our nation's culture, and how to bless people with truth and wisdom. This is a rare combination of gifts and talents. I expect David to be one of the people who will help the Christian community find its way through the maze of challenges and opportunities that await it. Such leadership is a huge gift from God, but we must appreciate that gift if we are to reap the benefit it represents.

Second, understand the depth and breadth of the objective research that forms the foundation of this book. Most of the books published about culture and faith are based on the author's personal opinions and a few idiosyncratic anecdotes. Such a basis for cultural evaluation is of limited value. David, on the other hand, has spent years collecting and studying reams of national survey data in an effort to truly grasp the big picture and its nuances. *UnChristian* is based on research, even though he has gone to great lengths to write the book in such a way that your eyes will not glaze over in response to an overload of statistics, charts, and tables. But that effort to make the research more digestible does not mean he has taken shortcuts. His effort is based on rigorous research and the difficult process of communicating statistics in everyday language.

Third, learn from the expert analysis and interpretation that David provides in relation to the perspective that our society has of American Christians and their faith. He has gone way beyond mere reporting of the data to dig deeper into the meaning and context of the findings. He has also interacted with numerous people to glean their insights into what the facts mean from their vantage point. What you are reading is a logical, carefully reasoned narrative about the past, present, and future state of society and the Christian faith.

Finally, I encourage you to pray. Pray that you will understand and be touched by the wisdom imparted in these pages. Pray for the Christian church, in all of its varieties, in America. Pray for your role in being the church to a culture that is gospel-ignorant, if not gospel-resistant. Pray for the leaders of the church, who must understand the arguments David has set forth in this book if they are to be strategic agents for the kingdom of God. And pray for your own influence for that kingdom in times that are changing, uncertain, and challenging.

One of the discussions that David and I have shared over the years is that God does not call leaders to be popular but only to be obedient to him. In that vein, I should warn you that David has written some things you will not like. So be it. Your job is not to anesthetize yourself with congratulatory prose about the state of the world or the church, but to deal with reality, even when it is embarrassing or hurtful. You don't have to like what he has written, but you do have to deal with it.

So I give my thanks to David for writing the truth, as best we can understand it. And I send my thanks to you for considering how these perspectives must affect your contribution to the kingdom of God and the world in which we serve him.

George Barna
Founder, The Barna Group
Chairman, Good News Holdings
May 2007

1

THE BACKSTORY

SEEING CHRISTIANITY FROM THE OUTSIDE

Christianity has an image problem.

If you've lived in America for very long, I doubt this surprises you. But it brings up important questions. Just what exactly do people think about Christians and Christianity? Why do these perceptions exist? Obviously, people believe their views are accurate (otherwise they would disavow them), but do their perceptions reflect reality? And why do people's perceptions matter—should they matter—to Christ followers?

I have spent the last three years studying these questions through extensive interviews and research. You may be astonished to learn just how significant the dilemma is—and how the negative perceptions that your friends, neighbors, and colleagues have of Christianity will shape your life and our culture in the years to come. Our research shows that many of those outside of Christianity, especially younger adults, have little trust in the Christian faith, and esteem for the lifestyle of Christ followers is quickly fading among outsiders. They admit their emotional and intellectual barriers go up when they are around Christians, and they reject Jesus because they feel rejected by Christians. I will describe how and why this is happening later in this book, but for the moment think about what this means. It changes the tenor of people's discussions about Christianity. It alters their willingness to commit their lives to Jesus.

If you are interested in communicating and expressing Christ to new generations, you must understand the intensity with which they hold these views. As Christians, we cannot just throw up our hands in disgust or defensiveness. We have a responsibility to our friends and neighbors to have a sober, reasonable understanding of their perspectives.

For some time I have had a sense of this image problem, yet I never fully realized its depth, not until an unlikely source pointed me in the right direction. The telephone call that began this adventure is still lodged in my memory. Let me explain.

"David, I am quitting my job."

I couldn't mistake my friend Gabe Lyons's self-assured voice. "Really? Are you crazy?" I blurted out.

"Probably," he said, with the rounded edges of his slight Southern accent. "But I am sure it's the right time, and I have a clear sense that it's now or never. And God has given me a vision for what I am supposed to be doing." He paused and then said matter-of-factly, "I can't do it here."

"Well, what are you going to do, Gabe? Where are you going to work? You must have a plan. Do you have a company in mind?" (As a professional researcher, rarely do I have trouble coming up with questions. This moment was no exception.)

"I am not going to work for another company. I am going to *start* my own organization. It's going to be a nonprofit. I know I'll have to raise funds to make it work, but I want—"

I interrupted him. "But you're leaving a great job! You're being mentored by a widely respected Christian leader. It pays well. You have a chance of really helping a lot of people spiritually." Trying to persuade my friend to reevaluate, I urged, "You should really think about this before you make such a big change."

When I finished, Gabe was quiet. *Good*, I thought. *He's thinking about my advice.* I felt a glimmer of pride. *It was solid feedback,* I reasoned. Then after a few moments, I broke the silence, "Gabe? You there?"

"David." He spoke my name slowly. I could hear the frustration. "I have thought and prayed about this more than you know. My family is behind this. I am going to do this. I don't look back once I make a decision." He paused. "Will you let me explain what I feel God has been leading me to do?"

I couldn't think of much to say. "Yes, of course . . . sorry."

"I am gonna sound crazy, I know, but I want to help a new generation of leaders understand the perceptions and images that young people
have of Christianity—what people really think of us." He spoke thought-
fully and deliberately. "People have a lot of opinions about our faith, and
every time I strike up a conversation with a friend or neighbor, it seems
like those perceptions are incredibly negative. Let's face it—what people
think becomes their reality, and although we may not deserve all those
images, some of their thoughts about us may be accurate."

"Well, you're right about the negative perceptions," I said, mentioning some research my company had done on the subject. "But what
do you think you can do?"

"I am still trying to get my head around this," Gabe replied. "I
believe that the image young people have of the Christian faith is in real
trouble. They hold stereotypes of Christians, and we make assumptions
about them. I don't understand what all that looks like, how that happened, or even whether it's something that can, or should, be fixed. But
I want to help start conversations and lead people to start thinking about
how to bridge this divide between us and them."

Then my friend Gabe spent some time describing his ideas in
greater detail.

"Wow," was all I could muster. "That's a big vision. You know me;
I hate to see you leave a great career, but this new direction sounds like
something you should consider."

Gabe laughed. "I already told you, David. I *am* doing it, not considering it."

I laughed too, as I thought about our different personalities bounc-
ing off each other again, as they had so many times in our friendship.

"But *how* I do it is another thing. There is lots to do," he said, his
voice trailing off. "Oh, and I have an important question for you."

"Yeah, what's that?" I asked, oblivious to how his request would
shape the next few years of my life.

"I am going to raise some money to fund a major research project
on this." He paused to let the moment hang out there. "And I would like
you to do that research."

That's how this book began.

AN UNEXPECTED JOURNEY

I get a chance to learn something with every research study our firm, The Barna Group, conducts. Yet I could not have imagined how much God would use this research to open my eyes. At first, I took on the project because I felt we would learn how Christians could connect more effectively with people outside the faith. If we understood outsiders' objections, I reasoned, perhaps we could better connect with them. But what we found was their perceptions are more than superficial image problems. Often outsiders' perceptions of Christianity reflect a church infatuated with itself. We discovered that many Christians have lost their heart for those outside the faith. The negative perceptions are not just "images" conjured up to debase Christianity. Yes, the issues are complex. No, it is not always "our" fault.

However, if we do not deal with our part of the problem, we will fail to connect with a new generation. We are not responsible for outsiders' decisions, but we are accountable when our actions and attitudes—misrepresenting a holy, just, and loving God—have pushed outsiders away. Often Christianity's negative image reflects real problems, issues that Christians need to own and be accountable to change. My purpose in writing this book is to pry open the hearts and minds of Christians, to prepare us to deal with a future where people will be increasingly hostile and skeptical toward us. A new generation is waiting for us to respond.

Three years ago, when Gabe first called to describe his job change, the research excited me. But the Barna team has the privilege of doing a wide range of fascinating research, so, frankly, I had no unusually high expectations for the project. For the most part, it just represented more deadlines!

Along the way, Gabe and I found that this project deeply shifted our perspectives about those outside of Christianity. We felt compelled to share these findings with you in this book. The things we were learning in this research started to spill out in other projects, writing, and conversations. Artists will tell you that, after a long creative session, they start to perceive the world through the lens of their medium. Research is like that for me. I don't see reality clearly until I have a chance to analyze it thoroughly through carefully constructed research.

What began as a three-month project has turned into a three-year study to grasp the picture God was revealing through the data. In that process, I have examined more than a dozen nationally representative surveys (reflecting thousands of interviews) and listened attentively to the stories of people who are on the outside of Christianity. A major component of the study was a series of interviews we did with a representative sample of sixteen- to twenty-nine-year-olds. We also interviewed hundreds of pastors and church leaders. And we probed the views of Christians to understand their thoughts on the issues and how much they are in tune with the image problem and the deeply rooted issues it represents. Through these surveys and interviews, the Lord has graciously helped me understand the experiences and in many cases the very real offenses, confusions, questions, discouragements, and disappointments that people have had when interacting with Christianity.

It's not a pretty picture.

WHY *UNCHRISTIAN*?

Using the lens of the careful, scientific research we conducted, I invite you to see what Christianity looks like from the outside. In fact, the title of this book, *unChristian*, reflects outsiders' most common reaction to the faith: they think Christians no longer represent what Jesus had in mind, that Christianity in our society is not what it was meant to be. I will describe this in greater detail in chapter 2, but for many people the Christian faith looks weary and threadbare. They admit they have a hard time actually seeing Jesus because of all the negative baggage that now surrounds him.

One outsider from Mississippi made this blunt observation: "Christianity has become bloated with blind followers who would rather repeat slogans than actually feel true compassion and care. Christianity has become marketed and streamlined into a juggernaut of fearmongering that has lost its own heart."

After thousands of interviews and countless hours studying non-Christians, I believe outsiders would want this book titled *unChristian*. Young people today are incredibly candid. They do not hold back their opinions. I want to capture outsiders' expressions and views in these pages. I don't agree with everything they say. Yet if I am going to be your guide to the hearts and minds of people outside Christianity—if you are going to really understand them—I feel compelled to represent their viewpoint fairly and candidly, even if it is uncomfortable for those of us who are Christians. To engage nonChristians and point them to Jesus, we have to understand and approach them based on what they really think, not what we assume about them. We can't overcome their hostility by ignoring it. We need to understand their unvarnished views of us. Therefore this book reflects outsiders' unfiltered reactions to Christianity.

So *unChristian* it is.

Even though some of the realities are uncomfortable, I have no intention of picking on Christ followers. Far from it. My purpose is not to berate Christians. You won't find here the names of any Christian leaders who have done wrong things. From time to time, I will use an anonymous illustration to show why some of the negative perceptions exist. Yet the point is not to pick on any particular person. Every Christ follower bears some degree of responsibility for the image problem (I'll explain that later); it is not helpful to assign blame to those who have made mistakes.

Still, for the things we can influence—our lives, our churches, the way we express Christianity to others—I hope that by helping you better understand people's skepticism, your capacity to love people will increase, offering them genuine hope and real compassion through Jesus Christ. Paul, the most prominent writer of the New Testament, says, "While knowledge may make us feel important, it is love that really builds up the church" (1 Cor. 8:1).

NEW DIRECTIONS

Along with describing the data and experiences of outsiders, this book includes the reactions from over two dozen Christian leaders and pastors, some well-known and others less so. As Gabe and I talked about the direction of this book, we felt that you should hear from these leaders. They are on the front lines of dealing with the hostility that Christianity faces, and you should understand what they are doing and how they are thinking. These men and women, in action and attitude, are helping to reshape the negative images. They are helping to articulate a "kinder, gentler" faith—one that engages people but does not compromise its passion for Jesus or its theological understanding of him.

I hope you will be challenged and inspired through the research and the contributors' thoughts.[1] The church desperately needs more people who facilitate a deeper, more authentic vision of the Christian faith in our pluralistic, sophisticated culture.

Before we dig in, allow me to describe some important details about this book. First, let me clarify some of the language. The main group we studied is "outsiders," those looking at the Christian faith from the outside. This group includes atheists, agnostics, those affiliated with a faith other than Christianity (such as Islam, Hinduism, Judaism, Mormonism, and so on), and other unchurched adults who are not born-again Christians.[2] According to the research, part of the problem is we often describe these people with derogatory labels and terms, which they often find offensive. Christians use terms like "pagans" or "the lost" or worse. Other phrases are also inadequate, such as "nonChristians" (which defines them simply by what they are not) as well as "nonbelievers" or "seekers" (labels that are not necessarily true of all outsiders).

Labeling people can undermine our ability to see them as human beings and as individuals. I am not entirely comfortable using the term "outsiders," since it seems to classify people by where they are not, but for the sake of discussing perceptions, we have to use something. And I do not believe that, in the sense we are using it, most outsiders would take offense.

I will also use two terms that relate to the primary generations we studied, Mosaics (born between 1984 and 2002) and Busters (born between 1965 and 1983). This book will focus primarily on the oldest Mosaics, those in their late teens up through age twenty-two, and the youngest Busters, primarily describing those under thirty. For the sake of clarity, unless I specifically describe otherwise, when I mention Mosaics and Busters, I am referring to the sixteen- to twenty-nine-year-old set. Keep in mind that identifying a "generation" is an analytical tool for understanding our culture and the people within it. It simply reflects the idea that people who are born over a certain period of time are influenced by a unique set of circumstances and global events, moral and social values, technologies, and cultural and behavioral norms. The result is that every generation has a different way of seeing life. Recognizing the generational concept as a tool, rather than as definitive for every person, means that exceptions are to be expected.[3]

Second, this book is based on the belief that God wants us to pay attention to outsiders because he cares about them. The Bible says he patiently gives everyone time to turn to him (see 2 Peter 3:9). He is described as a father who waits for the safe homecoming of his children, even if they have disappointed him (see Luke 15:11–32). As Christians, we should have this mindset toward outsiders.

And because of the sheer number of outsiders, we need to recognize their concerns. There are about twenty-four million outsiders in this country who are ages sixteen to twenty-nine. It is significant to note that outsiders are becoming less and less a "fringe" segment of American society. Each generation contains more than the last, which helps explain their growing influence. For instance, outsiders make up about one-quarter of Boomers (ages forty-two to sixty) and Elders (ages sixty-one-plus). But among adult Mosaics and Busters, more than one-third are part of this category, a number that increases to two-fifths of sixteen- to twenty-nine-year-olds.

If we want to influence new generations, we have to pay attention to the swelling group of outsiders.

The Outsiders—A Growing Part of Our Society

Generation	Age (in 2007)	Percent of generation who are outsiders to Christianity	Size of this segment in the United States
Adult Mosaics and Busters	ages 18–41	37 %	34 million
Older Mosaics and young Busters*	ages 16–29	40 %	24 million
Boomers	ages 42–60	27 %	21 million
Elders	ages 61 +	23 %	12 million

*This book focuses on the sixteen- to twenty-nine-year-old segment, that is, the leading edge of the Mosaic generation and the trailing half of the Buster cohort.

Third, Christianity's image problem is not merely the perception of young outsiders. Those inside the church see it as well—especially Christians in their twenties and thirties. I was unprepared for the research showing that Mosaic and Buster Christians are skeptical of present-day Christianity. There are a number of reasons for this, which we will explore in the chapters to follow, but we must grasp the idea that young people in our churches are also feeling the heat of these negative perceptions.

They are bringing up some of the same challenges, questions, and doubts facing those outside the church.

A fourth detail is to remember the size and scope of Christianity in America. Yes, there are many "flavors" of the Christian faith, and it may not dominate society, as some secularists declare. Yet everyone has to deal with the massive numbers of people who are part of the Christian tradition: the vast majority of Americans identify themselves as Christians; most adults in this country say they have made a personal commitment to Jesus Christ that is still important in their life; and nearly half are relatively active churchgoers. Of course, the depth of most Christians' faith leaves much to be desired, but the fact is Christianity leaves an enormous footprint in America.

You have to keep the overwhelming size of American Christianity in mind because part of the reason that people agitate against the Christian faith is due to the real—and perceived—position of influence it has had. It is not a good time to be the favored team. It's in vogue to be different, under the radar, and independent. Christianity feels like none of these things.

As Christians, we have to avoid being defensive about the culture's push to remove Christianity's power in society. This book never advocates that we try to become more popular. Our task is to be effective agents of spiritual transformation in people's lives, whatever that may cost in time, comfort, or image. Yet we have to realize that if the enormous number of Christians in this country has not achieved the level of positive influence hoped for, it's not the fault of a skeptical culture.

Finally, this book is designed to be a mirror for you to see yourself and your faith reflected more clearly. Through this process, God rolled up the blinds so I could see my own capacity for spiritual pride and how often self-absorption inhibits my ability to see people for who and what they really are. My prayer is that God will reveal your attitudes and stereotypes as you ponder this research. I hope you will more carefully consider how firmly people reject—and feel rejected by—Christians, and that you come away feeling inspired with ways you can make a difference.

While I expect most readers will be Christians, I also hope that those outside of Christianity will find this book to be positive, affirming, and representative of their perspectives. If this describes you, my goal is to help you reconsider the person of Jesus Christ. Christians make a lot of mistakes, and often those costly errors and arrogant attitudes undermine a deep desire that Jesus would become vividly real to you. (I can think of conversations I've had that stole a part of God's reputation because I reduced the Christian message to a "who-is-more-right" argument.)

Jesus is so much more than a logical proof. His life is the starting point where our lives can really begin. Perhaps as you read this book, you will discover a more complete picture of Jesus, a transcendent yet personal God who loves and accepts you perfectly, who wants to shape you and give your life deep meaning and purpose. This is the Jesus I want to describe, even if the actions and attitudes of Christ followers have not always represented this to you.

Still, whether insider or outsider, you need to understand just what the Mosaic and Buster generations think about Christianity. Are you ready to take a look?

2

DISCOVERING *UNCHRISTIAN* FAITH

Several months ago, I was browsing the religious section at a bookstore. As I stood there, checking out the titles, two young men and a young woman wandered into the same section. It was obvious that the three twentysomethings were not searching for books. They were hanging out, discussing life, and joking as friends do.

I was not particularly tuned in to their conversation, not really aware of what they were talking about until one of them said, "Oh, check this out. It's a Bible with a metal cover!" That caught my attention.

The young woman said, "What? What are you talking about?"

"Yeah, look. It's a Bible encased in metal."

"Huh? What's that for?"

"How the heck should I know? Maybe it's supposed to be indestructible. Let's see if it is." Then I heard the Bible hit the floor.

"I guess not!" They laughed, stuffing the battered book back on the shelf. I saw them shuffle off to another part of the store. Their conversation had already moved to a new topic.

My bookstore experience illustrates that Christianity's image problem is partly fueled by the unique characteristics of two new generations of Americans: Mosaics and Busters. Young adults enjoy challenging the rules. They are extremely—you might say innately—skeptical. Today's young people are the target of more advertising, media, and marketing than any generation before. And their mindset is both incredibly savvy and unusually jaded.

I draw these conclusions not simply based on personal experiences but through my vantage point as a researcher. During my time at The Barna Group, our firm has studied social trends, lifestyles, and public opinion among more than two hundred thousand Americans.[1] In this substantial amount of information, one of the most consistent findings is the gap between generations, and specifically the divide between those in their twenties and thirties and older adults. Clearly some generational differences are life-stage issues—natural chronological differences that affect virtually every generation at the same time during their development and maturation (such as the way parenting changes a person's perspectives and lifestyle).

Yet I would caution you not to underestimate the widening gap between young people and their predecessors. Those who think that in due time Mosaics and Busters will "grow up" and look like everyone else should prepare to have unfulfilled expectations.

Rather than looking for an end to the generation gap, it is important to recognize its existence, because it can help us understand the thoughts that Mosaics and Busters have about Christianity. Let me describe the contours and complexities of emerging generations.

In many ways, young people perceive the world in very different terms than people ever have before. For example, the lifestyles of Mosaics and Busters are more diverse than those of their parents' generation, including education, career, family, values, and leisure. Young people do not want to be defined by a "normal" lifestyle. They favor a unique and personal journey. Many young people do not expect to be married or to begin a family as a young adult (if at all), though this may have been the expectation in the past.

For both Mosaics and Busters, relationships are the driving force. Being loyal to friends is one of their highest values. They have a strong need to belong, usually to a tribe of other loyal people who know them well and appreciate them. Still, under their relational connectedness lies fierce individualism.

Even though they esteem fair-mindedness and diversity, they are irreverent and blunt. Finding ways to express themselves and their rage is an endless pursuit. Being skeptical of leaders, products, and institutions is part of their generational coding (Busters tend to express skepticism layered with cynicism, and Mosaics do so with extreme self-confidence). They do not trust things that seem too perfect, accepting that life comes with its share of messiness and off-the-wall experiences and people.

Americans of all ages are inundated with media and entertainment options. Yet Mosaics and Busters consume more hours of media from more sources than do older generations. Many enjoy immensely the latest hot movie, music, website, or pop culture buzz. Technologies connect young people to information and each other—and power their self-expression and creativity—in ways older adults do not fully appreciate.

Young people engage in a nearly constant search for fresh experiences and new sources of motivation. They want to try things out themselves, disdaining self-proclaimed experts and "talking head" presentations. If something doesn't work for them, or if they are not permitted to participate in the process, they quickly move on to something that grabs them. They prefer casual and comfortable to stuffy and stilted. They view life in a nonlinear, chaotic way, which means they don't mind contradiction and ambiguity. They may tell someone what that person wants to hear, but then do whatever they desire.

Spirituality is important to young adults, but many consider it just one element of a successful, eclectic life. Fewer than one out of ten young adults mention faith as their top priority, despite the fact that the vast majority of Busters and Mosaics attended a Christian church during their high school years. Most young people who were involved in a church as a teenager disengage from church life and often from Christianity at some point during early adulthood, creating a deficit of young talent, energy, and leadership in many congregations. While this is not a uniquely Buster or Mosaic phenomenon—many Boomers did this too—our tracking research suggests that today young people are less likely to return to church later, even when they become parents.

I could go on (and I will explore generational differences throughout the book), but this provides a snapshot, the context in which the new generations think about and interact with Christianity.

HOSTILE TAKEOVER

One of the generational differences is a growing tide of hostility and resentment toward Christianity. In 1996, our firm released the report "Christianity Has a Strong Positive Image Despite Fewer Active Participants." The study showed that Americans, even those on the outside looking in, possessed widespread respect for Christians. Among outsiders—atheists or agnostics, those of a faith other than Christianity, or unchurched individuals with no firm religious convictions—we discovered that 85 percent were favorable toward Christianity's role in society. And the perceptions of the youngest generations mirrored this finding.

That was then.

Now, a decade later, the image of the Christian faith has suffered a major setback. Our most recent data show that young outsiders have lost much of their respect for the Christian faith. These days nearly two out of every five young outsiders (38 percent) claim to have a "bad impression of present-day Christianity."[2] Beyond this, one-third of young outsiders said that Christianity represents a negative image with which they would not want to be associated. Furthermore, one out of every six young outsiders (17 percent) indicates that he or she maintains "very bad" perceptions of the Christian faith. Though these hard-core critics represent a minority of young outsiders, this group is at least three times larger than it was just a decade ago.

Outsiders direct their skepticism toward all things Christian: the faith itself, the people who profess it, the Bible, *and* Jesus Christ. Frankly, their feelings toward all of these are interwoven. Still, don't assume that each of these four elements is perceived on equal footing—young outsiders are most likely to be frustrated with present-day expressions of Christianity, followed by their aggravation with Christians.

Their impressions of the Bible are mixed: most think it has good values, but only three out of ten believe that it is accurate in all the principles it teaches. And Jesus draws an interesting set of reactions. Jesus receives outsiders' most favorable feelings, but even the clarity of his image has eroded among young people. They are more likely than previous generations to believe he committed sins; they are also more likely to believe that people can live a meaningful life without him.

Since Christianity is such a diverse community, our research zeroed in on various "slices" of the Christian faith in America. Christians come in a variety of shapes, so we wanted to examine a few of the most significant and recognizable segments. In particular, do Mosaic and Buster outsiders possess unique reactions to "born-again" and "evangelical" groups?

We learned that outsiders are more familiar with the phrase "born-again Christians" than they are with the term "evangelicals." People perceive born-agains in about the same way as they think of Christianity itself—most say their impressions are indifferent or neutral, but among those who expressed an opinion, negative outnumbered positive perceptions of born-agains by more than a three-to-one ratio (35 percent to 10 percent).

We discovered that outsiders express the most opposition toward evangelicals. Among those aware of the term "evangelical," the views are extraordinarily negative (49 percent to 3 percent). Disdain for evangelicals among the younger set is overwhelming and definitive. Think of it this way: there are roughly twenty-four million outsiders in America who are ages sixteen to twenty-nine. Of these, nearly seven million have a negative impression of evangelicals; another seven million said they have no opinion; and ten million have never heard the term "evangelical." That leaves less than a half million young outsiders—out of the twenty-four million—who see evangelicals in a positive light.

How Outsiders Perceive Evangelicals and Born-Again Christians

percent of outsiders, ages 16 to 29 (N* = 440)

	Christianity	Evangelical Christians	Born-Again Christians
Know of/aware of	NA	57 %	86 %
Have bad impression**	38 %	49 %	35 %
Have neutral impression**	45 %	48 %	55 %
Have good impression**	16 %	3 %	10 %

*sample size   **percent of those aware of each group

We did not define "evangelical" or "born again" for respondents; we simply asked if they had ever heard of the groups and, if so, to describe their opinions. As we probed these young peoples' perceptions, we encountered a great deal of confusion. For instance, many outsiders thought born-again Christians were former believers who had left the church and subsequently returned, hence, born again. Evangelicals were often thought to be Christians who are political activists. But beyond misunderstanding the terms, most young outsiders pay little attention to the specific theological perspectives that comprise the evangelical or born-again groups. Don't get me wrong. Most outsiders are familiar with the story of Christianity—that Jesus was God's Son who came to die to take away our sins if we believe in him. As you will see later in this book, the premise of Christianity is not a mystery because the vast majority of outsiders have been to Christian churches and have heard the message of Christ.

The primary reason outsiders feel hostile toward Christians, and especially conservative Christians, is not because of any specific theological perspective. What they react negatively to is our "swagger," how we go about things and the sense of self-importance we project. Outsiders say that Christians possess bark—and bite. Christians may not normally operate in attack mode, but it happens frequently enough that others have learned to watch their step around us. Outsiders feel they can't let Christians walk over them.

One of the surprising insights from our research is that the growing hostility toward Christians is very much a reflection of what outsiders feel they receive from believers. They say their aggression simply matches the oversized opinions and egos of Christians. One outsider put it this way: "Most people I meet assume that *Christian* means very conservative, entrenched in their thinking, antigay, antichoice, angry, violent, illogical, empire builders; they want to convert everyone, and they generally cannot live peacefully with anyone who doesn't believe what they believe."

WHY SO NEGATIVE?

Why would present-day Christianity inspire such unfavorable reactions? Our studies explored the nature of the perceptions about Christianity—not just pro or con but the *substance* of how people feel about Christians and Christianity. The central goal was not just to determine *if* people feel negatively but *why*. What are we known for?

One crucial insight kept popping up in our exploration. In studying thousands of outsiders' impressions, it is clear that Christians are primarily perceived for what they stand against. *We have become famous for what we oppose, rather than who we are for.*

Think back to the outsider's comment. What is her image of Christians? Entrenched-thinking, antigay, antichoice, angry, violent, illogical, empire-building, convert-focused people who cannot live peacefully with others. We are known for having an us-versus-them mentality. Outsiders believe Christians do not like them because of what they do, how they look, or what they believe. They feel minimized—or worse, demonized—by those who love Jesus.

How common are these perceptions? It is one thing to encounter a person on the street who says audacious, brash things about Christianity, but quite another if these perceptions broadly define the Christian faith among young people.[3] In our national surveys with young people, we found the three most common perceptions of present-day Christianity are antihomosexual[4] (an image held by 91 percent of young outsiders), judgmental (87 percent), and hypocritical (85 percent). These "big three" are followed by the following negative perceptions, embraced by a majority of young adults: old-fashioned, too involved in politics, out of touch with reality, insensitive to others, boring, not accepting of other faiths, and confusing. When they think of the Christian faith, these are the images that come to mind. *This is what a new generation really thinks about Christianity.*

Yet not all reactions are negative. As part of our research, we found that many outsiders embrace favorable perceptions of present-day Christianity as well. They express conflicted attitudes about the faith—maintaining significant doubts, negative images, and concerns while experiencing positive associations. The most common "favorable" impression is that Christianity teaches the same basic idea as other religions; more than four out of every five young outsiders embrace this description. Three-quarters believe that Christianity has "good values and principles," and most outsiders indicate that present-day Christianity is "friendly." Outsiders were split down the middle when it came to the following images: a faith they respect, a faith that shows love for others, something that offers hope for the future, and people they trust. Only a small percentage of outsiders strongly believe that the labels "respect, love, hope, and trust" describe Christianity. A minority of outsiders perceives Christianity as genuine and real, as something that makes sense, and as relevant to their life.

Outsiders' Perceptions of Christianity

Question: Here are some words or phrases that people could use to describe a religious faith. Please indicate if you think each of these phrases describes present-day Christianity.

(N = 440)

	Outsiders, ages 16 to 29	
Unfavorable Image	a lot	a lot or some
antihomosexual	66 %	91 %
judgmental	57	87
hypocritical—saying one thing, doing another	54	85
too involved in politics	46	75
out of touch with reality	37	72
old-fashioned	28	78
insensitive to others	27	70
boring	27	68
not accepting of other faiths	22	64
confusing	19	61
Favorable Image		
teaches same basic idea as other religions	28	82
has good values and principles	26	76
friendly	18	71
a faith you respect	16	55
consistently shows love for other people	16	55
offers hope for the future	19	54
people you trust	9	52
seems genuine and real	11	41
something that makes sense	9	41
relevant to your life	10	30

How can people hold both positive and negative images at the same time? On balance, young people possess deeply ambivalent feelings about Christians and Christianity. Their reactions to the faith are widely divergent. What people say about Christianity depends on their experiences and when and where you talk with them. Their aversion is punctuated as often by indifference as it is by hostility. While some young adults are openly hostile to Christians, an equally common reaction is to blow us off.

When outsiders claim that we are unChristian, it is a reflection of this jumbled (and predominantly negative) set of perceptions. When they see Christians not acting like Jesus, they quickly conclude that the group deserves an unChristian label. Like a corrupted computer file or a bad photocopy, Christianity, they say, is no longer in pure form, and so they reject it. One-quarter of outsiders say that their foremost perception of Christianity is that the faith has changed for the worse. It has gotten off track and is not what Christ intended. *Modern-day Christianity no longer seems Christian.*

SIX BROAD THEMES

Do the negative images that people have of Christians get your blood pumping? Keep in mind, the terms and concepts that outsiders throw at us are loaded. Sometimes the criticism is meant to push our buttons, but that is not always the case.

These are important issues because often they reflect very real ways in which the Christian community has mistakenly portrayed itself to a skeptical generation. This book explores our research in six broad themes—the most common points of skepticism and objections raised by outsiders. Those six themes are as follows:

1. *Hypocritical.* Outsiders consider us hypocritical—saying one thing and doing another—and they are skeptical of our morally superior attitudes. They say Christians pretend to be something unreal, conveying a polished image that is not accurate. Christians think the church is only a place for virtuous and morally pure people.
2. *Too focused on getting converts.* Outsiders wonder if we genuinely care about them. They feel like targets rather than people. They question our motives when we try to help them "get saved," despite the fact that many of them have already "tried" Jesus and experienced church before.
3. *Antihomosexual.* Outsiders say that Christians are bigoted and show disdain for gays and lesbians. They say Christians are fixated on curing homosexuals and on leveraging political solutions against them.
4. *Sheltered.* Christians are thought of as old-fashioned, boring, and out of touch with reality. Outsiders say we do not respond

to reality in appropriately complex ways, preferring simplistic solutions and answers. We are not willing to deal with the grit and grime of people's lives.

5. *Too political.* Another common perception of Christians is that we are overly motivated by a political agenda, that we promote and represent politically conservative interests and issues. Conservative Christians are often thought of as right-wingers.

6. *Judgmental.* Outsiders think of Christians as quick to judge others. They say we are not honest about our attitudes and perspectives about other people. They doubt that we really love people as we say we do.

The next six chapters of this book explore these six critical perceptions, describing how outsiders arrive at these viewpoints and how these viewpoints affect their understanding of Jesus. Each chapter also articulates a desirable new perception—a biblical vision for how Christians should be known. This desirable perception is not an effort to be popular or merely to accommodate outsiders, but to engage them with the life-changing Jesus rather than an unChristian version of him.

Let me reiterate that you may not agree with the views of outsiders, but you should not ignore them. We have to deal with Mosaics and Busters as they are—candid, irreverent, and brazen. If we do not, it makes their criticism even more forceful because it goes unanswered.

COMPLEX BACKGROUND

One of the responses to this research that we often encounter is blaming the negative perceptions of Christianity on people's spiritual denial. But Christianity's image problem with a new generation is not due merely to spiritual resistance on the part of outsiders, although sometimes this plays a role. Certainly it's easier for people to rationalize their rejection of Christ if they believe Christianity doesn't deserve respect. But you would be dead wrong to conclude that people discard Christ for a simple set of factors or just to avoid feelings of spiritual guilt. You will be surprised to learn, as I was throughout this research, how often someone's aversion is based on a complex set of background factors that include the following elements.

☐ Perceptions are not formed in a vacuum or based on limited exposure. Most Mosaics and Busters in America have an enormous amount of firsthand experience with Christians and the Christian faith. The vast majority of outsiders within the Mosaic and Buster generations have been to churches before; most have attended at least one church for several months; and nearly nine out of every ten say they know Christians personally, having about five friends who are believers.

☐ People's impressions have been forged through a wide range of inputs: experiences at churches (59 percent of young outsiders said this influenced their views) and relationships (50 percent) are the most common ways their views are shaped, followed by the input they receive from other religions (48 percent) and what their parents have told them about Christianity (40 percent). At the core of this, young people said they formed their views of Christians based on conversations with others, often with Christians. This is significant because not only does it mean we have a great deal of responsibility in developing many of the perceptions that people hold, but it also suggests the possibility that our words and our lives can change these negative images.

☐ The "secular" media certainly do affect how outsiders view Christianity, but less than you might think. Books were mentioned by slightly less than half (44 percent), followed by visual media (movies and television—31 percent) and music (16 percent). On the subject of Christians being portrayed inaccurately in the media, only 9 percent of young outsiders and only one-fifth of young churchgoers (22 percent) said that Christianity has received a bad reputation from television and movies. Realize that young people are unaware of the "silent" shaping of media in their lives. People often underestimate the role of media in their thinking and behavior. Yet it is important to realize that young outsiders attribute their image of Christianity primarily to conversations and firsthand experiences.

☐ Painful encounters with the faith also have a strong influence on what a person thinks of Christianity. In fact, we discovered that one-fifth of all outsiders, regardless of age, admitted they "have had a bad experience in a church or with a Christian that gave them a negative image of Jesus Christ." This represents nearly fifty million adult residents of this country—including about nine million young outsiders—who admit they have significant emotional or spiritual baggage from past experiences with so-called Christ followers. Church leaders are not unaware of this issue. Among pastors of Protestant churches, three-quarters said they often encounter people whose negative experiences create major barriers to their openness to Jesus.

☐ Being hurt by Christianity is far more common among the young than among older outsiders. Three out of every ten young outsiders said they have undergone negative experiences in churches and with Christians. Such hurtful experiences are part of the stories of nearly one out of every two young people who are atheists, agnostics, or of some other faith. To put this in perspective, outsiders who are Mosaics and Busters are two and a half times more likely than older outsiders to say bad experiences have degraded their picture of Jesus. Whatever the reasons, compared to their predecessors, younger adults are forming greater resistance to Christianity in less time.

What's the point in focusing on these complex factors that shape outsiders' perceptions? I hope to shed light on critical reasons why young people are at odds with Christianity. They have had very personal experiences, frustrations, and hurts, as well as devastating conversations or confrontations. You probably know people who have gone through something like this. You may have had such an experience yourself, when people were so unChristian that you doubted Jesus. You will encounter such stories throughout this book. The important thing to remember is these experiences have deeply affected outsiders, and the scars often prevent them from seeing Jesus for who he really is. This should inspire our compassion for those outside our churches. We should be motivated not by a sense of guilt but by a passion to see their hurts healed.

HIJACKING JESUS

As we work to change the negative perceptions of outsiders, we need to avoid an opposite and equally dangerous extreme. Some Christians respond to outsiders' negativity by promoting a less offensive faith. The unpopular parts of Christian teaching are omitted or deemphasized. They hijack the image of Jesus by portraying him as an open-minded, big-hearted, and never-offended-anyone moral teacher. That is an entirely wrong idea of Jesus. He taught remarkably tough truths about human beings and about sin. You cannot read a passage like Revelation 19 (when his second coming is equal parts glorious and dangerous) or his time on earth (where he opposed religious leaders and spoke bluntly of people's spiritual fractures) and not see the strong, righteous side of Jesus. Softening or reshaping the gospel is an utterly wrong response to the objections people raise.

Consider two important reasons why hijacking Jesus happens in today's culture. First, theologically conservative people are increasingly perceived to be aloof. This causes them to seem isolated from dealing with a new generation's concerns, doubts, questions, and objections. Mosaics and Busters are the ultimate "conversation generations." They want to discuss, debate, and question everything. This can be either a source of frustration or an interest we use to facilitate new and lasting levels of spiritual depth in young people. Young outsiders want to have discussions, but they perceive Christians as unwilling to engage in genuine dialogue. They think of conversations as "persuasion" sessions, in which the Christian downloads as many arguments as possible.

Outsiders told us that the underlying concern of Christians often seems more about being right than about listening. There is an undercurrent of arrogance that outsiders perceive. This raises the implication that even the "correct" answers, if expressed in an unChristian way, are totally out of tune with a skeptical generation. If Christians are perceived as difficult to live with—and if they do not respond in godly, appropriate, and humble ways to people's questions and doubts—we permit the hijacking of Jesus, simply by leaving our voice out of the conversation.

Second, in the years to come, without major alterations to the unChristian faith, we expect that the hijacking of Jesus—this create-your-own-savior mindset—will become even more popular with young adults. That's because young Christians are also experiencing significant skepticism about unChristian ways of expressing the faith.

Among young adults who participate regularly in a Christian church, *many share some of the same negative perceptions as outsiders.* For instance, four out of five young churchgoers say that Christianity is antihomosexual; half describe it as judgmental, too involved in politics, hypocritical, and confusing; one-third believe their faith is old-fashioned and out of touch with reality; and one-quarter of young Christians believe it is boring and insensitive to others. These are significant proportions of young people *in Christian churches* who raise objections to the motivation, attitudes, and image of modern Christianity.

The Struggle of Young Churchgoers

Question: Here are some words or phrases that people could use to describe a religious faith. Please indicate if you think each of these phrases describes present-day Christianity.

(outsiders, N = 440; Christian churchgoers, N = 305; percent who say each term describes Christianity "a lot" or "some")

	Among Americans ages 16–29	
	Outsiders	Churchgoers
antihomosexual	91 %	80 %
judgmental	87	52
hypocritical—saying one thing, doing another	85	47
old-fashioned	78	36
too involved in politics	75	50
out of touch with reality	72	32
insensitive to others	70	29
boring	68	27
not accepting of other faiths	64	39
confusing	61	44

Even though young Christians are wrestling with the unChristian faith, many are trying to make the best of it. A cadre of Mosaics and Busters are feeling the brunt of the hostility toward Christianity, but they continue to work diligently to connect their peers with Jesus. Their realism is both sobering and encouraging. Consider the mindset of born-again Christians who are sixteen- to twenty-nine-year-olds:

☐ A majority said that when deciding how to spend their time, they try to choose activities that will help bring people closer to Christ. Most young Christians indicate that they intentionally build friendships with other people so they might get a chance to explain their faith in Jesus.

☐ Young born-again Christians realize that the negative image of Christianity actually affects their relationships with peers. Two-thirds of young born-again Christians say they believe that most outsiders have a negative image of Christianity. Another one-third admit that the way Christians act and the things they say make them embarrassed to be a Christian.

☐ They are also sensitive to the way in which Christians engage a broken world and are often frustrated by the poor image that Christianity has. We heard many young believers say that in some circumstances they are reluctant to admit they are Christians. They don't fear being unpopular, but they feel that raising the Christian flag would actually undermine their ability to connect with people and to maintain credibility with them. This is a major indictment of unChristian faith, that to bring those around them closer to Christ, they must distance themselves from the current "branding" of Christianity. They have to put aside unChristian ways of doing things to connect people with the depth and power of the Christian message.

Despite the challenges facing Christianity, there is good news. This research project led Gabe and me to discover thousands of young people who want nothing more than to elevate the relevance of Jesus to our culture. These young believers are very concerned about how Christianity looks to outsiders. They see holes in present-day Christianity, but they do not want Jesus to be hijacked, either by reinventing him or by those whose lives and words do not adequately represent a holy, just, compassionate, and loving God. These young Christians feel disconnection between their lives today and the way Jesus lived—a mission to bring the kingdom of God into sharp focus for all people, especially those who have the deepest needs. These young adults worry that the unChristian message has become one of self-preservation rather than one of world restoration.

One thirty-five-year-old believer from California put it this way: "Christians have become political, judgmental, intolerant, weak, religious, angry, and without balance. Christianity has become a nice Sunday drive. Where is the living God, the Holy Spirit, an amazing Jesus, the love, the compassion, the holiness? This type of life, how I yearn for that."

Jesus was called a friend of sinners, relentlessly pursuing the downtrodden. What an irony that today his followers are seen in the opposite light! How can people love God, whom they can't see, if those of us who claim to represent him don't respond to outsiders with love?

Young Christians are asking questions like this because their desire to connect with outsiders conflicts with the us-versus-them mentality.

DO PERCEPTIONS MATTER?

Gabe and I frequently encounter the idea that Christians should not care what outsiders think about us. After all, Jesus warned that the "world" would hate us. Scripture even promises persecution for those who follow Christ.[5]

Keep in mind that part of the reason Christians possess a bad reputation is because our faith perspectives grate against a morally relativistic culture. Mosaics and Busters find that Christian perspectives run counter to their anything-goes mindset. Although outsiders don't always understand us, we have to be very careful about not tossing aside the biblical motivations that contribute to these perceptions. For instance, Christians are known as judgmental because we address sin and its consequences. Christians should be involved in politics because faith weaves itself into every aspect of our lives. Christians should identify homosexual behavior as morally unacceptable because that is what Scripture teaches. Christians should be pursuing conversations and opportunities that point people to Christ because we are representatives of life's most important message. And Christians should strive for purity and integrity even if that makes us appear sheltered.

As Christ's representatives, we have to articulate the reality that there is a holy Creator who holds us to a standard that exists beyond our finite, cracked lives. Our awareness of a transcendent being should alter who we are and how we think.

However, before you dismiss the unChristian perception as "just Christians doing their duty," realize that the challenge runs much deeper. The real problem comes when we recognize God's holiness but fail to articulate the other side of his character: grace. Jesus represents truth *plus* grace (see John 1:14). Embracing truth without holding grace in tension leads to harsh legalism, just as grace without truth devolves to compromise. Still, the important insight based on our research is that

Mosaics and Busters rarely see Christians who embody service, compassion, humility, forgiveness, patience, kindness, peace, joy, goodness, and love.

Should we care what people think? Gabe and I began to realize that the more important question was *What if young outsiders are right about us?* What is missing in our portrayal of the Christian faith to new generations? If we have failed to represent the grace that Jesus offers—if we have been poor representatives of a holy and loving God—then, absolutely, what they think about us matters. If we have been unChristian, then we bear responsibility for the problem—and the solution.

In trying to understand people's reactions to Christianity, there are four reasons why perceptions matter.

1. *What people think about Christians influences how they respond to us.* Many people make a conscious choice to reject the message of Christianity, or to avoid churches, because of their views about the faith. *People's attitudes drive their actions.* For instance, our firm has done community-based research for hundreds of churches. Many congregations are perceived in the same negative terms: judgmental, boring, insincere, arrogant, old-fashioned, irrelevant, and so forth. Typically these images are based on specific experiences that outsiders have had in that particular church. So the negative images are not just "made up" or "out there." Young outsiders are choosing to avoid churches and reject allegiance to Christianity because the faith seems at odds with the type of people they want to associate with.

2. *What people think about Christians should help us be objective.* Outsiders kept telling us that Christians are not realistic or transparent about themselves. An important perspective we should embrace is "You are what you are, not what you tell people you are." As Christians, however, we need to make continual, honest evaluations of ourselves so that we can uncover the ways in which our lives do not accurately reflect what we profess. Then we might be more discerning about the things we say and how we say them. We might realize that people don't change their perceptions just because we disagree.

3. *What people think of Christians can change.* Another reason Christians should care about the image of their faith is that people's

attitudes are constantly in flux, particularly in a society that is as fluid and dynamic as ours. Just a decade ago the Christian faith was not generating the intense hostility it is today. If the Christian faith has image problems today, the ever-changing environment means we will have opportunities tomorrow to change those perceptions. This won't happen if we try simply to make ourselves look good. The reputation of the Christian faith should never be managed or spin-doctored, but we can change how we're known by becoming more Christlike.

4. *What people think about Christians reflects personal stories.* The *unChristian* faith affects your life, perhaps more than you realize. As you interact with your friends, the labels "hypocritical," "conversion-happy," "antihomosexual," "sheltered," "too political," and "judgmental" are welded to what many people think about you. You do not have to like this, but it's a fact of our complex world.

If you are a pastor, your church has to deal with the image of Christianity each time you send a mailing, in each instance of interacting with city officials, and every time you invite unchurched individuals to your church. If you are a professional working in other industries, such as science, education, the media, and so on, your job and your witness are affected by the image that people conjure up when they hear you are a Christian. This is important because, as much as I want to help you understand the national patterns, it is ultimately your task to interpret those trends for your context and for the decisions you make each day about how you represent Christianity to others. Is there an appropriate balance between grace and truth in your life? Jesus was concerned about the reputation of his Father in heaven. Are you? Your life shows other people what God is like.

If I have still not convinced you to care about unChristian faith, I wish you could read and hear the thousands of interviews we did. Some of the stories will appear in this book, but the brief written excerpts give you only a glimpse of their potency. It is easy to say you don't care that Christians are known as judgmental, but then you hear a kind, soft-spoken single mother describe what Christians said to her about her parenting abilities. You can biblically defend the fact that Christians should be against homosexuality; then you interview a young person who describes how her experience in churches led her to believe that Christians have absolutely no compassion or answers for her gay friend.

If you are skeptical that perceptions matter, my request is that you read these pages prayerfully. Then spend time listening to outsiders in your life. What have they experienced? What do they think of *you*? The depth and force of unChristian faith will start to hit you, as it did Gabe and me.

A WAKE-UP CALL

Are you starting to wrap your heart and mind around all of this? Millions of young outsiders are mentally and emotionally disengaging from Christianity. The nation's population is increasingly resistant to Christianity, especially to the theologically conservative expressions of that faith. Of course we have always had detractors, but now the critics of the faith are becoming bolder and more vocal. And the aversion and hostility are, for the first time, crystallizing in the attitudes of millions of young Americans. A huge chunk of a new generation has concluded they want nothing to do with us. As Christians, we are widely mistrusted by a skeptical generation.

This is difficult to take. Our research findings are a punch in the gut to Christians, and they are particularly challenging to theologically conservative Christians. Are you feeling defensive, dismissive, angry, challenged?

I urge you to stick with me here. There is much more we have to understand about outsiders if we want to represent Christ effectively to this culture. We are at a turning point for Christianity in America. If we do not wake up to these realities and respond in appropriate, godly ways, we risk being increasingly marginalized and losing further credibility with millions of people.

Perhaps you wonder if things are really so bad. Perhaps you rarely interact with young people who seem so negative. First, realize that one person's experiences are a poor "sample" for describing a generation. The skeleton of this book is based on careful, scientific polling, which makes it representative of the nation's population. Second, your experience may include a disproportionate number of Christian young people, who, despite their own frustrations, are still working hard to believe the best about the faith.

RESPONDING TO *UNCHRISTIAN* FAITH

Young outsiders and Christians alike do not want a cheap, ordinary, or insignificant life, but their vision of present-day Christianity is just that—superficial, antagonistic, depressing. The Christian life looks so simplified and constricted that a new generation no longer recognizes it as a sophisticated, livable response to a complex world. Young outsiders are exposed to and can choose from virtually limitless options in life; from their perspective, why would they need Jesus?

Mosaics and Busters deserve better than the unChristian faith, and they won't put up with anything less. And, unlike any previous generation, they will not give us time to get our act together. If we do not deal with unChristian faith, we will have missed our chance to bring a deep spiritual awakening to a new generation.

It would be easy for Christians to dismiss outsiders' critiques by quoting the Bible: "Satan, who is the god of this world, has blinded the minds of those who don't believe. They are unable to see the glorious light of the Good News" (2 Cor. 4:4).

But if unbelievers can lose sight of Jesus, isn't it possible—likely, in fact—that Satan would try to degrade Christians' efforts to portray Christ? Wouldn't it be in his interest to undermine our lifestyles and even our very methods of representing Jesus, so that outsiders do not really see a compassionate Savior? Paul, the writer of the New Testament letters to the Corinthian church, even alludes to this: "I fear that somehow your pure and undivided devotion to Christ will be corrupted, just as Eve was deceived by the cunning ways of the serpent" (2 Cor. 11:3).

You have choices. You can deny the hostility, you can refute its causes, you can harass those Christians who are trying their best to represent Jesus in a completely new context, or you can deal with the increasing hostility of outsiders in ways that honor God. Jesus pioneered this approach. He listened to the Holy Spirit so he could point people to his Father. He engaged his culture and its people with respect and love. He was *in* but not *of* the world.

That doesn't sound like unChristian faith at all.

3

HYPOCRITICAL

Everyone in my church gave me advice about how to raise my son, but a lot of the time they seemed to be reminding me that I have no husband—and besides, most of them were not following their own advice. It made it hard to care what they said. They were not practicing what they preached.

Victoria, 24

PERCEPTION **Christians say one thing but live something entirely different.**

NEW PERCEPTION **Christians are transparent about their flaws and act first, talk second.**

What does it mean to be a hypocrite?

At the core of the perception that Christians are hypocritical lies a debate about what hypocrisy means. In the most basic terms, hypocrisy occurs when you profess something that you do not really believe. For instance, it is not hypocrisy when a pastor preaches against a sin with which he is personally struggling.

Yet if you ask Mosaics and Busters, they rarely apply logic or technical definitions to their complaints about hypocrisy. Hypocrites are people who are two-faced or who have double standards. Anyone who says one thing and seems to do another is subject to the label.

Part of this stems from immersion in a mean-spirited and fault-finding society. Having been the target of countless advertisements and thousands of messages and lectures, Mosaics and Busters recognize word games and are sensitive to inconsistent lifestyles. They are skeptical of what others say—even if they have little reason to be wary.

Yet whether we like it or not, the term "hypocritical" has become fused to young people's experience with Christianity. Eighty-five percent of young outsiders have had sufficient exposure to Christians and churches that they conclude present-day Christianity is hypocritical.[1] And as I have pointed out, negative perceptions also bleed into the perspectives of young churchgoers—half agreed that Christianity is hypocritical (47 percent).

Mosaics and Busters contend that this is so, not merely because the failures of prominent leaders have been broadcast across their television screens, but also because they are quick to recognize holes in the lives of people with whom they live and interact.

Jake, age thirty-two, one of the young outsiders we interviewed, made this comment: "My former pastor used to teach baptism by immersion, then he got a better job with the Presbyterians and now teaches baptism can be done by sprinkling. What you believe depends on where the paycheck is coming from, I guess."

Amber, age twenty-two, said that her mom used to work the angles with the churches they attended: "She was a single mom, and our family needed help. I still remember her trying to get in close with the leaders of the church—kinda pretending to be spiritual—at least that's what I thought of her. I still have major doubts that she's as spiritual as she tries to make herself out to be."

Preston, age twenty-three, is a Mormon. Here was his comment about his Christian friends: "The message about talking to Mormons with love seems hollow. Especially when I've heard them joking about us. It would be like exclaiming you'll feed the starving in Ethiopia but then laugh about how scrawny they are. . . . I don't find either very funny."

Erin, age thirty, said her husband abused her, "even though he taught Bible studies about how husbands should love their wives." Now she is divorced; her faith has taken a beating.

Victoria is a twenty-four-year-old single mom. She described the impact of hypocrisy this way: "Everyone in my church gave me advice about how to raise my son, but a lot of the time they seemed to be reminding me that I have no husband—and besides, most of them were not following their own advice. It made it hard to care what they said. They were not practicing what they preached." She is not currently attending a church.

First, notice that many of these outsiders were former insiders. And, second, realize that what they see from Christians creates their ideas about the reality and authenticity of following Christ. By our words and actions, are we boosting the reputation of Christianity, or are we unwitting accomplices in presenting an *unChristian* faith to outsiders?

WHO CARES?

Despite the perception of hypocrisy, here is an unexpected revelation of our research: Mosaics and Busters are not bothered by the image as much as you might think. They have learned not to care. In large part this is because they have come to the conclusion that people cannot be counted on, that one should expect to be disappointed. I was surprised how frequently young outsiders simply blew off the hypocrisy issue. One example: "Yeah, everyone is hypocritical at some point. It is not a general failing of Christianity that its practitioners are prone to the same faults as the rest of us." Or this: "Hypocrisy is a common occurrence in most people's lives. It happens. Get over it."

Yet, more subtly, young outsiders have also come to expect everyone to play the angles and make themselves look as good as possible. Our culture considers having a good image to be one of the highest goals in life. Whether it's enhancing their MySpace identity with that "perfect" photo, playing mind games with their friends, shifting the way people think about them to gain an advantage, telling white lies to cover themselves, or boosting their credentials on a résumé, young people have become adept at shaping their own version of reality. This mindset to preserve image is fueled in large part by the hyper-individualism of Busters and Mosaics. Everything around them, from parents and teachers to media and marketing, has reinforced their sense of individuality and self-worth.

This image-driven, self-oriented mindset has woven itself into the minds and perspectives of young adults. For instance:

☐ Facing a moral or ethical dilemma, young adults are significantly more likely than older adults to say they do whatever feels comfortable or whatever causes the least amount of conflict. Young adults are more likely than their predecessors to believe that sometimes the rules have to be bent to get by in life.

☐ More than four out of five young adults said they are totally committed to getting ahead in life, compared with three out of five Boomers.

☐ By a wide margin, the top life priorities of eighteen- to twenty-five-year-olds are wealth and personal fame. Objectives like helping people who are in need, being a leader in the community, or becoming more spiritual have much less traction among young Americans than they do among older adults.[2]

These statistics paint a stark picture of young people. Think about how this relates to their views of hypocrisy. In most cases, the dreaded H-word is perceived to be a simple reality of modern life.

They see Christianity through the same protect-your-image-at-all-costs lens. Like their own choices and priorities, they believe that everyone says and does whatever is necessary to get ahead. Mike, age twenty-nine, made this comment: "You could say I am a lot like Christians—I have gotten good at telling people what I think they want to hear. I see why Christians do it. They want to look good. I guess I don't really see the harm in it."

Don't misunderstand: hypocrisy is not considered a distinctly favorable profile. Busters and Mosaics do not aspire to be two-faced or want to spend time with hypocritical people. When they criticize Christians for being hypocrites, they are not excusing it. Yet they have become so jaded by the holes in people's lifestyles that they are no longer shocked to find incongruence between words and actions.

This gives the critique that Christianity is hypocritical even more potency. We are not known for the depth of our transparency, for digging in and solving deep-seated problems, but for trying to project an unChristian picture of having it all together. Young outsiders believe that rather than being able to help them sort through the image-is-everything world, followers of Christ are playing *the very same* mind games that they are. They perceive us as employing the same tactics as everyone else to preserve an appearance of strength.

THE HYPOCRISY CHALLENGE

How and why does the H-word undercut our efforts as Christians? Of course, there are times when outsiders simply throw up the "hypocrisy excuse"—essentially deflecting attention from their own decision to reject Christ. This is a little like catching someone on a technicality so that you feel better about yourself.

Some have this reaction to Christianity, but I want to explore a deeper, more common issue: how the perception of hypocrisy among outsiders has created very real barriers to hearing and understanding the message of Christianity. Based on what we have learned in our research, I believe Christians can change their reputation in appropriate ways.

Of course, during his time on earth, Jesus experienced criticism too. But the negative perceptions he inspired seem fundamentally different from what we deal with in America today. I imagine Jesus and his early followers were much more likely to be perceived as lunatics, radicals, rebels, and cultists than to be thought of as hypocritical.

The hypocritical perception is most acute not when a religion is on the fringes of society, but when it has become a dominant part of the culture. At the time of Christ, it was the religious people who were most likely to be perceived as hypocritical. Jesus saves his sharpest condemnation for self-righteous individuals, those who feel secure in their religious trappings (described in Matthew 23): "Outwardly you look like righteous people, but inwardly your hearts are filled with hypocrisy and lawlessness" (v. 28). And this: "You are so careful to clean the outside of the cup and dish, but inside you are filthy—full of greed and self-indulgence" (v. 25).

In his criticism of these leaders, Jesus actually points out how deep-seated hypocrisy produces spiritual barricades: "What sorrow awaits you teachers of religious law . . . hypocrites! For you shut the door of the Kingdom of Heaven in people's faces. You won't go in yourselves, and you don't let others enter either" (v. 13).

Think about the young people introduced in this chapter—Jake, Amber, Preston, Erin, Victoria—and the tens of thousands their stories represent. Our research suggests hypocrisy has been at least partly responsible for separating them from the purposes of God in their lives.

LIFESTYLE GAPS

So how did Christians acquire a hypocritical image in America today? Let's start with the most obvious reason: our lives don't match our beliefs. In many ways, our lifestyles and perspectives are no different from those of anyone around us.

In one study conducted by our firm, we explored more than one hundred variables related to values, behaviors, and lifestyles, including both religious and nonreligious areas of life. We compared born-again Christians to non–born-again adults. We discovered that born-agains were distinct on some religious variables, most notably owning more Bibles, going to church more often, and donating money to religious nonprofits (especially a church). However, when it came to nonreligious factors—the *substance* of people's daily choices, actions, and attitudes—there were few meaningful gaps between born-again Christians and non–born-agains. Christians emerged as distinct in the areas people would expect—some religious activities and commitments—but not in other areas of life.[3]

You might be thinking that I am simply referring to the broad group of self-identified Christians, who account for more than four out of every five Americans. Actually, I am talking about born-again Christians, a more narrowly defined group, accounting for about two out of every five adults nationwide. It is important that you understand how we define these people. In our research we do not ask people if they consider themselves to be born again. We probe the nature of their commitment and belief in Jesus Christ. I gave our definition in chapter 1, but let me repeat it here. To be classified as a born-again Christian, a person has to say he or she has made a personal commitment to Jesus that is still important and that the person believes he or she will go to heaven at death, because the person has confessed his or her sin and accepted Christ as Savior. That's it. After the survey is done, we put people into the born-again category based on their responses to these questions. It is not a perfect solution—only God knows people's hearts—but it's a method for understanding and examining the group of people who have professed faith in Christ and confessed their own sinful nature.

In virtually every study we conduct, representing thousands of interviews every year, born-again Christians fail to display much attitudinal or behavioral evidence of transformed lives. For instance, based on a study released in 2007, we found that most of the lifestyle activities of born-again Christians were statistically equivalent to those of non–born-agains. When asked to identify their activities over the last thirty days, born-again believers were just as likely to bet or gamble, to visit a pornographic website, to take something that did not belong to them, to consult a medium or psychic, to physically fight or abuse someone, to have consumed enough alcohol to be considered legally drunk, to have used an illegal, nonprescription drug, to have said something to someone that was not true, to have gotten back at someone for something he or she did, and to have said mean things behind another person's back.[4]

No difference.

One study we conducted examined Americans' engagement in some type of sexually inappropriate behavior, including looking at online pornography, viewing sexually explicit magazines or movies, or having an intimate sexual encounter outside of marriage. In all, we found that 30 percent of born-again Christians admitted to at least one of these activities in the past thirty days, compared with 35 percent of other Americans. In statistical and practical terms, this means the two groups are essentially no different from each other. If these groups of people were in two separate rooms, and you were asked to determine, based on their lifestyles alone, which room contained the Christians, you would be hard-pressed to find much difference.

To give you a balanced view of the data, there were a handful of areas that showed slight divergence in behavior. For instance, born-again Christians were less likely than non–born-agains to use profanity in public (26 percent versus 38 percent) or to have bought a lottery ticket (26 percent versus 34 percent) in the last thirty days. Recycling was less common among born-again Christians (68 percent versus 79 percent), but they were slightly more likely to say they had helped a poor or homeless person in their community (53 percent versus 45 percent). This represents a mix of good news and bad—there are some areas of distinction, but in practical terms these differences are not very large. Again, if you were asked to pick out Christians based on these factors alone, the presence or absence of these behaviors would be of little help.

Here is what all of this boils down to—and, I believe, one of the most important findings of our research for this book: among young outsiders, *84 percent* say they personally know at least one committed Christian. Yet just *15 percent* thought the lifestyles of those Christ followers were significantly different from the norm. This gap speaks volumes.

Few Young Outsiders See Difference in Christian Lifestyles

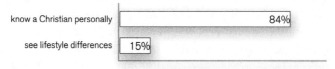

know a Christian personally — 84%

see lifestyle differences — 15%

To the casual observer, it is all too easy to call us hypocrites, because, well, we often fit the bill. I am not trying to hammer born-again believers; it deeply troubles me that our witness—including my own—waters down the image of Jesus. Of course there are millions of born-again Christians who are remarkable people, being transformed by their faith, serving their communities, and changing the lives of people around them. The witness of these rare individuals is often confounded by the rest of us—and by many other Americans who identify with the Christian faith in many ways but do not follow Christ and all that he requires.

So we cannot simply dismiss the criticism of hypocrisy by saying, "Christians are not perfect; they are sinners just like anyone else." True or not, young adults have seen our lifestyles and heard our excuses, and they still land on the label "hypocritical."

That's just half the problem.

WHAT'S THE MESSAGE?

There is a twist—a deeper reason why the perception of hypocrisy exists. It's not just our lifestyles that have gotten us in trouble; *it's the very way in which we convey the priorities of being a Christian.* The most common message people hear from us is that Christianity is a religion of rules and regulations. They think of us as hypocritical because they are measuring us by our own standards.

The most compelling research we did on this is a recent study in which we asked Christian adults to identify the priorities Christians pursue in terms of their personal faith. We did not prompt any answers; respondents were able to mention anything that came to mind.

What do you imagine was the *most* common response?

It was lifestyle—being good, doing the right thing, not sinning.

Christians describe their main faith priority in these terms. Indeed, Christ calls us to be different people, reflected in our lifestyle, so the fact that people are mentioning this is not inherently wrong. Scripture makes it clear that we are to prioritize the "fruit" or outcomes of people's lives as a measure of their faith (John 15:1–8). The writer James points out that without some way of measuring the reality of our faith (our deeds), faith is nothing more than a series of empty beliefs (James 2:20–26). Remember that spiritual transformation means becoming more like Christ, which includes both living in a holy manner and having the humility to admit we're not innately good or holy.

Nevertheless, given the pervasive perception that Christians are hypocritical, it is telling that "being good" is the primary way we define what being a Christian is all about. It is also sobering to see how other important passions of a Christ follower are way down the list. The "lifestyle" priority was more frequently mentioned than discipleship—learning about the Bible and about Christ. It was more often included in the definition of being a Christian than were evangelism, worship, or relationships. Serving others and the poor was identified as a main concern by just one-fifth of believers. Thoughts of stewardship or nurturing family faith were almost nonexistent as faith priorities.

The research also pointed out that "lifestyle" indicators are more significant to born-again Christians over age forty (41 percent) than they are to Mosaic and Buster believers (23 percent). Because this is a new question that we have not asked in our surveys before, we do not know if Christians become more focused on purity as they get older, or whether it is a true generational difference (that is, Boomers have always been more focused on lifestyle). But it does suggest that Mosaic and Buster Christians face a generation of older believers who put a high priority on avoiding sin as a measurement of faith. In a moment we will see how difficult they are finding it to live up to those standards.

The fact that lifestyle is the most common priority of Christians suggests a related difficulty: the temptation to give a false pretense of holiness. When avoiding sin is the main concern and is not balanced by other important priorities of faith, it sets up the conditions in which we project a got-it-together image. We want to make ourselves look as though we have tamed our struggle with sin. First John 1:8 says, "If we claim we have no sin, we are only fooling ourselves and not living in the truth."

The Priority of Being a Good Person

Question: What would you say are the two or three most important priorities for Christians to pursue in terms of their faith?

	Born-again Christians
lifestyle—doing the right thing, being good, not sinning	37 %
discipleship—learning about Christ, learning about the Bible	31
evangelism—explaining/sharing your faith, leading people to Christ	25
worship—worshiping God, singing	25
relationships—loving others, making and keeping friends	23
service—helping others, helping the poor, serving people	18
stewardship—giving money, time, or resources to others, blessing others	4
family faith—discipling your children, shaping family faith	1
other	2
not sure	10

The evidence that born-again Christians prioritize "avoiding sin" is compelling. First, realize that most Americans believe you can earn a place in heaven if you do enough good things for others or if you are a decent person. One-third of the people who qualify as born-again Christians embrace this idea as well. That is, even among people who believe they are personally being saved by faith in Jesus, they think of salvation as a multiple-choice test, with many reasonable possibilities: while they believe their own spiritual destiny is secure through faith in Christ, they also believe that others *could* be saved through being a good person or because of God's benevolence.

Second, we can also look at the views of churchgoers for evidence. In a study we conducted for Freedom in Christ Ministries, we explored the perspectives of those who attend church in a typical month. More than four out of every five agreed that the Christian life is well described as "trying hard to do what God commands." Two-thirds of churchgoers said, "Rigid rules and strict standards are an important part of the life and teaching of my church." Three out of every five churchgoers in America feel that they "do not measure up to God's standards." And one-quarter admitted that they serve God out of a sense of "guilt and obligation rather than joy and gratitude." These are the actual phrases we used in our surveys, which makes it quite startling to see how much these terms resonate with church attenders.

Our passion for Jesus should result in God-honoring, moral lifestyles, not the other way around.

MORAL STEREOTYPING

Now, here is how this discussion relates to outsiders. One of the fascinating outcomes of this mindset is reflected in Christians' stereotypes of outsiders. Our research shows that Christians believe the primary reason outsiders have rejected Christ is that they cannot handle the rigorous standards of following Christ. There is a nuance here that allows Christians to feel like they're better than other people, more capable of being holy and sinless. We rationalize that outsiders don't want to become Christ followers because they can't really cut it.[5]

The truth is that few outsiders say they avoid Christianity because the moral standards are too restrictive. Only one-quarter of young outsiders are convinced Christianity would limit their lifestyle and options in life. Instead, outsiders said they have never become a Christ follower for a number of other reasons: because they have never thought about it, because they are not particularly interested in spirituality, because they are already committed to another faith, or because they are repelled by Christians.

When the primary way we measure our faith is based on lifestyle, it is easy to assume that the missing ingredient for outsiders is virtuous, moral living. Again, moral issues are not inherently wrong priorities. God deeply cares about our actions, as should we. Yet don't our priorities seem backward?

The gospel—the Good News of Jesus—is that God has released us from the endless striving to measure up to God's standards, let alone the expectations of other human beings. In a culture where moral values are slipping with a new generation, we assume the best way to right the ship is to fix the morals.

In this context, what are Christians known for? Outsiders think of our moralizing, our condemnations, and our attempts to draw boundaries around everything. Even if these standards are accurate and biblical, they seem to be all we have to offer. And our lives are a poor advertisement for these standards. We have set the game board to register lifestyle points; then we are surprised to be trapped by our own mistakes. The truth is we have invited the hypocrite image.

Paul, one of the writers of the New Testament, specifically warns the early Christians that trying to be good by their own efforts will fail. "How foolish can you be? After starting your Christian lives in the Spirit, why are you now trying to become perfect by your own human effort? . . . So Christ has truly set us free. Now make sure that you stay free, and don't get tied up again in slavery to the law" (Gal. 3:3; 5:1).

Then Paul emphasizes his point in clear-cut terms: "For you have been called to live in freedom, my brothers and sisters. But don't use your freedom to satisfy your sinful nature. Instead, use your freedom to serve one another in love. For the whole law can be summed up in this one command: 'Love your neighbor as yourself.' But if you are always biting and devouring one another, watch out! Beware of destroying one another" (Gal. 5:13–15).

The unChristian faith—hypocritical, judgmental, and full of empty moral striving—is what Paul warned his readers about! And it is part of the reason we are known as hypocrites.

INSIDE LOOK

Another reason we should care about the issue of hypocrisy is that young people in our churches are showing major cracks in their moral perspectives. Despite being exposed to teaching on morals and ethics—more so than any other topic—young churchgoers do not seem to be getting the message. While older believers are being tempted to convey Christianity as primarily about lifestyle standards, young believers are struggling with issues of purity. Mosaics and Busters are facing significant difficulties with their character and moral compromises, even within the church.

In some ways this is a classic tug-of-war between generations, but there are new levels of tension. In our studies we discovered young Christians currently embrace the acceptability of many behaviors older believers staunchly reject. For example, a majority of born-again adults in their twenties and thirties currently believe that gambling, cohabitation, and sexual fantasies are morally acceptable. There are also huge gaps between young believers and older Christians when it comes to the acceptability of sex outside of marriage, profanity, drunkenness, pornography, homosexual sex, and illegal drug use. The only two areas of statistical similarity between older and younger born-again Christians are views on abortion and using the f-word on television.[6]

Young Christians Do Things Their Way

	Born-again Busters (23–41)	Born-again older adults (42+)
	Percent who believe each is morally acceptable	
cohabitation	59 %	33 %
gambling	58	38
sexual thoughts or fantasies about someone	57	35
sex outside of marriage	44	23
using profanity	37	17
getting drunk	35	13
looking at pictures of nudity or explicit sexual behavior	33	19
having an abortion	32	27
having a sexual relationship with someone of the same sex	28	13
using drugs not prescribed for you	16	8
allowing the "f-word" on broadcast television	7	6

It is fascinating to see that television decency standards—the one area virtually everyone agrees is wrong—are perhaps *least* connected to deep matters of the heart. Of all the moral issues to have nailed, young Christians are most resistant to the f-word on television, while adopting moral license in many other areas of life.

Here is another interesting point of comparison: just 5 percent of born-again Busters say they have recently given someone "the finger." But compared to this vulgar gesture, *born-again Christian* young people are *three times* more likely to have had sex outside of marriage in the last month (18 percent), *five times* more likely to have gotten drunk (24 percent), and *five times* more likely to have purchased a lottery ticket (25 percent). They hold up their middle finger *much less* frequently than they use profanity in public (36 percent), view explicit sexual content in a magazine or a movie (36 percent), or say mean things about others (40 percent).[7]

It pains me to discuss this research, because it is not flattering to young people in churches, yet we have to be realistic about the snapshot of life being portrayed by born-again Busters. Young people—even in churches—are reshaping moral and sexual rules. This gives the unChristian perception even more potency, because many young believers are living out their Christian faith with enormous moral laxity.

This creates a wicked double jeopardy: older born-again believers may be emphasizing lifestyle and avoiding sin as a means of measuring faith maturity, but the behavior and perspectives of young Christians only intensify the perception that Christians are hypocritical. Older born-agains need to look more carefully at what Jesus teaches, that spiritual maturity is demonstrated in a life as an *outcome* of the condition of a person's heart and soul, that behavior follows belief. And younger born-again Christians need to take an honest assessment of their lives and realize that they are increasingly poor witnesses of a life and mind transformed by their faith. Embracing personal integrity and rejecting compromises to personal purity are crucial goals for young believers. We cannot hope to shed our hypocritical label if our lifestyles offer no proof of the "fruit" of Christlikeness. These are tough realities to think about, but we must do so if we hope to shift our reputation from unChristian to Christian.

SHIFTING GEARS

Another significant antidote to hypocrisy (in addition to integrity and purity) is transparency. On one level, hypocrisy is failing to acknowledge the inconsistencies in our life. It is denial. It is, as the Bible describes it, trying to remove a speck from someone else's eye when you have a log in your own. Living with integrity starts with being transparent.

Young people talk these days about the need for authenticity, for "keepin' it real"—not pretending to be something you are not, being open about your faults. Young people are searching for this type of person, this kind of lifestyle. In one survey we found that "doing what you say you are going to do" was among the characteristics young people most admired.

Did you realize that some of the major corporations in America are now intentionally advertising their imperfections, sometimes even pointing out in their ads the unvarnished view customers have of their brand? Ford did a series of online films that describe some of the challenges their company faces. They are trying to connect with skeptical people by being straightforward and clear about how consumers really feel. The April 2007 cover of *Wired*, a magazine about trends and technology, featured the headline "Get Naked and . . . Rule the World." The story explained the trend this way: "Smart companies are sharing secrets with rivals, blogging about products in their pipeline, even admitting to their failures. The name of this new game is Radical Transparency, and it's sweeping boardrooms across the nation."

Will Christians learn this lesson? We should have a head start. Transparency simply means admitting what the Bible says about us: we are fallen people who desperately need God in our lives—every day. David Crowder sings about this in "Rescue Is Coming": "There is darkness in our skin; our cover is wearing thin." Romans 12:3 says we should have an honest estimation of ourselves, measuring our worth by God's purposes for our life. Transparency means not merely trying to act right, but being honest about our own lives—even being open about the problems our lifestyles have created.

Here is an example: Josh, one of my college roommates, is a pastor in the Los Angeles area. He proposed doing a five-week series of talks that he called "Confessions of a Sinful Church." Other leaders in the church needed some convincing, but it happened. To promote the events, his team passed out postcards at local college campuses.[8] The postcard said:

April 5—Apology #1   We're Sorry for Our Self-Righteousness and Hypocrisy

April 12—Apology #2   We're Sorry for Our Endorsement of Slavery

April 19—Apology #3   We're Sorry for Our Mistreatment of Homosexuals

April 26—Apology #4   We're Sorry for the Medieval Crusades

May 3—Apology #5   We're Sorry for Saying the Earth Is Flat

Free Event—Bring friends, neighbors, acquaintances, enemies, siblings, strangers who are college age. We are serious about our need to confess to you. It is not a joke.

Josh described what happened in an email: "I think just giving out several thousand postcards at several universities was a success. Most of the comments we got from people on the campuses were to the effect of, 'Wow! I admire that.' We had visitors during those weeks, but one of the main goals was just to break down some of the stereotypes and walls people have toward the church. Those who visited received a heartfelt apology and a message of truth about what the Bible teaches on this topic. I figured that people wouldn't listen to us until we got off our high horse and became real with them. We needed to recognize where there have been faults and sin. Then maybe people would be disarmed to the point of actually listening to the true message of Christ."

Josh's talks also attracted attention from several journalists. The *San Francisco Chronicle* interviewed him about a related issue. Another reporter from a university newspaper attended one night and wrote an article for the paper. Josh spoke with him extensively afterward. Josh wrote in his email to me: "Someone even called me after reading that article and asked for a CD of the talk."

Transparency disarms an image-is-everything generation.

TRUE VISIBILITY

Still, even transparent people have boundaries.

☐ First, there are situations in which caution makes sense—such as times when your confession may cause younger believers to be tempted in their faith. Don't misunderstand: young people want—and need—to experience transparency in their leaders, but this is not synonymous with graphic detail. Being transparent and authentic requires real balance, and we err too often on the side of being fake and superficial.

☐ Second, keep in mind that the basis of transparency is Scripture's clear teaching that we do not attain perfection in this life. This is a standard we can all live up to, and it is a unique truth of the Christian faith. Humans are not capable of ever reaching God's standards, and we will be in constant tension with this elusive goal. This so perfectly addresses our condition—trying hard but often failing—that we should fuse it to the very way we express Christianity to outsiders. This is the message of grace: we can accept ourselves and others unconditionally, just as God has accepted us. The adage "Christians aren't perfect, just saved" is a cop-out, compared to what the Bible teaches about this. Scripture looks at the deep fractures of our heart and tells us to admit that we can never prove our worth; Jesus made us worthy by his sacrifice. This part of the message of Christianity will help a young generation that is trying to understand the constant struggle between loving God and trying to please him.

☐ Third, the motivation of transparency is important. The culture teaches people to be candid and blunt, but this usually revolves around self-centeredness—you have a right to express your true feelings and your rage. This is transparency for the sake of shock value and personal entitlement. Instead, the Christian way to approach transparency is to realize our candidness should be motivated by a desire to have a pure heart before God and others. My friend Josh was motivated to confess the problems of a sinful church because he wanted to make connections with people who feel deeply that the church is unChristian.

☐ Fourth, the outcome of our transparency should be restoration. It should produce more of what God wants in our lives. One of the writers of the New Testament put it this way: "Confess your sins to each other and pray for each other so that you may be healed" (James 5:16). Instead of pretending to have all the answers, godly transparency is oriented toward helping people get their lives back in line.

As an example, consider the difficult subject of abortion. For many women, it is easier to keep the "problem" hidden than to be candid. It doesn't make the situation easier for young women who feel they have no other option. But what better place to deal with the difficulties of these pregnancies than within the church? Are we openly and honestly talking about sexual issues in our churches? Or are we hiding behind religious pretenses, pushing people away who have deep hurts and needs? Are we helping people understand the gravity of their choices but also displaying a clear process to restoration, including providing financially for women and adoptive families? Do we wait until a person is forced to anguish over abortion, or do we nurture soft-heartedness and transparency in her life? Have we created relationships and expectations within our churches in which older women are accessible and transparent with younger women about their struggles—not just occasionally, but in ongoing, real-life ways?

Based on our research, Christians are not defined by such transparency but by adherence to rigid rules and strict standards.

I urge you to consider transparency in your life—with your family, neighbors, and co-workers—and begin to ask yourself how you believe you should address significant moral issues. God's laws are important, and he is just as concerned with our inner thoughts and attitudes as he is with our behaviors. What concerns you? Major moral issues—pornography, sexuality, addiction, integrity, homosexuality, abortion, profanity, selfishness, and so on—are symptoms of deeper issues. Every human being struggles with immorality, because at our core is our heart's rebellion against God.

As a Christ follower, does your response to these moral issues reflect their complexity? Are you honest with yourself about your own struggles? Do they motivate you to turn your heart—and that of others—toward God, seeking his ways to handle these issues? Or are you focused on maintaining the rules and regulations?

One thing this discussion brings up is the consequence of sin. Being transparent about sin—and being willing to restore people—does not negate the effects of our actions. For instance, having children outside of marriage simply is, by virtue of enormous amounts of sociological data, a more difficult way to raise children. As Christians, we should articulate the reality of a situation, but we must be careful to choose the appropriate time and manner to address it.

Think back to the story of Victoria, whose encounters with hypocritical churchgoers frustrated her and left her outside the church. Spirituality is not measured just by the number of sermons we hear, the piety of our lives, or the goodness of our actions. As people relying on Jesus's grace, we should know this. But it's easy to miss the fact that so much of our lives is made up of the simple conversations and interactions we have with people—what is said in the hallway after church, the tone of voice someone uses, the parties you are invited to (or not), the genuineness of people's concern, how people respond to you and your child. Victoria gave Christians a chance and found us hypocritical. The way we react to people and to their life circumstances is also a measure of our spiritual maturity.

This is important because some Christians actually believe that we should just ignore negative perceptions. To them, it doesn't matter that we are labeled hypocrites. They mistakenly assume it's mostly because outsiders don't really "get it."

Yet ask yourself about Victoria. Did she say we are hypocritical because she *chose* to reject the kindhearted help that Christians offered her? Did she misunderstand dozens of well-intentioned people? Was she oblivious to men in the church who were trying to help, perhaps by taking her son fishing or to basketball games?

I doubt it. Victoria watched, waited, and listened for people like you and me to embrace her needs, to restore her life—and that of her son's—to God's purposes. Did she make a mistake? Sure, she made one. But so did the Christians around her.

The unChristian faith says it is important to remind Victoria that a single-parent family is not as good as a married family. It tells us to keep giving her advice, without love or genuine interest, about how to raise her son. It leads us to believe we should know because we have it all together.

DEALING WITH THE DIRT

We can be defensive about the idea that we are hypocritical. We can ignore it. Yet what if culture's accusations of hypocrisy are God's way of waking us up to the overwhelming needs of others? What if he is using our culture to make us aware of our hollow religiosity and empty answers?

Busters and Mosaics are searching for authenticity. They want to find people to trust and confide in, but they often find more transparent, authentic people outside the church. We have opportunities to help outsiders—if we are willing to put aside our unChristian ways of interacting with them.

Philip Yancey, in his book *What's So Amazing about Grace?* makes his own candid conclusion:

> Having spent time around "sinners" and also around purported saints, I have a hunch why Jesus spent so much time with the former group: I think he preferred their company. Because the sinners were honest about themselves and had no pretense, Jesus could deal with them. In contrast, the saints put on airs, judged him, and sought to catch him in a moral trap. In the end it was the saints, not the sinners, who arrested Jesus.[9]

If only our view of outsiders were more like that of Jesus. And if only we condemned hypocrites the way he did: "They crush people with impossible religious demands and never lift a finger to ease the burden" (Matt. 23:4).

Think of the overwhelming perception among young outsiders that we are merely hypocrites. Does your life point people to a life in Christ that bursts with freedom to love, restoration, purity, and transparency?

Or are you burying people—insiders and outsiders—under the weight of a self-righteous life? Do you lift a finger to help?

As a Christian, it's my duty to ask: Are you lifting a finger now? Which one?

CHANGING THE PERCEPTIONS

IT'S OKAY NOT TO BE OKAY

Many young adults view Christians as hypocrites, meaning we say one thing and do another. They're right. But hypocrisy isn't the issue. We all believe certain things and then act in ways that are contradictory to our beliefs. One person declares the beauty of the simple life on the balcony of the half-million-dollar home with a new Cadillac Escalade in the garage. Another rants against all things corporate with a latte from Starbucks in hand. I'm a Dallas Cowboys football fan, but I root *against* Terrell Owens as he plays *for* the Cowboys—I need therapy.

The problem is not fundamentally hypocrisy. We're all hypocrites at some level. The problem is the air of moral superiority many of us carry around. We stop acknowledging imperfections in our lives. We forget where we came from and all God has done in our lives. I don't see in Jesus's teaching a call to fake moral superiority. I'm a sinner following him. I don't have it all together, and that admission is precisely what tweaks the perception of hypocrisy. In our faith community we say, "It's okay not to be okay." We talk about how we as human beings have a lot in common no matter where we are on our faith journey. At the most basic level, we all share the human condition with all of its brokenness. And we have the hope that Jesus can really transform lives and redeem the future.

The perception of hypocrisy also emerges when we start fighting the "culture war"—meaning we attack people's behavioral patterns rather than love them as people. Or we lobby to legislate morality. In

Las Vegas, where I live, the culture war is over. We lost. Let me repeat: WE LOST. Now our calling is to love and accept people one-on-one, caring for them where they are. Our role is subversive as we carry the light and love of Jesus into the casinos, clubs, and streets of our city. We're trying to flip the perception of hypocrisy by being honest and straightforward about our faults and our hope for transformation in Jesus. And we're joining our community in a different culture war—one that attacks poverty, crime, addiction, and pain. We're active in helping the homeless, we've declared war on child hunger in the Vegas valley, and we are showing our faith by our actions, even if imperfectly.

Jud Wilhite
pastor, Central Community Church, Las Vegas
author, *Stripped*

WE NEED HELP

We're labeled hypocritical because we are. I know I'm a hypocrite, and I'm *not* sorry for it. I have this thing called sin, which is like a disease—or at least it gives me a lot of dis-ease—woven into the fabric of my being. I didn't ask for it; I don't want it. More often than not, the sin manifests itself in the form of self-destructive behavior. So if I look a little inconsistent on the outside, you can only imagine what's going on inside!

As for dealing with the perception, I think we've got to get honest with ourselves and others and admit not just to the hypocrisy but to the fact that we need help. I know in my own life, I've opened myself up to friends (even when it stings) pointing out my hypocrisy. Slowly, it's helping, but I have a long way to go.

A recent entry from my blog reads:

I thought that becoming a follower of Jesus would help me kick the sin habit, providing the inoculation I needed, but in some ways the symptoms just grew worse. I realized how much I was infected and how it was affecting my attitude, my relationships, my life. So the truth is that I'm fighting. I'm fighting sin with everything I've got. Some days I fare better than others. Odds are that if you're calling me a hypocrite, then you caught me on one of my worst days.

I am sorry. I'm sorry that I let you down and disappointed you. But the truth is that I'm not giving up or letting go. I've encountered a God who promises that the battle ends in victory—life instead of death. So call me crazy—but I'm holding on to that promise. I'm also trying to uphold the standards God has set. They're pretty high, and some days I just find myself laying on the ground, staring at the ceiling. But then I feel an urge, an energy, to get up and fight once again.

I could use your help. The next time you see me behaving like a hypocrite, pull me aside and gently let me know. I'd really appreciate it.

Margaret Feinberg
author and speaker

FALLING IN LOVE WITH THE STREETS

There is a separation between church and neighborhood. And hypocrisy—talk without action—plays a part in this divide.

I have spent my life living and working in the urban centers of Philadelphia and Atlanta. In these communities, you will find an abundance of churches. In my current Atlanta neighborhood there is one on every block. Then you consider that on the very same street corner reign drug activity and prostitution. It is not out of the ordinary to watch drug deals on the church steps. The institution has made its own quiet and unspoken deal with the vendors who make their living there. People who most need the church are sitting outside, waiting to feel worthy enough to come.

For the young who grew up on the streets, it's an age-old story: the drug kingpin knows their name, and the pastor does not. The teachers at school don't think they can learn, but they conquer the "street classes" just fine. The street culture always pursues and welcomes them, but the doors of the church are open only on Sunday. The church wants them neat and clean, but the streets take them as they are.

For the past eighteen years I have worked with young adults in missions programs. These usually involve college-aged followers of Jesus coming into these same neighborhoods, ready and eager to represent the church to hurting people. They want to be the hands and feet of the gospel. So they move into the city and get to know their neighbors. They serve in summer camps and after-school programs. They become tutors and mentors. And they come ready to find support in their local church, plugging into whatever they're already doing in the neighborhood.

Young adults with full hearts are ready to serve and listen to the voices of the rarely heard. They set out to bring Christ's love outside the church's walls. These young adults quickly discover a loyalty to their new neighborhood. They fall in love with the streets and all those who live there.

This should be a match made in heaven. But it isn't. Instead it turns out to be a sharp gust of wind, extinguishing the flame of trust that these young adults kept lit for their vision of "church." Their new church is not ready for the neighborhood kid who comes to youth group for the first time without a Christian foundation. The homeless men really smell when they come to services. The building fund, pew fund, and organ fund lose their importance when you encounter hungry people daily. Those who have put in a year or more living with families in pain, people on the street, and victims of injustice, quickly lose respect for the church.

I believe that today, young adults are starting to see the church as a place that has not dealt well with the poor and the outcast, whether it be a homeless man in the city of Atlanta or a suburban teen who struggles with pornography.

Young people will not communicate with and seek help from parents, pastors, and teachers whose lifestyles and passions do not match their words and faith. They will go to those who will embrace relationship with them; those who are also hurting and who are willing to share it.

Young adults are turning away from a modern church that they see as nothing more than hypocritical. Standards and rules without sacrifice and solidarity is hypocrisy. Christian rhetoric without tangible acts of love is hypocrisy. Churches on every corner with hurting people outside is hypocrisy.

A large building with little connection to the streets is essentially empty.

Leroy Barber
president, Mission Year

REDUCING SPIRITUALITY TO MORAL BENCHMARKS

Without question, one of the principal stumbling blocks the world has when it comes to the Christian faith has to do with Christians themselves, and specifically the question of hypocrisy.

And rightfully so.

The word *hypocrite* is taken from an old Greek word that refers to the wearing of a mask. In ancient Greece, actors often wore masks according to the character they played. Their character's appearance on the stage was a facade, an "act." Hypocrites, then, are mask-wearers. They appear to be one thing, but it's all a front—behind the mask they are someone else.

The only way this will be addressed is if Christians themselves get a grip on what it means to follow Christ, and then convey that authentically to the world. What is behind many—not all, but many—charges and accusations against the character and integrity of Christians is the demand for perfection in the life of anyone who claims to be a Christian and urges others to consider Christianity as well. This is not, of course, the true meaning of a hypocrite, but even more to the point, it is not an accurate understanding of what it means to enter into the Christian life.

Yet the world holds us to it, because we hold ourselves—and others—to it. We fall prey to the charge of hypocrisy because we have reduced spirituality to a list of moral benchmarks coupled with a good dose of judgmentalism.

The only way to regain our footing is to remind ourselves—and others—that an authentic Christian is simply someone who has made the decision to believe in Jesus as his forgiver and then attempt to follow him as his leader. But *nowhere* in this series of events is perfection *or* sinlessness. Rather, there is simply the intentional effort and sincere desire to recognize God as, well, God.

And then we must convey that to the world. Authentically. I am reminded of the words of the great nineteenth-century Russian novelist Leo Tolstoy, who wrote in a personal letter,

> Attack me, I do this myself, but attack me rather than the path I follow and which I point out to anyone who asks me where I think it lies. If I know the way home and am walking along it drunkenly, is it any less the right way because I am staggering from side to side!

Simply put, we must stop presenting ourselves as the message and begin presenting Jesus as the message. There will be disappointment with Christians as long as there are imperfect people. Since all Christians are imperfect, there will always be disappointment. So we must stop having the message of Christ tied to our butchered efforts.

Jim White
author

4

GET SAVED!

Christians are too concerned with converting people. They are insincere. All I ever hear is "Get saved!" I tried that whole "Jesus thing" already. It didn't work for me before, and I am not interested now.

Shawn, 22

PERCEPTION **Christians are insincere and concerned only with converting others.**

NEW PERCEPTION **Christians cultivate relationships and environments where others can be deeply transformed by God.**

The doorbell rings. You aren't expecting anyone. You quickly shuffle through the house, glancing at the mirror in the hallway to make sure you're halfway presentable. You crack open the door and glimpse two young men in white shirts and ties. Uh-oh. You hardly have to check for the other visual clues, but as you do, they confirm your suspicions. Backpacks. Name tags. Each of them has a book in hand. *Mormons.*

They smile at you. You know what's coming before they say a word. They are there to introduce the "other" testament of Jesus's life, the Book of Mormon. They want to win your spiritual allegiance.

Our research among outsiders shows that Christians have a reputation similar to that of the Mormon evangelists. When it comes to matters of faith, young outsiders feel they know what Christians want before any words are uttered. Although Mosaics and Busters generally resonate with spiritual topics, they don't like feeling "cornered" into conversations about faith. A generation reared in a marketing-drenched world is quick to sniff out what they believe to be the underlying motivations and superficialities.

This type of comment is fueled in large part by generational skepticism. Of course every generation has its share of cynics, but Mosaics and Busters have been raised in an environment in which certainty is up for grabs. Among young adults, process trumps product and the journey is more important than the destination. This skeptical viewpoint affects how they think about belief and conversion.

In John Mayer's bestselling album *Continuum*, the twentysomething musician epitomizes the generational perspective. His song "Belief" raises questions about people's motivation and how much they recognize the complexities of their perspectives. One of the lyrics slices to the heart of this idea; "Belief is a beautiful armor, but makes for the heaviest sword."

Realize that skepticism has both positive and negative implications. One of the favorable outcomes is that Mosaics and Busters are reluctant to be "salesperson pushy" about their faith and are highly sensitized to what other people think and feel. Yet this also means young Christians are less likely than older adults to feel compelled to share their faith in Christ with others. Young people are also more likely to believe one can live a meaningful life without accepting Jesus Christ. It's also interesting that Mosaics and Busters are less likely to embrace the "once-saved-always-saved" perspective, that is, that a commitment to Christ permanently alters one's eternal destiny.

Now, consider how this affects young people outside the faith. Young outsiders generally do not get the impression that Christians have good intentions when it comes to trying to "convert" them. Most reject the idea that Christians show genuine interest in them as individuals. This was one of the largest gaps in our research: most Christians are convinced their efforts come across as genuine, but outsiders dispute that. When it comes to matters of faith, young outsiders are skeptical of "the Jesus shtick." This is a key finding of our research. Only one-third of young outsiders believe that Christians genuinely care about them (34 percent).

And most Christians are oblivious to these perceptions—64 percent of Christians said they believe that outsiders would perceive their efforts as genuine. This is especially significant because Christians were very accurate in anticipating many of the negative perceptions of outsiders, but being perceived as insincere surprised believers. Showing genuine interest in someone is hard to fake.

Just as Christians are skeptical about Mormon evangelists, outsiders are skeptical about our motives. Even if our intentions seem pure to us, outsiders often feel targeted, that we merely want another church member or a new notch in the "get-saved" belt. While we are trying to convey the most important message in human history—that Jesus offers a new life through faith in him—something gets lost in translation.

When outsiders question our motives, it neutralizes their interest in Christianity. Only one-quarter of young outsiders firmly perceive that Christianity offers them "hope for the future" (23 percent), and only one out of every seven strongly believes Christianity is "genuine and real" (15 percent). Despite the fact that most young outsiders say that Christianity has good values and principles (79 percent), a majority say that the Christian faith teaches pretty much the same basic ideas as other religions (81 percent).

In asking about how Christians come across to people, we interviewed Steven, a thirty-four-year-old who moved to New York from Phoenix. During the interview, he described his initial excitement when he met a peer in an unfamiliar city. "A young guy approached me in a subway station once, friendly, full of questions, interested in talking. He seemed really nice, and I couldn't believe a New Yorker was being so, well, nice! We exchanged numbers and said we'd hang out sometime. Next time I heard from him, he invited me to a Bible study, and that was all he wanted to talk about. When I said, 'No thanks,' I never heard from him again." Rather than being genuinely interested in people for their friendship, we often seem like spiritual headhunters.

Many of the young people we interviewed also pointed out how hard it is to take Christians seriously in light of some of their tactics. In all of the interviews we did, we heard no favorable comments about so-called street witnessing, where Christians intercept unknown passers-by to share the Good News. "People stalk you and verbally berate you. I'm like, do I know you? Why should I care what you are saying?" was one comment.

And outsiders expressed particular disdain for methods that "trick" people into paying attention. One respondent called this "the con of conversion." She said, "Christians want you to pay attention to their message about Jesus, yet somehow I don't think Jesus would be happy about being turned into a gimmick."

Outsiders are skeptical and savvy. In the vast majority of cases, rather than creating spiritual depth in people, these methods create unChristian barriers—mental and emotional obstacles—to Jesus.

MISCONCEPTIONS

In a dozen years at Barna, I have conducted significant amounts of research about evangelism and faith-sharing activities. Our firm has had the chance to help explore the effectiveness of many of the nation's most popular evangelism programs and resources, from videos to Bibles, from congregational programs to other forms of training and events. Based on this large body of research, we have identified a number of myths about how and why people become Christians. These misconceptions enable Christians to be in a state of denial about their conversion efforts. And these myths often inhibit the kind of relationships and environments in which people can be deeply changed by their faith in Jesus. Let's explore a handful of these that relate to understanding outsiders.

Myth: The best evangelism efforts are those that reach the most people at once.

Reality: The most effective efforts to share faith are interpersonal and relationship based. When we asked born-again Busters to identify the activity, ministry event, or person most directly responsible for their decision to accept Jesus Christ, 71 percent listed an individual—typically their parent, a friend, another relative, or a teacher. A majority of those decisions were described as conversations and prayer, while about one-third were instances in which their friend or family member took them to a church service or an evangelistic event. In an era of mass media, it is easy to believe that the more eyeballs, the more impact. But radio, television, and tracts accounted for a combined total of less than one-half of 1 percent of the Busters who are born again. The clear implication is that most young people come to Christ because of people they know very well, usually in the context of "everyday" interaction.

Myth: Anything that brings people to Christ is worth doing.

Reality: When you're talking dollars, there is no price too high for a soul. But the problem isn't just cost. In our research with some of the leading "mass evangelism" efforts, we found that *often these measures create three to ten times as much negative response as positive.* In other words, imagine your church is considering mailing Bibles or videos or other Christian materials to homes in your community. Our research shows that the "collateral damage" of doing so—those whose impressions of your church and of Christianity would be *more* negative as a result—is significantly greater than the positive impact on those who will respond favorably to these efforts. Moreover, such mass evangelism efforts are most effective with marginally churched adults, while outsiders are usually the ones who respond most negatively.

As Christians, we have to keep in mind that response rates are not the ultimate goal but rather the wise and careful stewardship of the image of God. Today's media and technology create unparalleled opportunities, but they also wield the potential to harm the Christian image among many outsiders. If you create more barriers with outsiders because of your tactics, you have not been a good steward of the gospel. How we choose to share Christ is as important as our actually doing it.

Myth: We cannot worry about the possibility of offending people when sharing the truth about Jesus.

Reality: Obeying the command to make disciples does not give us license to offend people, especially when those offenses are actually inhibiting us from fulfilling that very commandment. Jesus used strong language, but who was he most likely to offend? Religiously arrogant people, not outsiders. Yes, the cross is offensive to people, but that gives us no extra motivation to be harsh or spiteful. True respect for people is a key factor in effective evangelism. The Bible specifically addresses this: "The Lord's servants must not quarrel but must be kind to everyone. . . . They should gently teach those who oppose the truth. Perhaps God will change those people's hearts, and they will believe the truth" (2 Tim. 2:24–25). This Scripture also reminds us that people commit to Christ because God changes their hearts.

Myth: People embrace Christianity because of logical arguments.

Reality: Most people, by personality, are not logical thinkers and are not likely to change their beliefs because of elegant argumentation or apologetics. Of course, some outsiders are wired this way, and thoughtful responses are particularly important for articulating Christianity's remarkable ability to address all aspects of life. Culture is shaped by ideas and worldviews, so do not underestimate the proper role of good thinking, logic, and intellectual engagement. However, most people do not become Christians because of the overwhelming evidence. And since Mosaics and Busters are more likely to possess a nonlinear, fluid way of processing life, they are increasingly comfortable with subtlety, nuance, ambiguity, and contradiction. So even if you are able to weave a compelling logical argument, young people will nod, smile, and ignore you.

When we asked outsiders what the most important factor is in their faith, they said it is something that "feels right to them personally" (69 percent of outsiders said this was an important facet of their spirituality). Before you start lamenting this reliance on feelings, you should realize that 67 percent of *Christians* between the ages of sixteen and twenty-nine said this was important as well. Among young people, whether we like it or not, their sense of individualism, their loyalty to peers, and their emotional and experiential outlook on life guide their spiritual pursuits.

Myth: Everyone has an equal chance of becoming a Christ follower.

Reality: Based on extensive research on this topic, our data points out clearly that the faith trajectory of the vast majority of Americans is mapped out before they become adults, often before they even reach adolescence. In fact, for every one hundred people who are not born again by the time they reach age eighteen, only six of those individuals will commit their lives to Christ for the first time as an adult. Of course, we have to always assume the best about people's spiritual potential. God can do anything in anyone's life at any time, and he often does. But consider how likely it would be for you as an adult to be persuaded to convert to another religion right now. You have to admit, it would take a lot to change your views so dramatically.

Think of the implications of this. First, it underscores that Christians should prioritize the faith development of children, a unique time in human development when the vast majority of us "pick" a faith. Second, it implies that we must work hard to strengthen the often-tenuous faith of teenagers, because this is when their faith is gelling (more on this in a moment). Finally, it reminds us why respect for other people's faith is so crucial. We are not likely to change another adult's spiritual trajectory by a comment here or a small dose of Jesus there. If we really want to help outsiders see the unique freedom available through Christ, a simplistic get-saved message is an insult to their intelligence. We may think people just need a quick spiritual transaction, but this kind of overhaul does not happen without a person's permission and the activity of the Holy Spirit.

Myth: We just need to help outsiders find a connection with God.

Reality: While it's true that God's presence is life changing, most outsiders admit they are reluctant to have anything to do with this type of experience. Nearly half of young outsiders (42 percent) said they are skeptical and distrustful of faith and religion. Part of that skepticism is fierce independence. They don't want to be whipped up into a state of emotionalism and reliance on faith. Only one-quarter of outsiders said they are looking for a faith that helps them connect with God. By comparison, this was the top motivation of young Christians, which confirms that this is a huge area of dissonance between those of us on the inside and those outside the church. We have experienced the presence of a living God, but outsiders are wary of feeling brainwashed or manipulated.

FORGETTABLE FAITH

Another mistake Christians make is not realizing how much experience and background with the Christian faith most outsiders have. Most outsiders have "been there, done that." Rather than being something new and untested for most outsiders, Christianity seems blasé and commonplace. It has become an ignorable part of their daily existence. Eric, age twenty-nine, made this observation: "Christianity seems like an old, broken-down building that I have to drive by every day. I don't even notice it any more."

That's partly because, in America, the vast majority of people (even outsiders) are exposed to the message of Christianity many times throughout their lives—in churches, via media, through their friendships, and so on. For instance, among nonChristians ages sixteen to twenty-nine—that is, atheists, agnostics, those undecided about their faith, and individuals affiliated with other faiths—more than four out of every five have gone to a Christian church at some time in their life (82 percent). Most of these attended for at least three months. And two-thirds of nonChristians (65 percent) said they have had conversations in the last year with a Christian friend about their faith views. More than half (53 percent) said they have been specifically approached in the past few years about becoming a Christian.

The opportunities that outsiders have to hear about Christ and know Christians are nothing short of astounding. For nearly two decades, the Barna team has been exploring church participation among American teenagers. We consistently find that the vast majority of teenagers nationwide will spend a significant amount of their teen years participating in a Christian congregation. Most teenagers in America enter adulthood considering themselves to be Christians and saying they have made a personal commitment to Christ. But within a decade, most of these young people will have left the church and will have placed emotional connection to Christianity on the shelf. For most of them, their faith was merely skin deep. This leads to the sobering finding that the vast majority of outsiders in this country, particularly among young generations, are actually *de*-churched individuals.

In spite of the fact that many of them are currently disconnected from a church, most Americans, including two-thirds of all adult Mosaics and Busters (65 percent), tell us that they have made a commitment to Jesus Christ at some point in their life. This is slightly lower than the percent of older adults who have made such a commitment (73 percent). This is an amazing fact about our culture. The vast majority of Americans, regardless of age, assert they have already made a significant decision to follow Christ!

Of course, this raises the question of the depth of their faith. If that many Americans have made decisions to follow Jesus, our culture and our world would be revolutionized if they simply lived that faith. It is easy to embrace a costless form of Christianity in America today, and we have probably contributed to that by giving people a superficial understanding of the gospel and focusing only on their decision to convert.

At Barna we employ dozens of tools to assess the depth of a person's faith. Let me suggest one for our discussion: a biblical worldview. A person with a biblical worldview experiences, interprets, and responds to reality in light of the Bible's principles. What Scripture teaches is the primary grid for making decisions and interacting with the world. For the purposes of our research, we investigate a biblical worldview based on eight elements. A person with a biblical worldview believes that Jesus Christ lived a sinless life, God is the all-powerful and all-knowing Creator of the universe and he stills rules it today, salvation is a gift from God and cannot be earned, Satan is real, a Christian has a responsibility to share his or her faith in Christ with other people, the Bible is accurate in all of the principles it teaches, unchanging moral truth exists, and such moral truth is defined by the Bible.

In our research, we have found that people who embrace these eight components live a substantially different faith from other Americans—indeed, from other believers. What we believe influences our choices.

Getting back to the issue of spiritual depth, if two-thirds of young adults have made a commitment to Jesus before, how many do you think possess a biblical worldview? Our research shows only 3 percent of Busters and Mosaics embrace these eight elements. That is just one out of every twenty-two young adults who have made a commitment to Christ. (Although older adults are more likely to have such a perspective, it is also a small slice—only 9 percent—who do.)

This means that out of ninety-five million Americans who are ages eighteen to forty-one, about sixty million say they have already made a commitment to Jesus that is still important; however, only about three million of them have a biblical worldview.

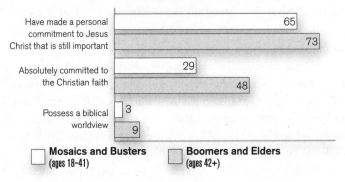

Wide but Not Deep—Americans' Commitment to Christianity

Have made a personal commitment to Jesus Christ that is still important
- Mosaics and Busters: 65
- Boomers and Elders: 73

Absolutely committed to the Christian faith
- Mosaics and Busters: 29
- Boomers and Elders: 48

Possess a biblical worldview
- Mosaics and Busters: 3
- Boomers and Elders: 9

☐ **Mosaics and Busters** (ages 18–41)   ☐ **Boomers and Elders** (ages 42+)

I do not mean to discourage you but to provoke your attention toward spiritual depth. At Barna we use research and information to catalyze leaders to address problems in the church. Here is one of those challenges we face: we will not be effective with Busters and Mosaics if we do not address the problem of superficial faith.

Our firm has spent a great deal of time and energy studying worldviews, but our efforts certainly are not the final answer for defining or assessing biblical perspectives. What does your definition of a biblical worldview look like? There may be other elements you would add or subtract. Ultimately, of course, faith is not getting a bunch of questions right on a survey.

It is much deeper than that.

How deep is the faith you convey to outsiders? What type of depth are we asking our friends and neighbors to have? A get-saved approach ignores the fact that most people in America have made an emotional connection to Jesus before; now they need much more than a one-dimensional understanding of him.

More of the same lightweight exposure to Christianity, where a decision for Christ is portrayed as simple and costless, will fail to produce lasting faith in young people. We have to decide what our measures of success will be over the next decade. Where will we be more effective—trying to increase the number of young adults who make emotional commitments to Christ or facilitating significant growth in the 3 percent who have a biblical worldview?

Our research indicates that we have let discipleship languish in far too many young lives. Our enthusiasm for evangelism is not matched by our passion for and patience with discipleship and faith formation.

GENUINE AND REAL?

Let's go back to a few of the statistics I brought up earlier. They bear repeating now that you know more of the story. Only one out of seven outsiders describes Christianity as something that seems genuine and real. Just one-third believe that Christians show genuine interest in them. These are not perceptions derived in a vacuum or from seeing Christians negatively portrayed in the media. Most outsiders have grown up around Christians; many have given the "Jesus thing" a thorough test drive; a majority have tried churches and found them desperately lacking relevance.

Outsiders' familiarity with Christianity creates the fascinating condition of people actually having *too much* background in the faith. Most young people have already formed their conclusions about Christianity. These people have heard about Jesus, they can recite concepts and stories found in the Bible, and they believe they pretty much "get it." It is a daunting task to break through people's preconceptions when they think they've seen the movie before.

In some instances, familiarity breeds strong contempt. Some outsiders have well-developed, well-reasoned objections to the faith. These are not without flaws, but the key point is that these individuals have spent an unusual amount of time studying and considering Christianity and coming to the conclusions they hold. Even though their viewpoint is not pro-Jesus, these individuals often display greater familiarity with Scripture than their Christian peers, a fact that gives them particular disdain for Christians who "ignorantly follow Christ." Unfortunately, these outsiders are not entirely wrong about the paper-thin beliefs of many Christians.

All of this leads to a stunning finding among those under age thirty. Even among those who have never made a commitment to Christ, nearly half (45 percent) said they have considered becoming a Christian before, with the other half saying they have never given the notion much thought. These two groups represent vastly different experiences! In the latter case, these are young people who have never given consideration to "converting." Many of them have Christian friends and acquaintances, and most say they generally understand the basic story of Christianity, but they are either too devoted to a different faith perspective or too disinterested in matters of spirituality to give Christianity much thought. This is a little like asking a Yankees fan if he or she ever considered pulling for the Red Sox. They know about the other team, and they certainly have no shortage of perceptions about that team, but they aren't interested in switching allegiances.

The other group includes people who have thought about, considered, and rejected the message of Christ. Conversing about Christianity with these individuals is, for them, like being served leftovers. They may be spiritually hungry, but the menu is not appetizing.

Our research confirmed that many of these young people actually went through a time when they were searching for faith. They were probing the Christian faith, trying it on for size, but they couldn't get past some of the mental, emotional, or spiritual barriers—often heightened by their experience of an unChristian faith—so they gave up. This should be a major wake-up call for us. Mosaics and Busters have been coming to our churches and to our homes, but we have largely missed their moments of spiritual openness. Most end up disengaging without much lasting connection with Jesus. We simply cannot continue to squander the enormous number of opportunities we have to minister to Mosaics and Busters.

Here is a story that describes this idea of lost chances. About the time this project began, we interviewed Rachel, a pleasant, poised twenty-one-year-old. At the time, she was a nursing student in Kentucky. She calmly, almost apologetically, explained her experience. "There was this transitional period, I guess, in my personal faith, where I wasn't quite certain of all that was going on, but I was starting to lean where I am right now, where I don't really believe in religion as much. I would go to churches, and they would be like, 'You're a Catholic? Well, you can't be a Catholic and come to this church. You need to convert.' And I just think it shouldn't matter. It shouldn't matter what brand of this you are, or what belief you have on individual, tiny topics . . ."

We did a videotaped interview with Rachel, so whenever I explain her story, I picture her with a polite smile, seeking a small measure of acceptance from the interviewer. I have deep compassion for this young woman and the individuals her story represents. She went looking for help, with her life open to input. But because of the get-saved mentality of the church's leaders, she is now further away from comprehending God's grace. Like Rachel, many outsiders actually miss the chance to experience true life in Christ because we cheapen the message of Jesus to church membership or denominational loyalty. Rachel admitted she wanted guidance. Couldn't things have been handled much differently? As a result of her experience, she is now receiving *no* guidance from the Christian community. Rachel's faith is a casualty of our unChristian approach to converting people.

EXPLORING TRANSFORMATION

Scripture is clear that there is a basic starting point to the Christian faith: admitting that we need Jesus. When Jesus was dying on the cross, the criminal crucified next to him says simply, "Jesus, remember me when you come into your Kingdom." And Jesus responds with equal simplicity: "I assure you, today you will be with me in paradise" (Luke 23:42–43). In the book of Acts, people accept the message and then enter the Christian faith without any hoops to jump through (see Acts 2:37–41).

Yet the point of the research I have presented is to clarify when the simple starting point becomes a substitute for Christian discipleship. Intentionally or not, we promote the idea to outsiders that being a Christ follower is primarily about the mere choice to convert. We do not portray it as an all-out, into-the-kingdom enlistment that dramatically influences all aspects of life. Perhaps you are thinking that you *do* describe it in these terms. Then why are so many millions of young people missing the point, failing to develop the basic elements of a biblical worldview? Our research shows that most of those who made a decision for Christ were no longer connected to a Christian church within a short period, usually eight to twelve weeks, after their initial decision. In a get-saved culture, too many of the conversions become either "aborted" believers or casual Christians. How do we convey to people both the gravity and buoyancy of the decision to follow Christ?

To change the perception that we are focused only on converts, we have to embrace a more holistic idea of what it means to be a Christ follower. This requires us to focus our attention on spiritual transformation—or spiritual formation, as some describe it. In the last two years, we have completely reengineered the Barna organization around this concept—that the church must become a catalyst and environment for genuine and sustainable spiritual transformation. Consequently, more research on this crucial subject is forthcoming from our team. Still, here are some of the things we have learned thus far.

DEFINING TRANSFORMATION

Most people do not have a clear sense of what spiritual transformation is or what it should look like. This is partly understandable because it is an elusive topic. By definition, spiritual formation is about depth rather than simplistic formulas. Yet it is hard to pursue something that is not defined.

One way of looking at spiritual formation, though certainly not the only way, is to examine the passions that should define a Christ follower. In our work at Barna, we examine these seven elements:

- ☐ worshiping God intimately and passionately
- ☐ engaging in spiritual friendships with other believers
- ☐ pursuing faith in the context of family
- ☐ embracing intentional forms of spiritual growth
- ☐ serving others
- ☐ investing time and resources in spiritual pursuits
- ☐ having faith-based conversations with outsiders[1]

If you think back to the chapter on hypocrisy, I showed research reflecting these seven passions of a believer. You may recall that we asked born-again Christians what they believe the priorities of the Christian life should be. Their answers were primarily focused on lifestyle and avoidance of sin. It is sobering to realize that most born-again Christians have very little understanding of what their priorities or passions should be as Christ followers. Perhaps outsiders would realize that we're not just about conversion if our faith provided a more well-rounded and holistic picture of following Christ, pursuing these seven passions.

HAVING CLEAR OUTCOMES IN MIND

The ultimate goal of transformation is to become like Christ. Paul writes in Galatians, "What counts is whether we really have been changed into new and different people" (Gal. 6:15). But what else should spiritual transformation produce in the lives of Christ followers? Here are three outcomes we should consider.

☐ *Thinking.* Our research shows that one of the most consistent influences on behavior is how a person thinks.[2] People who have a biblical worldview are much more likely to act like Jesus because they see such things as life, people, and crises differently than most people do. Romans 12:2 is perhaps the most famous Scripture on this subject: "Don't copy the behavior and customs of this world, but let God transform you into a new person by changing the way you think."

We are learning that one of the primary reasons that ministry to teenagers fails to produce a lasting faith is because they are not being taught to think. This gets to the core of the get-saved perception: young people experience a one-size-fits-all message that fails to connect with their unique sensibilities, personality, or intellectual capabilities. Young people desperately need to be taught to process the rich complexities of life, to probe and test and stretch their faith from the perspective of a Christ follower.

☐ *Loving.* If we are being transformed by our faith, the way we perceive and love people, including outsiders, will change. Scripture continually addresses love. God is described as love, and Jesus moves love to the forefront of his commandments, teaching that we should love God with everything we are; we must love each other sacrificially; we must be defined by love (see Mark 12:30; John 11:35–36; 13:34; 1 John 4:16). Just because a person believes the right things about Jesus—that is, he or she has a highly developed biblical worldview—does not automatically make the person loving. A deep shift is needed from the sin-altered, me-first, and consumer-minded perspectives that so often plague us as Christians in America. Because Christ says we will be known for love, and because it is the clearest way we can show Jesus to people, this is one of the ways that Satan wants to diminish and tarnish the church. I think the unChristian faith is potent primarily because of this disconnect between our knowledge of God and our ability and willingness to love people. We do not look like Jesus to outsiders because we do not love outsiders as Jesus does.

☐ *Listening.* A third outcome of transformation is the ability to listen—to God and to others. In my dozen years as a research professional, I have come to the conclusion that the most important character quality is soft-heartedness. This involves listening to what God is telling us, within the context of Scripture, prayer, crises, and relationships. God is constantly communicating with his people. How can we orient our efforts as Christians to learn and respond to the ways he speaks? Knowing the right answers is not sufficient; we have to be able to apply what we know. The first step is realizing what we *don't know.* Listening to God, through the Bible and often through other people, is how we learn. The better we listen, the more productive we become for God's purposes. The biblical image of a vineyard captures this idea: "I am the true grapevine, and my Father is the gardener. He cuts off every branch of mine that doesn't produce fruit, and he prunes the branches that do bear fruit so they will produce even more" (John 15:1–2; see also 1 Cor. 3:18).

FITTING A GENERATION

Most people in America, when they are exposed to the Christian faith, are not being transformed. They take one step into the door, and the journey ends. They are not being allowed, encouraged, or equipped to love or to think like Christ. Yet in many ways a focus on spiritual formation fits what a new generation is really seeking. Transformation is a process, a journey, not a one-time decision. This resonates with Mosaics and Busters. The depth and texture of Christianity ought to appeal to young people, but the unChristian notion strains life in Christ into mere mental allegiance to a religion. The truth is that when a person makes a commitment to Christ, it is just the first step into a much larger reality. When people become Christians, we must describe appropriate expectations for them; engage them in significant, accountable relationships; and fashion environments where deep life change can take place.

CHANGING OUR PRIORITIES

What difference does transformation make? It changes our ideas of spiritual effectiveness. We should measure success not merely by the size of our church or the number of baptisms or decisions, but also by the depth and quality of spiritual growth in people's lives.

When Christians live out what the Bible teaches, we have an influence on our culture, as salt does on food or as light reveals a dark room (see 2 Cor. 2:3; Matt. 5:13–16). We are actively representing Christ to a needy world. As we go about our daily lives, with stale religion being pushed aside, God's words and actions flow out of us.

Christianity must reverse its current image and become dynamic, genuine, and real. If we can prevent the message from being watered down by casual Christians, outsiders will begin to experience believers who have been (and are being) transformed by their faith and who are working in humble and respectful ways to transform the culture. In the Bible Paul puts it this way: "This should be your ambition: to live a quiet life, minding your own business and working with your hands, just as we commanded you before. As a result, people who are not Christians will respect the way you live" (1 Thess. 4:11–12). There is nothing more powerful than the Christian life lived out in obedience; there is nothing worse than a flat, self-righteous form of faith that parades around in Christian clothes.

How does this relate to outsiders? Shifting the get-saved perception happens when we learn that relationships are the key—not just in leading people to Christ but also in helping them be transformed. We can create an environment in which relationships facilitate spiritual formation. In your interaction with outsiders, do you take time to understand their spiritual history? Does your church point people toward faith in Christ based on a firm understanding of each person's needs, perspectives, learning styles, and experiences? Helping people consider the Christian way of life is extremely hard work, but there is no greater reward when it is done in a way that honors God and builds lasting faith in people.

STICKING WITH IT

In the face of the criticism that we are too decision oriented, Christians cannot lose our motivation or heart for connecting outsiders to Jesus. When outsiders are outraged because we encourage people to make a decision to follow Christ, we can't respond by simply going home. Some believers forget what it means to be compelled by the message of freedom and grace we receive only through Jesus. Some people contend that Christians should not talk about Jesus at all or send missionaries anywhere, since that might somehow offend people. This is a serious threat to Christianity because it essentially says evangelism can be traded for the path of minimal resistance.

The opposite reaction is to become more vocal and "in your face" about decisions, but then the critique of outsiders has even more traction. Why should the most important message in human history be perceived as a cheap marketing gimmick? If outsiders stop listening, we cannot just turn up the volume.

The middle ground between these extremes suggests that we focus on cultivating relationships with people and developing environments that facilitate deep spiritual transformation.

A few years ago, on a business trip to present data to one of our clients, I was waiting to check out of my hotel. It was the end of a long day, and I was eager to get home. My client had arranged my ride to the airport. They sent a former pastor who was working with the organization, a well-spoken man who didn't seem perturbed by doing the taxi gig. The desk clerk, a young man probably in his early twenties, was processing my hotel bill. Clicking away on the hotel computer, he asked about my profession. I explained that I research the spiritual lives of Americans. I don't recall, but I probably mentioned something about studying Christianity. Already drained from my day's efforts, I wasn't really ready for what happened next. He started talking in great detail about his spiritual background. His comments revealed that he used to be a regular churchgoer, that his mom had pushed him to attend, and that now he was making up his own mind about things. Reflecting his newfound independence, he described a "great book" he had recently consumed, a text that was apparently not complimentary toward Christianity.

Perhaps not coincidentally, *I* had just read a great book—a short, winsome volume that described Christianity in a fresh way. I asked him, "Would you be open to reading another book, one that may help you think about Christianity differently?"

"Sure. But you have to read my book too."

"Okay. Here, write the title on this paper. I'll check it out." I wasn't enthusiastic about adding to my reading pile, but I intended to follow through with it. "If you want, here's my email address," I offered. "You can let me know what you think, and I'll do the same."

"Yeah, okay. Here is mine," he said, as he scribbled his digital identity onto the scrap of hotel paper.

As my friend and I slipped out of the hotel, I prayed for the clerk, but then my next thought was how I couldn't wait to fall asleep on the plane.

There are two details you should know about this story. The first was my Christian friend's comment: "I really liked your technique back there, how you got him to read a book by promising to review the one he suggested." Frankly, I was just too tired to explain that it wasn't a technique at all, that it just seemed like the right way to connect with the young man. I also did not tell the driver that his comment struck me as superficial, that it made what was a natural spiritual conversation feel like some sort of formula.

But now, several years later, after studying the lives of outsiders, having seen the negative baggage of Christians who mean well but often come across as insincere, I should also convey another detail of the story. On my trip home, I lost the email address.

 Listen to Gabe Lyons and Chuck Colson discuss the challenges of a faith solely focused on conversion at www.unchristian.com/fermi

CHANGING THE PERCEPTIONS

THE GOSPEL IN ITS FULLNESS

The good news is summarized in 1 Corinthians 15: "Christ died on the cross for our sins," so that we can be redeemed. That is the narrow definition that most evangelicals embrace. I think we are wrong in limiting it to that. If you read the first twenty-seven words Jesus spoke in Mark, it's clear that he announced the kingdom. He said that the kingdom of God had broken through into history. He was saying that we would be seeing in his life a picture of the kingdom yet to come. It is a picture of what the Hebrews called shalom, or peace, or wholeness, extending to every facet of life: the sick healed, the captives freed, the oppressed released, right relationships restored with God and humanity.

Then later, in Acts 4, you see this incredible story of the community of believers coming together. No one was in need because people were sharing their wealth; they were praying and studying the Bible. They created a community that absolutely dazzled the world right after the time of Jesus. They provided a foretaste of the kingdom yet to come in Revelation 22 and 23.

So, I'm one of those who believes that while the gospel is most accurately defined by evangelicals as the "good news," it goes beyond that. For instance, Catholics take it beyond that. The defense of human life is a part of the gospel because it matters greatly to God. I think Catholics have a really good point in this. When we think about Jesus ushering in the kingdom, as we pray, by the way, "thy kingdom come, thy will be done on earth as it is in heaven," I think we begin to see the gospel in a much broader context.

The local church has to be responsible for "making the invisible kingdom visible," as Calvin said. When the local church is doing what the church is called to do—preaching the gospel, administering the sacraments, and exercising discipline—inevitably the surrounding culture will be affected. In other words, if we are really living as Christians, the church expands exponentially.

Consider the rise of the Christians during the Roman era. People were drawn to Christians, not because of evangelistic outreaches or crusades, or through mass media—those didn't exist. The church grew because Christians were *doing* the gospel and had a community—a local church—where people really loved each other. During the great plagues that swept Rome in the second century, all of the doctors fled, but the Christians stayed and took care of the sick. They embodied what Christians are called to do. Although many Christians died because they took care of the sick, pagans were drawn to Christ because they saw both the love of Christians and Christianity itself as a better way of life. When Constantine declared Rome the Holy Roman Empire, people thought he did that for political reasons, but he didn't. It was already Christianized; he just recognized the realities of what really happened.

One of the things I do when I meet people is ask them, "What is Christianity?" Undoubtedly half will respond, "A relationship with Jesus."

That is wrong. The gospel cannot be merely a private transaction. God didn't break through history, through time and space, to come as a babe, be incarnated, and suffer on the cross just so you can come to him and say, "Oh, I accept Jesus and now I can live happily ever after." That's not why he came. . . . Jesus came as a radical to turn the world upside down. When we believe it is just about Jesus and yourself, we miss the whole point.

I even dislike using the words "accept Christ" anymore—because it is so much more than that. Christianity is a way of seeing all of life and reality through God's eyes. That is what Christianity is: a worldview, a system, and a way of life. I believe that when you truly see the gospel in its fullness, it's so much more. It is the most exciting, radical, revolutionary story ever told.

Chuck Colson
founder, Prison Fellowship Ministries

DON'T PUT THE CART BEFORE THE HORSE

I understand why most nonChristians believe that Christians are only concerned with converting people and getting them into heaven. If you are part of my generation, you remember the crusades, revivals, and worship services that ended with invitations to come forward and be *saved*. Those who did were immediately paraded across the front of the church and declared *Christians*. For a couple of generations, the emphasis was placed solely on that conversion moment.

In some ways, this is understandable. Christians know that salvation is important. But the truth is, we have put the cart before the horse. We have communicated that we want people to believe something that is critical to their lives before they know us, have experienced us, or have received anything from us . . . and before we know them.

If we were able to rewrite the script for the reputation of Christianity, I think we would put the emphasis on developing relationships with nonbelievers, serving them, loving them, and making them feel accepted. Only then would we earn the right to share the gospel. Their acceptance by us would not be predicated on their willingness to accept Christ. After all, God loved us before we were lovable; God loved the whole world before the world knew anything about him. This should be our model.

Here's my advice to Christians who want to change culture's perception of Christianity: "Let your light shine before men, that they may see your good deeds and praise your Father in heaven." In other words, do something that causes people to look favorably in God's direction.

I still believe that everybody spends eternity somewhere. If that's the case, getting this right isn't a marginal issue. It is *the* issue.

Andy Stanley
senior pastor, North Point Ministries, Atlanta, GA

INSUFFICIENT INFORMATION

In trying to communicate the gospel to the masses, the message was eventually reduced to a partial story: humans are sinful and need Jesus in order to go to heaven. This made Christianity lose some of its life because the full description of God's activity—such as his creation, his plans for restoration, his sovereignty—was left out. It was ultimate reduction, "renounce your sins and place your hope in Jesus." This phrase is not wrong per se. But it is insufficient, particularly as our culture becomes more and more pluralistic. As a result of this mindset, one can easily accept Jesus and Buddha and a form of Wicca and have not the slightest problem with the significant contradictions. By reducing the gospel to a *what's-in-it-for-me* message, people feel Jesus exists for their benefit.

The greatest problem with this model of communication is that God does not have to honor it. Just because someone prayed a prayer does not mean they put their faith in Jesus, were regenerated by the Spirit of God, and became a new creation in Christ. It may be a helpful tool for some, but it could be a point of departure and confusion for others.

Sometimes we believe the greatest Christian virtue is leading someone else to Christ. Scripture teaches followers of Christ that they should love their neighbors and make disciples along the way. Making disciples is a long process. Don't get me wrong, I believe it is important that people make decisions to follow Jesus—I just believe it needs to happen in a context of love and not be reduced to feed the consumer's mindset of finding spiritual comfort. The Gospels portray a grand, multifaceted picture of Jesus. I think we should really inter-act with this portrait in sharing Christ with others. Read through the Gospels with them and let them encounter the person rather than the formula. I just think that asking someone to commit to a major way of life like following Christ deserves much more respect than simple spiritual formulas.

The sad thing is that when we (Imago Dei Church) go out and love people in Portland without an agenda of getting a "return" for our time—this is considered revolutionary. I think this should be the norm, and we have so much to learn in doing it better. If we share the gospel and people reject Jesus, do we quit loving them?

Rick McKinley
pastor, Imago Dei, Portland

5

ANTIHOMOSEXUAL

Many people in the gay community don't seem to have issues with Jesus but rather with those claiming to represent him today. It's very much an "us-versus-them" mentality, as if a war has been declared. Of course each side thinks the other fired the opening shot.

Peter, 34

PERCEPTION **Christians show contempt for gays and lesbians.**

NEW PERCEPTION **Christians show compassion and love to all people, regardless of their lifestyle.**

"So, David, do you still think I am going to hell because I am gay?"

My friend's question caught me off guard.

After spending the day visiting some of our firm's research clients, I was having dinner with Mark. Exhausted by a day of meetings, I was eager to catch up with one of my longtime pals. Mark has been a friend since high school. We went our separate ways during college, and about that time Mark came out of the closet. He started telling people he was gay.

We had not talked about the issue much. He knew I was a Christian and that I believed homosexual acts were sinful, but I could not remember what I had said to Mark prior to our dinner that would have initiated his question.

Apparently Mark remembered, because an hour or so of friendly conversation led to his provocative question about hell.

I sat there, in silence for a minute, searching his face for some clue or insight. Finally, I got up the courage to ask, "Did I *really* say that?"

"In so many words. Is that what you still think?" His face flashed frustration and also some hurt, and his question was still hanging out there, waiting for me to respond.

My mind raced through a dozen possible responses. *I should have been ready for this,* I thought. "Well . . ." I began, catching an extra second to think as I sipped my coffee.

I will finish the story about Mark later in this chapter, but first let me describe what outsiders think of Christians in light of this hotly debated issue. In our research, the perception that Christians are "against" gays and lesbians—not only objecting to their lifestyles but also harboring irrational fear and unmerited scorn toward them—has reached critical mass. The gay issue has become the "big one," the negative image most likely to be intertwined with Christianity's reputation. It is also the dimension that most clearly demonstrates the unChristian faith to young people today, surfacing a spate of negative perceptions: judgmental, bigoted, sheltered, right-wingers, hypocritical, insincere, and uncaring. Outsiders say our hostility toward gays—not just opposition to homosexual politics and behaviors but disdain for gay individuals—has become virtually synonymous with the Christian faith.

The severity of the perception surprised me, but it began showing up right from the start of our research. During our initial exploratory interviews, the issue of Christians' treatment of homosexuals kept coming up. The first interviews were qualitative in nature, that is, primarily a series of anecdotes that do not provide "hard data." At first, I assumed the frequency of the comments was just a blip on the radar.

Then we did our quantitative interviews, providing representative data about outsiders' perceptions, and we found that the early interviews were not an aberration.

Out of twenty attributes that we assessed, both positive and negative, as they related to Christianity, the perception of being antihomosexual was at the top of the list. More than nine out of ten Mosaic and

Buster outsiders (91 percent) said "antihomosexual" accurately describes present-day Christianity. And two-thirds of outsiders have very strong opinions about Christians in this regard, easily generating the largest group of vocal critics. When you introduce yourself as a Christian to a friend, neighbor, or business associate who is an outsider, you might as well have it tattooed on your arm: antihomosexual, gay-hater, homophobic. I doubt you think of yourself in these terms, but that's what outsiders think of you.

Of course homosexuality is an electric topic. Most people have strong feelings about it. And the issue is incredibly complex, affecting families and children and influencing media and culture. Gay activists have been aggressive in their attempts to change Americans' perceptions, and media has played a significant role in shaping young people's attitudes and values on this topic. We cannot underestimate how a morally relativistic generation, along with sophisticated media and political strategies, have created a tinder box for Christians' reputations in this regard.

Yet Christians have often responded to this environment in unChristian ways. Though this chapter is not a comprehensive guide to all the issues, we will explore some of the complexities of homosexuality and try to unravel what a new generation really thinks about us.

Even though the challenges are unique and emotions are charged, we must not fail to understand what is happening in the hearts and minds of young people. Both inside and outside the church, they are telling us to wake up to this issue, to see ourselves objectively. When most of us engage homosexuals, we come across as arrogant, self-righteous, and uncaring—the opposite of how Jesus engaged outsiders. Rather than articulating a biblical perspective and living out a biblical response to homosexuals, the research demonstrates how inconsistent and uncompassionate—how unChristian—we have been.

And outsiders have been paying close attention. Here are a handful of examples pointed out by outsiders:

- ☐ Christians believe events like 9/11 and Hurricane Katrina are God's judgment on homosexuals.

- ☐ Public comments from pastors and other Christian leaders are often perceived as unduly berating gays.

☐ Another outsider pointed out how Christians oppose gays in public office: "Why should they be any less qualified to serve in government?"

☐ Christians use coarse jokes and offensive language to describe homosexuals, such as "fags," "sodomists."

☐ Some outsiders we interviewed pointed to God-hates-gays websites. One such website juxtaposes a list of Bible verses condemning homosexuality alongside a cartoon man holding a yellow sign condemning gays with two stick figures in a sexually suggestive gay pose. The outsider's comment: "What more do you need to see that Christians hate gay people?"

Are these just extreme examples? Perhaps most Christ followers would be ashamed by these stories, but our inconsistencies and biases run deeper than we imagine. Consider these realities:

☐ Born-again Christians are more likely to disapprove of homosexuality than divorce. The vast majority of Christians say that homosexuality should not be considered a legitimate lifestyle and strongly reject church-sanctioned weddings for same-sex unions. However, a minority of born-again believers (39 percent) embrace Jesus's teaching that divorce is a sin except in cases of adultery (see Matt. 5:32). Even among evangelicals, just three out of five describe divorce as a sin, well below their opposition to gay marriage.

☐ Most born-again Christians have a hard time knowing how they should respond to the lifestyles of homosexuals as well as how to respond to the political efforts of gay and lesbian activists. For instance, many believers advocate legal restrictions on homosexual behavior. A majority of born-again Christians, including more than four out of five evangelicals, say that homosexual relations between two consenting adults should be illegal.[1]

☐ Millions of Americans, including two out of every five churchgoers, say that school boards ought to have the right to fire teachers who are known homosexuals. Of course the issues are complicated, but Christians are fueling the idea that gays and lesbians should not be allowed to work in public schools.[2]

☐ Many Christians continue to be very skeptical about donating to HIV/AIDS causes, even overseas, despite Christians' generosity in many other arenas. In one poll we found that just 14 percent of born-again Christians say they would be highly motivated to help HIV/AIDS orphans overseas.[3] In another study we discovered that two out of every five born-again Christians, including the same proportion of evangelicals, admitted they have more sympathy for people who have cancer than they do for people with HIV/AIDS.[4] In probing people's attitudes, we find this perspective typically springs from the idea that the disease is deserved. They believe God is punishing these people—or that their decisions and lifestyle deserve this outcome.

As you will see, our criticism of gays and lesbians is not only ineffective, but also it repels many Busters and Mosaics. As one survey respondent put it, "I cannot imagine Jesus actually treating gays and lesbians like Christians do today." When you have read this chapter, my prayer is that you will be inspired and challenged to reverse this image in your own life and community. God intends to use your life as a conduit of his grace and compassion toward outsiders—gay, straight, bisexual, or transgender.

Outsiders are getting the message loud and clear that Christians reject the gay lifestyle, and they say that Christians' disdain for homosexuals is unmistakable. I realize this topic is controversial, but to deal with unChristian faith, we have to take a look at the tough realities of our *antihomosexual* label. We have to help a generation that has few sexual or moral boundaries understand and embrace the deep and rich truth of Christianity. My research leads me to conclude we have not been doing this.

WHAT DO YOU BELIEVE?

First, we should be clear about what we believe. Are there some crimes and sins that God cannot forgive? If you think so, you're not alone. Our surveys show that nearly one-third of Americans believe this, including one-quarter of born-again Christians.

The central teaching of the Bible, however, is that all sin is, at its core, rebellion against God. Shayne Wheeler, who writes a response to this chapter (found on pages 110–11), makes this observation: "There is not a special judgment for homosexuals, and there is not a special righteousness for heterosexuals." Another pastor put it simply: "The struggle of gays in being attracted to the same sex is no different than my struggle in being attracted to the opposite sex." We are all sinners. No one is any more likely or less likely to receive God's free gift of grace. All have fallen short of God's standards. The Bible says while we were still *enemies* of God, he made peace with us through the cross (Rom. 5:19). Because he *loved* the world, he sent his Son to die (John 3:16). Everything hinges on what a person decides to do with Jesus—commit to him or reject him. Regardless of the sin we commit, he still loves us.

Let me drive this point home as it relates to homosexuality. It's true that sexual sins are particularly destructive in people's lives, but this is true of all sexual sin. And frankly, when we recognize the complexity and significance of sin and sexual sin, it should engage our concern and compassion on the issue of homosexuality even more.

It is one thing to be *against homosexuality*, to affirm that the Bible rejects the practice of same-sex lifestyles,[5] but it is another to be *against homosexuals*, to let your disagreement with their behavior spill out in your feelings and words toward them as people. It is unChristian to lose your sense that everyone's fallen nature affects all aspects of his or her life, including sexuality, and to forget God's command to love people in order to point them to Jesus.

It is unChristian to focus our animosity on another human being, regardless of what they do or what they look like. Billy Graham, one of the most respected Christian leaders in American history, made this observation about homosexuality during a press conference: "I'm going to quote the Bible now, not myself, that it [homosexuality] is wrong, it's a sin. But there are other sins. Why do we jump on that sin as though it's the greatest sin? The greatest sin in the Bible is idolatry, worshipping other things besides the true and living God. Jealousy is a sin. Pride is a sin. All of these things are sins. But homosexuality is also a sin and needs to be dealt with and needs to be forgiven, and that's why Christ came and died on the cross."[6]

Our research shows that Christians struggle to offer a consistent and biblical response to homosexuality or to address the unique and significant challenges that emerge because of this lifestyle. We need to consider what the objectives of Christ followers should be. Do we really want government regulating the sex lives of its adult citizens? Our concerns about preventing the advancement of homosexual rights often translate into a desire for unrealistic boundaries on people's lives.

Here is an important clarification: I am not aware of any concerted effort on the part of a major Christian leader or organization to get laws passed that would make gay sex among consenting adults illegal, but many Christians would like to see such laws in place. Human beings are easily alarmed, and Christians often respond to their fears by exaggerating the danger and by seeking solutions that do not appropriately address the problems.

CLEARING THE AIR

One difficulty in communicating and connecting with homosexuals is how easy it is to misunderstand them. And, unfortunately, we encountered significant resistance among some Christians to having their views about gays and lesbians challenged. Apparently they have already made up their mind that they have nothing to learn. Consider some of the inaccurate assumptions Christians embrace:

Homosexuals are incapable of acting morally. We encountered this perspective consistently in our research among Christians: it is best to avoid homosexuals altogether because they are immoral. Facing a business decision, one young Christian described the advice he got from his pastor: "You cannot trust homosexuals to treat you fairly because they have no moral code." Christians take one look at a gay person's sexuality and assign stereotypes to other elements of their character.

Homosexuals are an organized movement with the purpose of subverting conservative Christianity. Another assumption is that all homosexuals are of the same mind regarding their political engagement as well as in their antagonism toward Christians. However, in our research we found that gays and lesbians have diverse feelings about, experiences with, and perceptions of Christianity. Compared with other segments of outsiders, some homosexuals are more skeptical of and hostile toward Christianity, but this is not true of all homosexuals. Our research shows that one-third of gays and lesbians attend church regularly, going to churches across a wide spectrum of denominations and backgrounds, including Catholic, mainline, nonmainline, and nondenominational churches. Most gays and lesbians in America align themselves with Christianity, and one-sixth have beliefs that qualify them as born-again Christians. Most have been active in a church at one time, such as this gay man: "Sometimes it's hard for me to reconcile the 'Christian movement' I see in politics today with the kind, generous people I knew from my own days in the church. I remember the Christians I knew (and once considered myself) to be students of God, who wanted to serve him and spread his good news and message of hope to a needy world." The bottom line: some gays are antagonistic to Christianity, but many are not.

Homosexuality is a simple issue. It is easy to assume the lives of gays are about simple choices (and it is especially easy to believe this without much interaction with homosexuals). But simplicity does not characterize many areas of human life. Many Christian psychologists and pastors consider human sexuality to be a complex puzzle of personality, our tainted sin nature, an individual's history, and personal needs. Some people draw their entire sexual identity from same-sex lifestyles, others struggle with homosexual feelings while living in heterosexual relationships, and some have gone through a period of same-sex experimentation in their past for which they continue to feel shame. Some people feel comfortable with their gay identity in public, while others live in secret or without being fully aware of their same-sex attractions.

The young outsiders we interviewed explained that most Christians seem to spend little energy in actually getting to know homosexuals or what happens in the lives of those who have some type of same-sex encounter or attraction. This lack of interaction leads Christians to misunderstand the complexity of the issues facing gays and lesbians. Also this is not a two-category conversation any longer. There is the increasing complexity of bisexual and transgender individuals. A new generation is exploring all sorts of sexual attitudes and experiences.

It is best to avoid any friendships with homosexuals. Many Christians believe that friendship with homosexuals should be avoided, yet Jesus did not seem afraid to hang out with all kinds of people. Religious people were scandalized by Jesus's choices of relationships. Ironically, when we make an effort to avoid homosexuals, we put up barriers for people to actually experience Jesus through us. One comment illustrated this: "My friend has a lesbian sister. Christians will come up to her and tell her that they want nothing to do with her or that lifestyle. My friend has been really hurt because it even affects *her* relationships with people, and she isn't even homosexual!"

In our research, one out of every thirty-three people in America admits to being gay, lesbian, or bisexual (3 percent). Our research among young adults demonstrates that in the high school or college years, most people will have personal friends who are gay, lesbian, bisexual, or transgender. So when we raise young people to shun their "different" peers, we are actually limiting the spiritual influence they can have, and we force them to create a false barrier that leads them to question their faith in more significant ways (more on this in a moment).

SHIFTING VALUES

To further understand why outsiders think of Christians as antihomosexual, let's look at what the new generation thinks about homosexuality. We may not like their morally relativistic attitude, but we have to understand what they think and why.

Americans of all ages remain deeply divided about gays and lesbians, but on the whole, most have a negative view. Conservatives sometimes take comfort in the fact that most Americans have no sympathy for the plight of homosexuals and reject their interest in marriage and adoption, among other things. In this context, political efforts have found traction, because antihomosexual initiatives generate a sufficient number of voters to win elections.

But when it comes to Mosaics and Busters, it's a completely different story. Their attitude about homosexuals is very distinct from that of their parents. A new generation of adults has significantly shifted its view and now accepts homosexuality as a legitimate way of life. While the general population has been slowly edging toward greater acceptance of gays and lesbians over the last twenty years, those under the age of twenty-six are much more likely to accept it without consideration. In the 1980s differences of opinion on this topic were rare across age groups, but since then there has been a widening gap between the views of young and older adults.[7]

Now most young adults endorse the idea of same-sex marriage, and a majority favor the legal rights of gays and lesbians to adopt children.[8] Also they generally believe that laws should be changed to provide more rights and protections to homosexuals. Most older adults soundly reject these alternatives.

And here is one more proof of changing attitudes. An important indicator of public opinion is not merely how many residents *endorse* an idea, but how firmly people *resist* it. Even in a country where the majority rules, a mobilized minority faction can make significant headway in getting society to accept their ideas. We have found, however, that opponents of homosexual rights have little influence on young adults—outside or inside the church. In fact, just one out of seven Mosaics (14 percent) and one-fourth of Busters (28 percent) said they strongly oppose changing the laws to grant homosexuals more freedoms, rights, and protections. Among older generations, more than two-fifths (42 percent) firmly oppose such legal protection for gays and lesbians. Not only are more young adults supportive of the homosexual community, only a small percentage want to resist homosexual initiatives.

The unconventional values of young adults will play an increasingly important role in shaping our society in the years to come, making it much more difficult for those with other views to achieve political traction in this arena. As these new generations begin to make up a larger share of the public, homosexuals will gain greater rights and protections—and widespread acceptance—in our culture.

CONFRONTING CHANGE

Christians, and particularly evangelicals, have relied primarily on two methods of dealing with the threats they perceive from the homosexual community: preaching and politics. Over the last twenty years or so, there has been a substantial increase in the percentage of churchgoers who have heard a sermon about homosexuality, with more than two-thirds of attenders in evangelical churches recalling such sermons.[9]

The second solution has been political engagement. Among those born-again Christians who have cast a ballot concerning same-sex marriage, nearly nine out of ten recall voting against it.

Most revealing, perhaps, is the comparative absence in the Christian community of any other approaches to addressing homosexuality. Although most Christians say they are concerned about homosexual lifestyles, just 4 percent of Americans (and 10 percent of born-again Christians) say they have engaged in any other nonpolitical means of addressing what they perceive to be a problem. Only 1 percent of Americans say they pray for homosexuals; a similarly miniscule proportion say they address the issue by donating money to organizations that help people dealing with the lifestyle or that they try to have meaningful discussions with people about it. This information was derived from a random, representative sample of 1,007 adults, among whom more than 600 said that the homosexual lifestyle is a problem facing America. As people described what they thought would help, just one respondent offered the word *love* as a potential solution. One other survey participant suggested "being sympathetic." Simply put, Christians think there is a problem but have no idea what to do about it.

CHANGING LOYALTIES

This absence of relational and spiritual solutions to the problem of the homosexual lifestyle has left the church particularly vulnerable. Mosaics and Busters are hardwired for relational connections, so when Christians overlook such solutions, they come across to younger adults as insincere and uncaring. We may not like this, but this is how they evaluate the reality of the Christian faith.

Even among Mosaic and Buster churchgoers, fewer than one-third believe that homosexual lifestyles are a major problem, compared with half of Boomers and nearly three out of every five Elders. This is significant because, despite more sermons on the subject from the pulpit and more emphasis on political engagement, Mosaic and Buster churchgoers remain unconvinced that the homosexual lifestyle is a problem for society. While most young churchgoers believe the Bible does not condone homosexuality, their conviction about this is waning, and they are embarrassed by the church's treatment of gays and lesbians. However, they have little insight or instruction in how a Christian should engage in meaningful friendships with gays, lesbians, bisexuals, or others with alternative lifestyles.

**Outsiders and Young Churchgoers: Similar Lack
of Concern about Homosexuality**

The percent who perceive the following
to be *major* problems facing America

	Homosexual lifestyles	Political efforts of homosexual activists
All adults	35 %	35 %
Mosaic and Buster outsiders	17	18
Mosaic and Buster churchgoers	29	33
Boomer churchgoers	46	44
Elder churchgoers	58	52

Based on several years of studying these issues, I cannot emphasize enough how churches and Christian leaders are not only missing the chance to address the sexual struggles of young people but are piercing the confidence of young believers by not offering a biblical response to the issue of homosexuality.

Here is an example: one seventeen-year-old churchgoer described her experience bringing a gay friend to church. "The youth pastor knew I was going to bring him, and even though his talk really had nothing to do with homosexuality, he still found a way to insert 'God created Adam and Eve not Adam and Steve' into his comments. I was sitting there, just dying. This happened more than once. My friend was at a point where he was interested in seeing what Jesus might offer, and the door was just slammed shut."

A few weeks ago I was chatting with Katie, who is a young journalist and a Christian. I mentioned how young people in churches are not sure what to do with homosexuality because they feel incredibly loyal to friends who are gay, and many churches have not given them any concept of how to deal with the topic, other than to feel awkward, embarrassed, or grossed out; to avoid the topic; and to fear for their gay friend's soul.

"You're telling my story," Katie said. "My best friend for the last eight years just told me that he is gay. I was shocked and really pretty upset about it. I know what the Bible says, but I also know what I feel about this guy. I have a hard time looking down on him for being gay. But I don't know what to think. I have not told my parents because they would just be too ... I don't know ... I have no idea what they would do."

These examples underscore a critical insight from our research: young people are facing a candid, sexually diverse world, often without assistance or biblical counsel from their churches or their parents.

And it is important to realize that Mosaic and Buster relationships have become a moral and spiritual compass—to a degree their parents wouldn't grasp. Let me explain how this works. Mosaics and Busters are intensely loyal to their "tribe," which is their network of relationships. This web of often fluid relational connections enables them to make sense of reality. Faced with a bevy of life choices, their peers become a filter for decision making. They determine right and wrong based partly on what makes sense given their experiences and their friendships. To their way of thinking, illegally downloading music is just peer-to-peer "sharing." Giving away products or services to friends, even if that would technically be stealing from their place of employment, is simply labeled "hooking up" their pals with free stuff. Being more accepting of gays and lesbians is the same thing as being loyal to the people they know best.

Mosaic and Buster loyalty is significant. It implies that the church can still find ways of connecting with these young adults in terms of accountability, community, transparency, purpose, and grace. But we cannot miss how deeply this loyalty affects the homosexual question. Mosaics and Busters really work at putting acceptance of people and lifestyles into practice. And they are very attuned to people's hearts and motivations. If they sense that Christians are being inconsistent, unwilling to learn, or uncaring, they are quick to conclude that Christians are just plain wrong. And this is one reason the gay and lesbian community is becoming more acceptable to outsiders. Right or wrong, because of their respect for others and relativistic viewpoints, young outsiders value what they perceive to be a more embracing and accepting mindset within the gay community.

As Mosaics and Busters move from tribe to tribe, Christians who show no compassion, kindness, or grace make them feel at odds with whom they want to be as people. Because it feels so condemning of gays, the unChristian faith does not offer significance and relevance to them. If some people interpret the Bible to make gays out to be abhorrent creatures, and if Christians make homosexuals feel like second-class human beings, young Christians start questioning their own loyalty to the faith. If Christianity is not the mixture of grace and truth that Jesus represents, they find it hard to reconcile it with their friendships.

Forced to choose, many young people would rather be loyal to their friends than adhere to the unChristian faith.

BIBLICAL RESPONSES

Because of our opposition to homosexuals, outsiders cannot picture the church as the loving community of believers Jesus envisioned. A pastor friend, Rob Brendle, had a high-profile gay man visit his congregation recently. This individual had opened up a crisis for the church by revealing an affair with one of the church's leaders. Here is how Rob explained why the church welcomed him so warmly, even after enduring such a painful experience. "One of the enduring truths of Christianity is to love people the world sets up as your enemies."[10]

How can we put the "enduring truth" of unhindered love into practice in our lives and churches? What is the biblical response that the Christian community needs to give? Here are some perspectives and responses to consider:

ACKNOWLEDGING THE COMPLEXITY

The biblical response to homosexuals should be to deal with the fundamental needs that all men and women have. We must acknowledge that everyone has sexual baggage but also has the potential for sexual wholeness. There are major problems across the spectrum of sexuality that the church needs to address. For example, a *majority* of born-again Busters believe that cohabitation and sexual fantasies are morally acceptable.

Being "against" gays and lesbians is not a flag to wave. Instead, develop a process within your church or within your life that allows people to work through sexual issues in a context of accountability, respect, and transparency. This process should begin as early as appropriate, especially as our culture pushes sexuality to younger ages. Sexuality should not be seen as dualistic—all good or all bad—but as a good part of our created nature that is constantly in need of repair. The process teaches people to be sensitive and soft-hearted to God and each other and does not end after a person is married, because sexual sin can invade every life. We must rely on spiritual solutions such as prayer, discernment, and other spiritual disciplines. Remember, Jesus raised the bar beyond skin-on-skin contact and said even a simple thing like sexual thoughts can defile us. Our approach should embrace this high standard of sexuality: it is ultimately a matter of the heart, and brokenness is as common in our private thoughts and attitudes as it is in our behaviors (see Matt. 5:28).

OPENING DOORS WITH CONVERSATIONS

A vital element of engaging homosexuals is to elevate the importance of conversations. Christians expect overnight results and are impatient with the need to cultivate deep, candid relationships and interactions of trust. Peter, a gay man we interviewed, made this comment: "Many people in the gay community don't seem to have issues with Jesus but rather with those claiming to represent him today. It's very much an 'us-versus-them' mentality, as if a war has been declared. Of course each side thinks the other fired the opening shot."

One effort to facilitate conversations came at the 2007 Sundance Film Festival, where filmmakers released *Save Me* and *For the Bible Tells Me So*, films intended to help demilitarize the Christian-versus-homosexual conflict. Our research demonstrates that conversations begin to open up avenues for spiritual influence. For instance, being willing to discuss HIV/AIDS has opened up doors for conversations with people who had sworn off having anything to do with conservative Christians.

TREATING OTHER CHRISTIANS WITH RESPECT

Christians need to downgrade the importance of being antihomosexual as a "credential," proving that we are more faithful to God than anyone else is. For example, a young Christian friend we interviewed said she has to be discreet about her attempts to minister to some gay people she has met at work. "If my church friends hear me talk sympathetically about gays, they get bent out of shape about it. It's interesting that our antennae don't go up when people admit to gluttony, lying, using pornography, or getting a divorce, but we seem fixated on homosexuality."

If we don't work at developing meaningful relationships with our co-workers, whether gay or straight, how can we expect them to respect us and our beliefs? When we get to know and love homosexuals because they are people, perhaps they will grow to love and appreciate us and maybe even listen to what we believe. We need to be more concerned about reaching those who need Jesus than "proving" our faith to those who already claim to know Jesus. Did Paul display a lack of faith in Athens when he acknowledged the unknown god? Or was he listening to the Holy Spirit to help connect a culture that needed Jesus? We need to trust our fellow believers, realizing that their love for Jesus and for others is greater than their fear of our disapproval.

HAVING THE RIGHT PERSPECTIVE

We should not give up channels of influence, such as in politics, just because our stand might cause negative perceptions, but we must pursue our efforts in these arenas with integrity, respect, and love for people. For instance, laws provide significant parameters that determine Americans' behaviors, so lawyers and legislators should work diligently to pursue a biblical perspective that achieves appropriate goals. It is necessary and appropriate for Christians to affirm that marriage is between one man and one woman. Nevertheless, even if we could "win" every legal, legislative, and political battle—a reality that will become increasingly difficult as Mosaics and Busters take center stage—the chasm between Christians and outsiders will only deepen. We cannot assume that politics is the only or best way to influence people.

Despite widespread mobilization over the last decade, most Christians have become even more isolated from homosexuals. However, gays and lesbians should not be surprised to find us working side by side with them to address HIV/AIDS and to end workplace discrimination in nonreligious settings. You change a country not merely by bolstering its laws but by transforming the hearts of its people.

EXPRESSING CONCERN FOR KIDS

As gays push for social rights, one of the important debates is whether they should be able to adopt children. Christians point out the importance of a father and a mother in child development and reject the claims that gay couples should be able to adopt. And, of course, I recognize that it's offensive to homosexuals to say that a child needs both a father and a mother; it's a difficult part of what Christians believe. However, though this is an important conviction, Christians have to avoid rhetoric that dehumanizes people, especially in interpersonal interactions. Our most important concern must be the response of young people to Christ, not merely what type of home they grew up in.

I realize that many Christians may be offended by this conclusion. Yet consider the ultimate goal of our lives: pointing people to Jesus. But if Christians attack gays and lesbians as if they are not worthy of dignity and respect, we tarnish the reputation of Christ. If the people of Jesus attack, mock, and criticize a child's parents, the chances that the child will ever commit his or her life to Christ are diminished.

This is unChristian faith in action—keeping people from Jesus. Instead of pitting ourselves in battle against these families, remember that true connection to people and to Christ happens most often when we love and serve them. If our concern is that loving and serving them might somehow condone their behavior, we probably do not love people the way Christ does. Being truly motivated by God's love always produces some sort of God-life in people, even if we do not see the results immediately. Read 1 Corinthians 13—the Bible's famous "love passage"—and then consider your concern for homosexuals. Paul writes that love is patient and kind. It does not keep a record of wrongs. It always believes the best. *Love never fails.*

HAVING COMPASSION

Dietrich Bonhoeffer, the German pastor who was executed for his opposition to the Nazi party, wrote this from a concentration camp: "Nothing that we despise in the other man is entirely absent from ourselves. We must learn to regard people less in the light of what they do or don't do, and more in light of what they suffer."[11] Christians should have this attitude toward homosexuals. We should think about what they go through. Do you imagine that they have been influenced by unChristian faith? What sorts of things do you think unChristian people have said, written, or emailed? Our words in an us-versus-them world can be weapons we use against outsiders, especially gays. This sheds new light on the writing of James: "If you claim to be religious but don't control your tongue, you are fooling yourself, and your religion is worthless" (1:26). It is easy to decry political correctness, but it is much more difficult to abide by the biblical concept of guarding our tongues and being accountable for what we communicate to others. It is easy to learn what words are offensive and simply avoid them; it is much harder to find meaningful ways to speak the truth in love. Do our language and actions communicate compassion to others? If our theology says homosexuality is wrong and sinful, is it still true that homosexuals have deep sexual needs, just like the rest of us? How can we not utter compassionate words and perform compassionate acts?

BACK TO MARK'S STORY

"So, David, do you still think I am going to hell because I am gay?"

"Well . . . I don't know what I said before. I am sorry if I said you were going to hell because you are gay. Here is what I believe. It all comes down to what you do with Jesus. I believe he was the Son of God. Not everyone believes that, but I would give anything for you to see the reality of Jesus. His life gives my life meaning and purpose. He can do the same for you."

I paused to let that sink in and thought about leaving it at that, but I ventured gently into the heart of Mark's question.

"No one goes to heaven for what they do or don't do. That's the message of Jesus. Every human sins, and we all deserve hell for that. But Jesus freely offers everyone his grace. I know it's not an easy part of Christian theology, but yes, I believe homosexual behavior is a sin, but it's no different than any other sin, no different than if I sleep with someone other than my wife or even have a momentary sexual fantasy. God created sexuality, so it is good, but it can be expressed in wrong ways. Every one of us, gay or straight or whatever, expresses sexuality in broken ways."

I glanced around, glad that the restaurant was virtually empty. Mark was looking at me intently. He did not seem particularly happy.

"You know what, though, I would give anything to see you come to know Jesus. I really would. I would die for that. Everything hinges on what you decide about Jesus."

I reached for my coffee again. My habit was to launch into long-winded answers with Mark (which was probably one reason why he had gotten mixed messages from our past conversations). But this time I felt that I had made my point.

"David, here is what you need to know about my life," Mark began. "I was incredibly lonely. I hated myself. I could not figure out what was wrong with me, and it was eating me alive. I almost dropped out of school. It was awful. I know guys who have committed suicide because of the deep conflicts that exist between who they are and what religion says is right and wrong."

"I don't think I had any idea what you went through, Mark," I said. "I am sorry I wasn't a better friend for you through all of that."

The waitress came up to the table to refill our drinks, and our conversation shifted to a new topic.

I wish I could tell you that Mark changed that night. I know that my views about homosexuals did.

 Hear an eighteen-minute Fermi Talk on *Homosexuality and the Church* with Chris Seay, Mike Foster, and Shayne Wheeler at www.unchristian.com/fermi

CHANGING THE PERCEPTIONS

THE FRACTURE IN OUR SOUL

During the Alexandrian plague (third century), Christians risked their lives in caring for the sick, taking a posture of grace that said, "I am here for you. I may die, but you will not be alone." The church embodied the gospel and the message was not forgotten.

In the 1980s, the AIDS epidemic hit the gay community. Otherwise healthy men were dying and nobody knew why. The only link seemed to be their sexuality. The church had opportunity to again speak grace and instead spewed venom. Rather than showing compassion, we self-righteously proclaimed God's judgment. The message came through loud and clear.

It was the wrong message.

And it has not been forgotten.

When Greg, who is gay, discovered I was a pastor, his demeanor changed. His wounds had history. After a few minutes of hyperbolic invective, I stopped him. "Tell you what, you don't assume I'm a gay-hating bigot, and I won't assume you're a pedophile. Deal? If we buy into stereotypes, we'll never be able to love one another."

Tears streamed down his face. He asked, "Are you *sure* you're a Christian?"

Now there were tears of my own.

Christians may say, "Love the sinner; hate the sin," but Greg and many other homosexuals hear, "God hates fags." It's unfortunate. It's wrong. And it's our fault.

It may look different from person to person, but sin has fractured *every* human soul (see Rom. 3:23; 5:12; 1 John 1:10). Aleksandr Solzhenitsyn said, "The line dividing good and evil cuts through the heart of *every* human being." It is time we lived and loved as though we really believed that.

At our church we say regularly, "As Christians, none of us have the freedom to live however we want. Man or woman, young or old, gay or straight—we are all under God's authority and called to conform our lives to Christ."

The Bible is clear: homosexual practice is inconsistent with Christian discipleship. But there is not a special judgment for homosexuals, and there is not a special righteousness for heterosexuals. For all of us, our only hope for the fracture in our soul is the cross of Christ.

Shayne Wheeler
pastor, All Souls Fellowship, Decatur, GA

PLANTING TREES

The finding that Christians are perceived as antihomosexual is not surprising to me. With the brutal culture war that has raged over the past decade, Christians certainly have been caught up in destructive rhetoric and bad politics and have strayed from Christ's commission to love. Unfortunately, GOD HATES FAGS banners have been waved vigorously all in the name of Christianity. This battle has been broadcast on the news channels, has been argued on the talk radio stations, and has radically polarized those in the Christian and gay communities. Both groups have suffered, and now those who have watched this ugly skirmish have come to some unfortunate conclusions about the Christian faith.

I would be the first to say that much of what has been represented in this culture war is an unfair representation of my faith and beliefs. I would often respond, "That's not me. Those people on TV are whack jobs. Why are they yelling, screaming, and viciously lobbying against gay marriage? I hate this!" And maybe that is your response too. But at some level, we must all own up to the fact that mainstream Christians, myself included, have stumbled in bringing forth an alternative message of love, compassion, and the Good News of Jesus to the gay community. We have remained woefully silent and have allowed those who scream the loudest to represent us. The beautiful gospel has been reduced to a hate-filled sound bite on the six o'clock news. And in my discussions with my gay friends, those sound bites matter to them and to many others. As Christians we have failed to speak up and passionately represent the true heart of Christ's message in our society.

My personal commitment to transforming this negative perception is that I have stopped letting political and religious organizations represent me on this issue. I have decided to represent myself, and in so doing I hope to accurately represent Christ. In my humble understanding of Jesus in the New Testament, I see a man who sought to restore relationships, not destroy them. A man of compassion who was crazy in love with what the religious of his day deemed the "wrong crowd."

French philosopher Albert Schweitzer once noted that example is not the main thing in influencing others; it's the only thing. If we are going to put forth a more accurate truth, then we must set the example in our own lives, starting today. We must be deliberate, introspective, and committed to taking personal ownership in redefining the perception. Our actions, responses, and relationships must consistently be filled with compassion, honor, and love. We must stop identifying people as "sexual beings" and instead identify them as "human beings." The change comes by sitting with our gay friends and family members at their dinner tables and in their living rooms. We go to their events and serve. We seek to do life together and find understanding. It is time for us to humbly serve and honor those we have been so effective at hurting in the past.

But we must keep this one thing in mind: it is critically important that we do this not because we feel compelled to "set the record straight" on Christianity but because it is the way of Christianity. Leaving agendas at the door, we engage with the gay community in a simple, truthful, and organic expression. We must not slip into making this a mission project or some cause. That would be disastrous.

An old yet relevant saying goes, "Someone is sitting in the shade today because someone planted a tree a long time ago." May you and I today begin to plant a new way of living, loving, and serving those in the gay community and in turn usher in a new kind of Christianity.

Mike Foster
president, Ethur
founder, XXXchurch.com

GOD LOVES THE HOMOSEXUAL

I have braved a few real-life conversations with homosexual friends. I distinctly remember how I felt on each occasion. Queasy mostly. Knowing that Christians often have a head start in the race to bigotry, I had no desire to win us any additional medals.

In each conversation, my Christian affiliation betrayed me. Hence, my homosexual friends gestured knowingly at the back pocket of my soul where I had temporarily stuffed the fact that homosexuality does not fit with my faith.

On one rare occasion, I even initiated the conversation . . . only because my friend hoped our Christian group would embrace his homosexuality and faith and perhaps join him in championing homosexuality as a non-sin.

Fearing he might be emotionally stir-fried in group, I offered a gentler "CliffsNotes" of the responses he might encounter.

This forced me to disclose the contents of my back pocket. To pull out, unfold, and display the wrinkles and stains on my evolving take on homosexuality and faith.

There were dozens of tangible traits I cherished about my friend, and I told him so. But—in a voice trembling with nervousness and compassion—I confessed I was afraid my friendship might seem insincere if I couldn't affirm what he held to be a central part of his identity: his sexuality.

"As far as I can tell," I gulped, "the Bible only introduces one kind of sexual union, and that is between a man and a woman. So, I have to believe this is the course that leads to the fullest life—the life the Creator intended for us."

When I spit out these defining sentences, I worried all my friend could hear was Blah-Blah-Christian-Blah-Blah.

But he stared back at me kindly, so I continued, thankful there were no microphones or flashbulbs as I struggled forward in my statement about homosexuality. "I want you to know I believe God loves every person deeply and equally. That includes the homosexual.

"It would be dishonest for me to pretend I agree with or understand the path you believe is right, but I accept that you are free to choose your own life course. That is not because I'm especially charitable or generous, but because God is."

I think the conversation changed me more than my friend, because it forced me to acknowledge parts of God's will I sometimes overlooked. To accept that God doesn't want me to do things even he does not choose to do—to control or hijack someone else's freedom.

I am not asked to impersonate the Holy Spirit but to live a life that gives off God's fluorescence. And I resolve to remember that God often allows us to learn just as much as we travel our chosen paths as we would have if we had walked only his lighted portions.

But wait, we protest, that is like saying that God allows learning even when we go the wrong way. But wait, we continue, now that we think about it, that sounds a whole lot like grace.

Sarah Raymond Cunningham
author, *Dear Church: Letters from a Disillusioned Generation*

WITHOUT CHRIST WE ARE INCAPABLE OF DEALING WITH OUR OWN SINS

Ecclesia is based in the Montrose district of Houston, which hosts one of the highest concentrations of gay people in the country. When we first bought this property as a church, I decided to walk the streets one night to better experience the dynamics of the neighborhood. As I walked closer to the place where our church was positioned, I realized there were three transvestite prostitutes working on the street corner. I decided to strike up a conversation with them, which led to me going inside and bringing them water. They were thirsty, so I gave them something to drink.

A few weeks later, our church was hosting an art festival. Two lesbians from the community attended and instantly connected with the art we were displaying. During the festival, one of the women approached me and, curious, asked, "Why all the Christian art?" I told her that I was a pastor, which immediately elicited the response—"No f—ing way." I told her about the story of Jesus, the gospel, and why I felt compelled to plant a church. She was enthralled and energized by this new view of life, all the while responding, "No f—ing way." That day, she began pursuing the journey.

I share these stories because I believe that one of the main contributing reasons that Christians have such a negative perception stems from our hyper-concern for morality. Instead of expressing what true Christianity is all about, we have put the cart before the horse and further alienate the people we should care for most.

This must change.

You can't possibly affect someone's morality without introducing them to Jesus. We must learn to tell the story of Jesus, which leads to a very different conversation, a completely different discussion.

In the conversation with my new lesbian friend, had I made morality the crux of the conversation, it would have been a much shorter one. She would have left offended and likely never begun a pursuit of Jesus.

The recent moral focus on homosexuality leads us to single out homosexuality as a "bad" sin, worse than all others. I find it ironic that so many are quick to point out the sin of homosexuality and its connection to AIDS but will gladly overlook the sin of obesity, which is directly linked to the disease of diabetes.

If we are compelled to deal with homosexuality in the way the Bible does, we must deal with it as we would any other sin. I think it has become easier to talk about homosexuality than to deal with the idea that God came for all of us since we all are sinners. We can't deal with sin apart from Christ. If people don't know Christ, they are incapable of dealing with their own sin. We at Ecclesia deal with sin when people are at a place where they are ready to follow God.

Christians need to be smart, wise, and educated. We should not be treating people differently based on their sins. Scripture is clear that no sin is greater than another. Grace is big enough for homosexuality . . . it just takes time. Redemption and sanctification don't take place overnight.

Chris Seay
pastor, Ecclesia, Houston

A HEALTHY PARTING

How Christians typically understand homosexuality is nature vs. nurture. We force ourselves to pick a side and identify the reason why someone is gay, which immediately places people into camps. This position is probably not the best place to start when engaging in a friendship with someone who is gay.

Imago Dei Church has a wide variety of people who attend who find themselves somewhere on the spectrum, struggling with homosexuality. As a church, we have to hold to what Scripture says is true about the practice of homosexuality—the acting out of same sex relationships is a sin. However, we are wondering if it is possible to experience same-sex attraction but give yourself to living a celibate lifestyle. What if we could provide intimate Christ-centered community and accountability for him or her in that pursuit? We believe that community is the answer to everyone feeling loved and human.

Recently, I spent a year with a guy who thought he was born gay. We spent time working through what I believed to be God's design for him. I believe God's design is clearly male/female union or heterosexuality, however, he concluded that God made him that way (homosexual) and wanted to embrace this lifestyle fully. Therefore, he left the church, but it was a healthy parting. I am not sure how you avoid this kind of messiness when building relationships and loving people who are struggling with sexual identification issues.

Rick McKinley
pastor, Imago Dei, Portland

A DEFINING MOMENT

I believe that almost every man who deals with homosexuality has a defining moment when he realizes that everything that is going on in his body, in his mind, and in the secret place of his heart is what is called "gay." It is an extremely frightening moment that is usually never forgotten.

I remember my moment clearly. I was sitting in my youth pastor's office in a counseling session with my father. I was fourteen years old, I had been kicked out of school, I had tried to kill myself twice, and no one knew how to help me or love me. I was acting out—I was hurting so severely. I didn't know why.

With the best of intentions, my youth pastor tried to get to the bottom of my issues. The result, instead, was that I realized I was gay, that it was something really bad, and as much as I loved church, I would never be accepted there.

In a way I was relieved, because the kids at my church called me "fag" or "queer" and rejected me, and so did the kids at my Christian school. Everywhere I went I ran into rejection . . . everywhere. Except with other gays.

I did not go back to church again. Not until about four years ago.

It took twenty years of depression, twelve years of drug addiction and dealing, and several suicide attempts to find myself searching for Jesus where I had wanted to be back when I was a teenager. There I met a compassionate God who loved me and understood me. When my search for answers was most desperate, my family, my friends, and my church were ill-equipped to handle my situation. Unfortunately, the hardest things for me to overcome were the hateful words and rejection that came from people who called themselves Christians.

Levi Walker

SEXUAL BROKENNESS

For ten years I led a New Life Counseling Clinic in Scottsdale, Arizona. I had four clients die of AIDS—all were gay. I am still saddened by their deaths because they were kind and caring people whom I got to know. They were like other people, but gay. I especially miss one young man who was full of life and talent. Of course, I disagreed with their sexual behavior, but I was also amazed and frustrated by how Christians treated these people.

I think one reason so many Christians are hostile toward gays is they have a difficult time figuring out how to view "gayness." Is it a sin, a sickness, a syndrome, or a simple choice? It reminds me of how thirty years ago society struggled with coming to terms with alcoholics. With time we came to better understand alcoholics and alcoholism. Now we need to come to terms with sexual brokenness, including homosexuality. Homosexuality is just one facet of a sexually broken society. We need to be clear that acting out on one's gayness is not acceptable, yet remain kind, compassionate, caring, and helpful with anyone struggling with their sexuality.

And I would add this caution: I have counseled many more straight Christians than homosexuals. Many believers are dealing with significant sexual issues, from marital unfaithfulness to pornographic addictions and other things you would not believe. Don't underestimate the power of sexual problems—gay or straight—to devastate even the best families and the best churches.

Rev. Alfred Ells
executive director, Leaders That Last Ministries

6

SHELTERED

Christians enjoy being in their own community. The more they seclude themselves, the less they can function in the real world. So many Christians are caught in the Christian "bubble."

Jonathan, 22

PERCEPTION **Christians are boring, unintelligent, old-fashioned, and out of touch with reality.**

NEW PERCEPTION **Christians are engaged, informed, and offer sophisticated responses to the issues people face.**

Think of America's biggest brands: Apple, McDonald's, Starbucks, Wal-Mart, Disney, Microsoft, Coke. What comes to mind when you think of the logo for each of these companies? Usually people have powerful, deep-seated reactions to these corporate entities, and these reactions differ broadly among people.

We asked outsiders to describe their images of Christianity. And although Christianity is not a brand, the reality is that people have a defined set of perceptions in their head about the Christian faith. When asked to describe what Christianity is like, outsiders offered provocative analogies:

The Titanic—a ship about to sink but unaware of its fate.

A powerful amplifier being undermined by poor wiring and weak speakers.

A pack of domesticated cats that look like they are thinking deep thoughts but are just waiting for their next meal.

An ostrich with its head in the sand.

A hobby that diverts people's attention.

These images capture an idea we repeatedly encountered in our research—Christians are sheltered. The perception that we are sheltered was expressed in diverse ways.

OUT OF TUNE

Outsiders think Christianity is out of tune with the real-world choices, challenges, and lifestyles they face. Only one-fifth of young outsiders believe that an active faith helps people live a better, more fulfilling life. Three-quarters of Mosaics and Busters outside the church said that present-day Christianity could accurately be described as old-fashioned, and seven out of ten believe the faith is out of touch with reality. Most outsiders and nearly half of young insiders say that Christianity is confusing. These perceptions are particularly distressing because Americans between the ages of eighteen and twenty-five believe their generation experiences a very different style of life than young adults did twenty years ago, and Christianity no longer seems in step with their fast-moving and ever-changing lives. A majority say they have better educational opportunities and higher paying jobs and they live in more exciting times than did people their age two decades ago, but they also admit that their generation is much more likely to have casual sex, resort to violence, and abuse drugs and alcohol than did their predecessors.[1] A reputation of being sheltered leaves Christianity coming across as antiquated.

LACKING SPIRITUAL VITALITY AND MYSTERY

Christianity is perceived as separated from real spiritual vitality and mystery. It seems like a religion of rules and standards. Surprisingly, the Christian faith today is perceived as disconnected from the supernatural world—a dimension that the vast majority of outsiders believe can be accessed and influenced. Despite outsiders' exposure *to* church, few say they have experienced God *through* church. It has no spiritual verve, they say. "Christianity is so predictable," one person we interviewed said with contempt. Two-thirds of young outsiders said the faith is boring, a description embraced by one-quarter of young churchgoers as well. The image of being sheltered means the Christian faith seems dull, flat, and lifeless.

INSULATED FROM THINKING

Many outsiders believe Christianity insulates people from thinking. Often young people (including many insiders) doubt that Christianity boosts intellect. We discovered a range of opinions on this, but Christianity is not generally perceived to sanction a thoughtful response to the world. One comment illustrates this image: "Christianity stifles curiosity. People become unwilling to face their doubts and questions. It makes people brain-dead." The vast majority of outsiders reject the idea that Christianity "makes sense" or is "relevant to their life." So part of the sheltered perception is that Christians are not thinkers.

LIVING IN THEIR OWN WORLD

Outsiders describe Christians as living in their own world. Even though outsiders generally have friends who are Christians, one of their complaints is that Christians are not speaking on the same level as everyone else. Nearly one-quarter describe Christians as using special words and phrases no one else can understand. And half of all young outsiders said that Christianity seems like a club only certain people can join. One person from Indiana described it this way: "Christians enjoy being in their own community. The more they seclude themselves, the less they can function in the real world. So many Christians are caught in the Christian 'bubble.'" Being perceived as sheltered makes Christians seem aloof and insulated.

A SURPRISING CONCLUSION

A new generation thinks of Christianity as devoid of spiritual vibrancy, parochial, small-minded, and ignorant. This "sheltered" impression of present-day Christianity is surprising for a number of reasons.

For one thing, Jesus is the legitimate path to a dynamic spiritual world that exists beyond our five senses. However, even after participating in Christian churches, this is not apparent to most young outsiders who see following Christ something like belonging to a social club that adheres to a nice set of life principles.

Another reason the sheltered image is surprising is that Christianity offers a sophisticated, livable response to the nature of the world and how we "work" as humans. As Christians, we understand that sin is everywhere and attached to everyone. We also know that humans are made in the image of God, capable of creating and doing good. Though a biblical worldview is not simplistic or always easy to understand, it enables us to make sense of creation and ourselves. Mosaics and Busters inside and outside the church have rarely been exposed to how well this worldview explains life as we know it.

Finally, a sheltered picture of Christianity is a relatively recent development in history. Yes, the church has an uneven track record of intellectual and political engagement, exposing a dark side in horrible excesses during the last two thousand years. Yet for centuries many Christians remained involved in shaping culture, not in being isolated from it. Major contributions to the fields of education, government, literature, music, art, medicine, science, and social justice have come from Christian thinkers and leaders.[2] These days young people could care less about Christianity's historical contributions and, from their perspective, they see little or no evidence of such engagement in today's world.

A faith that could be—and has been—influential is meeting only pedestrian expectations among Mosaics and Busters. How has this happened?

DISCONNECTED FROM THE "YOUNG" WORLD

If you have spent much time with people in their twenties or thirties, you know that Mosaics and Busters are the antithesis of "sheltered." This is one of the reasons Christianity, in its sheltered, clueless, nonintellectual form, makes no sense to them. Trained to believe they have control over just about everything and expecting to participate in reality, young adults don't resonate with a vision of cloistered Christianity. A faith that sidelines them is not tenable. Their existence is anything but bubble-bound.

Mosaics and Busters thrive on unexpected experiences and enjoy searching for new sources of input. Their lives consist of an eclectic patchwork of diversity, perspectives, friendships, and passions. A vast portion of their typical day is spent consuming media and exploring the burgeoning realms of the Internet. Movies, magazines, music, and television transport them into alternate realities with greater frequency and poignancy than any previous generation has experienced. They are exposed to and access more philosophies and ideas about life—and can get them at a faster pace—than any generation in history. They are a "pinch of this, pinch of that" generation, always willing to try a little of anything.

Along with their experimentalism, young people (particularly Mosaics) have grown up as one of the most "protected" generations ever, from car seats and air bags to public limits on smoking and other community safety standards. Overprotection seems to fuel their willingness to defy the "safe" life, the routine, and try something new, especially if it means they can break free from parental boundaries that may exist.

Another reason sheltered faith is unappealing is that young adults resist simplistic answers. Mosaics and Busters relish mystery, uncertainty, and ambiguity. They are not bothered by contradictions or incongruities. I was amazed in our research to see how comfortable young people are with nuance and subtlety, expressing awareness of context in complicated and intricate issues. A majority of Busters, including most born-again Christian young people, believe that the spiritual world is too complex and mysterious for humans to understand. Millions of young people admit that life itself is too complicated to really grasp. These ideas are twice as common among Mosaics and Busters as they were in their parents' generation.

Young people's perspectives about the world are not neat and tidy. They find themselves brushing aside those unwilling to explore life's intricacy and irony and idiocy, as they would say. A faith that does not effectively address convoluted and thorny issues seems out of tune with a generation asking big questions and expressing candid doubts. Spirituality that is merely focused on "dos and don'ts" rings hollow.

The diverse lifestyles and perspectives of young people mean that bubble-faith is out of kilter with their lives. Mosaics and Busters say they discuss morals as frequently as do older adults; the difference is they claim to be much less rigid about their perspectives and attitudes. Part of this is their immersion in a relativistic and ever-shifting world. Four out of five describe themselves as "adapting easily to change," a much more common self-perception than is true of Boomers. Another factor that makes them more flexible in their viewpoints is their desire for diversity. They enjoy being around people who do not share their take on life, in order to push and expand their opinions.

Young people are significantly less likely than older adults to limit their media content out of discomfort with the values or perspectives represented. Consider this fact: a majority of those ages forty-two-plus say that the content of movies and television is a major problem facing America; but that drops to just one-third of those eighteen to forty-one. Our initial research into this reality suggests a mix of two reasons: they don't care (they are not threatened by relativistic values), and they don't notice (they are not as likely to reject values that conflict with their own). For better or worse, few members of the Mosaic and Buster generations, including those within the Christian community, have the "hunker down" mentality to avoid media they deem offensive.

FRACTURED GENERATIONS

Finally, a sheltered faith seems out of touch with the intense challenges young people confront. Their world is coming unglued, and Christianity does not seem up to the challenge. Consider the world inhabited by young adults:

☐ Busters have grown up in a social setting more violent than that of their Boomer parents. Crime was three times more common in 1980 than in 1960, and violent crime was nearly four times more prevalent.[3] This violence affects the physical safety of millions of young people. In a 2005 study of high school students, one-third said they had been in a physical fight of some type in the last year.[4]

☐ Family structures have undergone dramatic change since the times when Boomers were growing up. Currently more than one-third of children born in the United States are born to unmarried mothers; in 1960 the ratio was just one out of twenty births. In some American metropolitan areas, as many as two-thirds of all infants are born to unmarried women.[5]

☐ Compared with Boomers, today's young adults are more likely to view sexually explicit magazines, movies, or websites. At least two out of every five Busters and Mosaics admit to viewing some type of pornography in a typical month. A majority of young adults say they have been exposed to Internet pornography sometime in their life.

☐ As the 1950s ended, 30 percent of young people approved of sex before marriage, compared to 75 percent now.[6] This change in attitude is reflected in their lifestyle. One-fifth of Busters and two-fifths of adult Mosaics say in the last thirty days they have had a sexual encounter with someone who is not their spouse.

☐ From the late 1960s to the late 1990s, the average age when a young woman lost her virginity had dropped from eighteen to fifteen.[7] And Busters are twice as likely as Boomers to have had multiple sex partners by age eighteen. By the time today's adults reach their midforties, women typically have had four sexual partners and men have had eight.[8]

☐ Young adults experience substance abuse more frequently than do older adults. In a typical month, about one-fifth of those ages eighteen to twenty-five have used illegal or nonprescription drugs; the same is true among roughly one-tenth of those ages twenty-six to thirty-four.[9] In the same thirty-day period, two-fifths of Mosaics and one-quarter of Busters have consumed enough alcohol to be considered drunk. Among teenagers, two out of five have consumed alcohol and one out of five have used marijuana in the past thirty days.[10]

☐ Profanity has become a natural part of conversation and self-expression of most young adults. Two-thirds of Mosaics and half of Busters say they have used expletives in public in the last month, compared with just three out of ten Boomers.

☐ Mosaics and Busters face other significant personal struggles and are aware of those challenges. One out of seven admits to dealing with an addiction. One-third describe themselves as overweight. One-sixth recognize they are already in serious debt. Almost one out of every four Busters who have been married has already experienced a divorce.

☐ Despite the centrality of relationships to this generation, nearly half of young adults say they are trying to find a few good friends. One-eighth are lonely. One-quarter feel unfulfilled in life. Nearly half say they are stressed out, which is double the proportion of Boomers.

☐ Their interpersonal skills are also unusually prickly. Mosaics and Busters are more likely than older adults to pay back someone who has offended them and to say mean things about people behind their backs.

☐ Many Mosaics and Busters live with an inner desperation that often leads to personal annihilation. Suicide is the third leading cause of death among people aged fifteen to twenty-four. In a 2005 study, one out of every six high school students had contemplated suicide during the last year, while one out of every twelve high school students said they had attempted suicide in the last year.[11]

I could go on, but the point is clear: young adults have significant needs, and they push the boundaries of conventional lifestyles.

I often encounter the argument that these are just the same struggles every generation endures and are certainly no different from those of Boomers when they were young. This line of thinking strikes me as odd. First, it is not generally supported by data. In those areas where comparable data exists, the Buster generation does seem to be more at risk than Boomers were at the same age. Second, even if the lifestyles *were* the same, this attitude seems to minimize the very real and present challenges young people face, as if young people ought to "make the best of things" because the Boomers did so.

These hurdles are not just passing fads. The activities that were on the *fringe* for Boomers now *define* the lifestyles of Busters. For instance, the 1960s may have brought the sexual revolution, but it was in many ways just the beginning of what is now part of the basic perspective of Mosaics and Busters—that sexuality can be recreational, that oral sex and other forms of sexual encounters are healthy and reasonable behaviors, and that there is no need for hiding behind formality or embarrassment when talking about sexual intimacy.

Even though the 1960s was defined by substantial social and sexual upheavals, there is no need to debate which generation has faced more problems. With an awareness gleaned from our extensive research, I urge you not to miss some of the fundamental changes that are significantly influencing younger adults today.

Busters and Mosaics need help.

ENGAGING PEOPLE

It would be easy to be discouraged about these facts and the lives of people they reflect. In the face of such pressing needs, how should Christians respond? Should we denounce the "moral compromises" of young people and shut them out of our lives?

Perhaps the challenges that were listed have made you reflect on your own life and you have realized, as I have, that a list like the one above does not just refer to "other people." As human beings, our lives are a mixture of surpassing highs and crushing lows. There is a very personal side to all such statistics, some of which we will see later in this chapter.

I think the research regarding Buster and Mosaic lifestyles should give us hope. There are remarkable opportunities for God to exert himself. He works best when people's lives are messy and out of whack. Yes, Mosaics and Busters face significant challenges, which cannot be minimized, but God has no use for people who (think they) have it all together. My prayer for my generation (Busters) and for Mosaics is that our desperate condition will provide us with clear pathways to God and to restoration through Christ. What a privilege it would be to see God working in the lives of Busters and Mosaics, transforming them in the midst of daunting circumstances!

As Christ followers, will we get excited about what God can do or will we turn to the unChristian response and shelter ourselves from a culture that offends us?

One thing that prevents us from engaging the world is the fact that our connection with outsiders dissipates as we enter the Christian enclave. In our interviews, a twenty-eight-year-old Christian described this lifestyle: "So many Christians are caught up in the Christian sub-culture and are completely closed off from the world. We go to church on Wednesdays, Sundays, and sometimes on Saturdays. We attend small group on Tuesday night and serve on the Sunday school advisory board, the financial committee, and the welcoming committee. We go to bar-beques with our Christian friends and plan group outings. We are closed off from the world. Even if we wanted to reach out to nonChristians, we don't have time and we don't know how. The only way we know how to reach out is to invite people to join in our Christian social circle."

Christians look inward for many reasons, some of which are en-tirely reasonable, even biblical! Balance is essential to a believer's life. For instance, pulling away from the distractions of life to recharge and refocus on God is entirely necessary. Some of Christians' most intimate and richest relationships come within the context of the Christian com-munity. Limiting children's exposure to media in age-appropriate ways that protect their young hearts and minds is a vital role of every parent. Avoiding a television program or movie because the content could ac-tivate your struggle with sin—sexual fantasies, profanity, materialism, anger, and so on—is a healthy and reasonable kind of sheltering. God wants us to be holy, which means to be set apart (1 Peter 1:15), and Scripture says we should think about things that are pure, lovely, and admirable (Phil. 4:8). Often Christians make God-honoring choices to reflect these goals.

The problem, however, is that our choices to live a sheltered life often leave us unable or unwilling to help people who need Jesus. Yet the Bible instructs mature, thoughtful believers to influence people and places around them—while maintaining their personal integrity and purity.

ACCEPTING RESPONSIBILITY

We are responsible to engage the world. Jesus uses many metaphors for this. We are the light of the world (that is, we offer guidance that points people to restoration); we are the salt of the earth (we help preserve people); and we are a city on a hill (we offer protection and hope for people) (see Matt. 5:13–16). Yet calling ourselves Christians does not mean that guiding, preserving, or protecting are easy and automatic. It's our duty to help remedy a broken world, but this takes effort. Our responsibility is to embrace this task with humility and energy, without expecting the world to come to our doorstep.

NOT BEING FEARFUL

Many Christians shelter themselves out of fear, trying to barricade themselves against any and every threat. But the Bible says we should not be driven by alarm, because perfect love dispels fear (1 John 4:18). We should be motivated by love and confidence (2 Tim. 1:7 KJV). Also, Scripture reminds us that nothing can separate us from the love of Christ, so whatever could cause trepidation represents no real peril to us (Rom. 8:38–39). We need to think about and disavow the fears that keep us sheltered from the world.

NOT BEING OFFENDED

Being offended is also the wrong response to the challenges of a new generation. Can you think of one time when Jesus was offended by people, especially by outsiders? It is not recorded in Scripture, except when he blasted self-righteous religious leaders and those who were desecrating the temple. In fact, he told his disciples to expect trouble. So if we are persecuted for our faith, we should not be surprised or offended (John 16:33). If we allow the actions and attitudes of outsiders to shock us, we become either isolationists or crusaders, and neither extreme will have much influence on outsiders.

And how can we be offended when outsiders are living out their true nature? Would we be that different if it were not for God's grace? When Paul visited the godless inhabitants of Athens (an episode described in Acts 17), rather than shock and rebuke, he creatively captured the Athenians' imagination, pointing them to Jesus. We too can learn how to engage outsiders in creative ways. Rather than allowing the sin we see in the world to make us withdraw, we can allow it to arouse our compassion and inspire us to make a difference.

HELPING THE DESPERATE

We have a responsibility to help people in desperate situations. At the end of his life, Jesus gave the first Christians instructions to go every-where—to the ends of the earth—with the life-changing message (Matt. 28:19–20; Mark 16:15; Acts 1:8). This instruction does not refer merely to geographical locations but also compels us to reach people we might otherwise consider unworthy. Jesus said he did not come for the healthy but the sick, not to help the righteous but sinners (Matt. 9:12–13; see Acts 10:30–48). God wants to use us in the gritty and raw places of people's lives, but our usefulness is hindered if we are more concerned about our protection *from* sin than the effects *of* sin in the lives of others.

BEING PREPARED

The lion's den made Daniel famous, but it wasn't just his being in the right place at the right time that determined his place in history. He was prepared. As a young man, Daniel had significant characteristics and readiness that enabled his rise to prominence. He was "showing aptitude for every kind of learning, well informed, quick to understand, and qualified to serve in the king's palace" (Dan. 1:4 NIV). He grew up in a Babylonian kingdom that was rebellious to God and self-indulgent (sound like America today?). But Daniel didn't hole up in his spirituality. He learned what lessons he could from an impure society, and through his abilities and his faithfulness to God, he became influential, eventu-ally administrating much of the Babylonian empire. When Christians shelter themselves, letting "someone else" answer the world's doubts and address its problems, they abdicate their biblical role to be spiritual influencers. It is incumbent on us to develop our hearts and minds so that we can fulfill our destiny as agents of spiritual, moral, and cultural transformation.

KEEPING A BALANCE

Christ calls his followers to be active missionaries to the culture. This culture is offensive, but we cannot take offense. It is increasingly hostile to Christians and to whom we claim to represent, but we cannot respond with anger when people express their skepticism, and we are not meant to be isolationists. Jesus described our role most succinctly: we are to be *in* but not *of* the world (see John 17:14–18).

There is one more important balance I have to mention. If it is possible to be overly sheltered, to hide in the Christian bubble, we can also undermine our influence when we do the opposite and try to fit into the world. Mike Metzger, an author and the founder of the Clapham Institute, describes this delicate balance:

> Being salt and light demands two things: we practice purity in the midst of a fallen world and yet we live in proximity to this fallen world. If you don't hold up both truths in tension, you invariably become useless and separated from the world God loves. For example, if you only practice purity apart from proximity to the culture, you inevitably become pietistic, separatist, and conceited. If you live in close proximity to the culture without also living in a holy manner, you become indistinguishable from fallen culture and useless in God's kingdom.[12]

As Christians, we should pursue both goals: purity and proximity—living in a way that honors God, but doing so in a way that can influence outsiders. What you do and what you learn should provide a lens to understand, interpret, and respond to a morally bankrupt culture. Mosaics and Busters need your compassion and attention. How does this affect the types of books you read or the movies you see? What types of friendships do you maintain as a result of this mindset? How do you cultivate your intellect and communication abilities? What career do you pursue? Where do you choose to live—what city, what country? What education should you pursue? How do you cultivate and protect your character? What risks do you take? How do you respond when an outsider does something that grates against your Christian sensibilities?

Your answers determine your purity and your proximity to the world—and ultimately your ability to have an influence on it. As a parent or a pastor, you should be addressing these crucial issues with the people in your charge.

ENGAGING THE WORLD

In thinking through how God wants to use his people, consider one of the most fascinating phenomena of our society: America is fragmenting into diverse subcultures. The "mainstream" experience, if there ever was such a thing, has now surrendered virtually all its gravitational pull. These days most Americans take their cues from a unique subculture, deriving meaning, values, heroes, self-expression, identity, and viewpoints from a unique segment of society. When people say that America is a mission field, it would be more accurate to say it is *many* diverse mission fields. And this phenomenon is particularly true among young people. The world of Mosaics and Busters is splintering into more subcultures than ever before.

My father, a lifelong pastor, asked about the changing dynamics of this world. "David, aren't relationships still possible with young people? I mean, can't we make friends with the young people you researched? Won't that influence them spiritually?"

"Well, yes, relationships are central to influencing Busters and Mosaics," I explained, "but it's not as simple as you think. You don't just 'make friends' with young people, and, bingo, they trust you. You'd have to make a commitment to being a part of their lives, to understanding what makes them tick and how they think," I continued.

"It really would be like quitting your job and going overseas to serve as a missionary. You truly immerse yourself in the lifestyles, decisions, relationships, and choices of a completely unique group of people. After the culture shock sets in, you have to be accepted into their 'tribe.' And it is a complex, strange world where even the best intentions may not be enough."[13]

The conclusion I hope you draw is that a fragmented world requires diverse means of engagement. God has given each of us a role in bringing Jesus to the people and places around us. Christianity begins to shift its sheltered reputation when Christ followers are engaged, informed, and on the leading edge, offering a sophisticated response to the issues people face.

In the last part of this chapter, let me describe people at two ends of the continuum who require our engagement: intellectual elites and the overlooked individuals in our society. What I am about to describe are a *few* examples of some of the various subcultures and the ways in which some young Christians are addressing these opportunities for engagement.

INTELLECTUALS

This may not surprise you, but the perception that Christians are sheltered is most significant among the subculture of intellectuals and influentials. Our research shows that upscale outsiders—those with advanced educational and financial profiles—are much more likely than average to express resistance and skepticism toward Christianity.[14] The sheltered perception—that Christians are ignorant and uninformed—is most common among young intellectuals. They were more likely than average to describe Christianity as judgmental, old-fashioned, out of touch with reality, and insensitive to others. In addition, they are also less likely to believe that Christianity is friendly, consistently shows love for others, offers hope for the future, is relevant to their life, and is trustworthy. In other multigenerational research our firm has conducted, we have arrived at the same conclusion: upscale outsiders, regardless of their age, maintain the most negative views of the Christian faith.

In our society, upscale adults are most likely to serve as leaders within the fields of business, politics, education, the arts, entertainment, science, and media. Christians who work in these arenas, or hope to, often have to labor against a stereotype that Christians are ignorant and sheltered. When they are introduced as a Christian, they face a credibility gap within their field of work.

As I have pointed out in other parts of this book, it's not just outsiders who feel this way about Christians. Many young insiders are also trying to deal with the out-of-touch perspectives in the Christian community. One of our interviews was with Ann, a thirty-year-old living in California. She began a career working for a prominent campus ministry, but after getting divorced, having her Christian friends "terminate contact," and entering a new career, she is particularly frustrated with the sheltered mindset.

"In my career choice—I work in geology and environmental research—I have been criticized repeatedly by Christians for choosing to go into a secular career rather than Christian ministry. I feel that I am, in fact, serving God by working to preserve his creation and take care of it. Instead, I've had conservative Christians criticize me for being involved in geology because it has incendiary connections to 'old earth' and 'evolutionist' views. I can't even count the times I've been harshly judged by Christians because I chose this job."

Ann is an example of a new (and yet not so new) impulse within America's Christian community. Instead of being separated *from* the channels of influence, many Christians are taking steps to be involved in these arenas. They realize that a sheltered faith has left intellectuals and culture shapers with no frame of reference about what a godly, respect-ful, and highly proficient Christian looks like. These Christians want to engage skeptical leaders within the channels of influence. Like the prophet Daniel, they want to be prepared. At Barna we expect to study these leaders more in the future, but here are some of the initial insights into their lives and perspectives that we have gained:

☐ These young Christian leaders realize that they must display ex-cellence at their craft. Their credibility as Christians depends on their ability to do a great job.

☐ One common element of this mindset is the pursuit of a first-class education (see Michael Lindsay's contribution at the end of this chapter). Also, many young Christian leaders find significant mentoring relationships and other forms of personal development. Our research leads us to conclude that their success is less about following a formula of education and career advancement and more about their hard work, appropriate mindset, and desire to continually grow.

☐ These young leaders define faith as their driving passion in life. And often this means they are confident enough in their faith that they do not have to keep restating this allegiance in robotic clichés. Sometimes they realize that because the people in their office or workplace have deep-seated defenses against Christians, these young leaders let their actions, not their association to the unChris-tian label, speak to their colleagues. And yet these young believers who are cracking the ranks of some of the highest positions of authority are careful to maintain a clear sense of their convictions. They are not hypersensitive and they are not compromising.

☐ The young leaders we have studied have a healthy respect for their peers and the differences of opinion and lifestyle these people represent. These young leaders relish the chance to break, with creativity and sensitivity, the unChristian stereotypes their peers hold.

☐ The motivation of these young leaders is to redeem rather than condemn the arenas in which they work. They realize it's easy to be a critic but far more productive to offer meaningful ways to improve the business or institution. In today's businesses and culture-shaping institutions, successful initiatives generate attention and further opportunities.

THE OVERLOOKED

On the other side of the spectrum from intellectuals and influentials are those individuals whom society overlooks. We have found remarkable stories of Christ followers pursuing people whom God loves, despite their status. These are important examples of Christians shedding their sheltered status.

LONERS

Individuals who are relationally or emotionally isolated—some might call them outcasts or loners—have difficulty fitting in, even within the Christian community. Their spiritual and relational needs are significant and often they are open to help, but they are not always easy to love, sometimes having personal needs or habits or appearances that give them a "reputation." Despite the clear teaching in Scripture that admonishes us to love this type of individual, several research studies we have conducted show that churches struggle to connect with loners in meaningful ways.

Stephen, a seventeen-year-old from New Hampshire, offered this gut-wrenching description of his life in one of our surveys: "What is God? Simply put, God is a figment of our minds grasping the sad fact that we have nothing else to believe in. I live alone. I am alone. I will always be alone. So why should I lie to myself about a God that lets me live a life where the only people I care for treat me like s——? I want to die every day; that is my one wish. I pray to God for that, sure, but it's only because

I need something. Every day I have to go through realizing that my life amounts to nothing. I quit."

Does this tear you up? Do his thoughts about God offend you, or do you see them for what they are: an expression of his deep hurt? What would it take to help him, to keep him from suicide, to really see and develop his potential to be a Christ follower? It would take more than a few nice conversations. It would take sincere, deep engagement over many months to deal with his depression and anguish.

SELF-INJURERS

Although the causes are complicated, one of the expressions of loneliness can be self-injury, which is defined as causing intentional physical harm to one's own body.

Consider Jamie Tworkowski—a Christ follower engaging the needs of self-injurers. On his website he describes his introduction to Renee, a nineteen-year-old woman whose deep need opened his heart to outsiders. "She takes a razor blade from the table and locks herself in the bathroom. She cuts herself, using the blade to write 'f—— up' in large letters across her left forearm. The nurse at the treatment center finds the wound several hours later. The center has no detox, names her too great a risk, and does not accept her. For the next five days, she is ours to love. We become her hospital, and the possibility of healing fills our living room with life. It is unspoken and there are only a few of us, but we will be her church, the body of Christ coming alive to meet her needs, to write love on her arms."

Renee was Jamie's doorway to seeing the needs of "cutters" and self-injurers. Now his ministry is called TWLOHA (to write love on her arms), and it raises awareness of the problem and connects sufferers to qualified treatment.[15]

Jamie writes about helping Renee finally check into a rehab center that can help: "She hands me her last razor blade, tells me it is the one she used to cut her arm and to prepare her last lines of cocaine. It hits me to wonder if this great feeling is what Christ knows when we surrender our broken hearts, when we trade death for life. We are only asked to love, to offer hope to the many hopeless. We don't get to choose all the endings, but we are asked to play the rescuers. We won't solve all mysteries, and our hearts will certainly break in such a vulnerable life, but it is the best way. We were made to be lovers, bold in broken places, pouring ourselves out again and again until we're called home."

FATHERLESS

Considering the statistics I gave earlier, it is no exaggeration to say that Busters and Mosaics are fatherless generations. When Christians talk about a heavenly Father who loves us and provides for us, it is a foreign concept to many, if not most, Mosaics and Busters. If you have not grown up without a father, it is hard to imagine the experiences of these individuals. Our research consistently underscores this reality: efforts to connect people to God are frequently undermined by the lasting negative influences of absent, abusive, or negligent parents.

My friends Jennifer and Dano offer a glimpse of redemption to the residents of their tough Seattle community. After earning the respect of the neighbors and young people, they started hosting a barbeque every week for youth, opening their home and lives to disconnected people. It has not always been easy. Jennifer has had her wallet stolen, and Dano has had to call the police when gang or racial tension has skidded out of control on their property. But they have discovered remarkable things in their faithfulness. Jenn emailed some of her insights: "I have learned kids want consistency. They are lonely and they don't trust you, especially if you are white and they are not. Dano and I feel a huge responsibility for how the kids see us interacting with each other and with our daughter. Many don't have parents who engage emotionally or with appropriate physical contact, so to see us showing love to each other, to see us disciplining our daughter and respecting her is new for many.

"I also know my daughter is learning a lot about treating all people with respect, whether they are homeless or a CEO. Fear among Christians causes us to miss many to whom Jesus ministered.

"I never thought we would live here five years, but now I could see us living here much longer. When you stay in a place, you build trust with others. And when you befriend those who differ from you, not only racially and ethnically, but socioeconomically, you become humbled and your stereotypes are broken. And in our case, we have been able to see God revealing himself to those who are not well-educated or well-off, and it has revived our faith."

DOING SOMETHING

There are other subcultures and challenges facing Mosaics and Busters. If we are going to engage this generation, we have to put aside sheltered lifestyles and perspectives and help them deal with life as it is. Without relenting our passion for purity and integrity, we have to come out of our cocoon and respond to the needs and confessions of a generation that needs our help.

Or maybe you can just cook like my friend Lauren.

She lives in Colorado Springs and works for a Christian organization. On the telephone last week, the twenty-four-year-old described how the Christian bubble—her friends, her work, her church—was swallowing her. So several nights a week, she clocks in to sell furniture and candles for a local import retailer. "At first, when I told my co-workers about my faith, people didn't know what to make of me. But now I think they trust me. They know I respect them, but we often have some lively discussions. It has been great to expand my thinking, and hopefully I am pushing theirs. Many of them come to my house every week for a meal."

"What?"

"Well, I like to cook," Lauren said, "and everyone at the store knows they are invited to my house. And a lot of them show up."

"You must make great food."

"It's not bad. But you know the best part? Most of the time my Buddhist friend from the store comes, and he gets to hang out with my Christian friend. I just think that's cool."

It is, because none of us as Christ followers—not Jamie, Jenn, or Lauren—are expected to disengage from generations that need Jesus. Maybe you're not a gourmet chef, but what could you do to shed a sheltered faith?

CHANGING THE PERCEPTIONS

TALK TO PEOPLE

Some days I feel as hip and trendy as a yellow banana hairclip. Living in Alaska doesn't help—the sense of distance can easily translate into disconnect—but following Jesus requires an awareness of not only our surroundings but also our world. So how do you stay connected when you're literally living a thousand-plus miles away?

Relationship. Talk to people. Anyone. Everyone. Ask questions. Lots. Listen closely to the answers. Open up your life to strangers, visitors, and friends of friends. Turn on the television; surf the Web. You don't need to become a full-blown couch potato or mouse potato to be aware. Oh yeah, and buy a subscription to the *New Yorker*.

Then wake up to the cold reality that you're part of the plan. You have a role in this generation, not only receiving the baton of faith but passing it on to the next generation. You have a role in preserving the earth, protecting the poor, defending the exploited. We need you. In particular, we need you to be aware, learn, grow—spiritually, relationally, culturally—because we can't do it without you.

Margaret Feinberg
author and speaker

DO SOMETHING

Eight out of ten students participate in church during their teenage years, but most of them will take a permanent detour from active faith at some point soon after they get their driver's licenses. That's right: only two out of ten of those celebrated teenage converts maintain Christian belief and practice between their teens and the end of their twenties.

The vast majority will cross over to the other side: pronouncing Christianity boring, irrelevant, and out of touch.

We've tried too long to educate their minds instead of engaging their lives. The more we try to change the way we do church so this generation will join us, the more they seem to stay away.

Although we've tried many ways to keep church from being boring, our best efforts are doing little to improve the image of the church.

Some of us are convinced the system is fundamentally flawed because we don't know what our goal is. We creatively market our programs, design innovative and relevant productions, and organize events that will capture the student imagination so we can get them into church. What if our goal should not be to get them *into* church? What if the same energy could be applied to mobilize them to *be* the church?

We have discovered a short window of time during the teenage years when students need to experience something beyond church as a spectator sport. If a young person is not challenged by hands-on personal ministry, their faith will likely be sidetracked and even sabotaged. For some, that hands-on experience is a mission project across the ocean. For others, it's a role in a family production or a place behind the ladle at a soup kitchen.

Students moving from the teenage years to their own college and post-college lives want to try out what they've been learning. They don't want to practice being better church people for when they grow up; they want to start now. We all know that our faith grows when our faith is challenged to *do* something.

Reggie Joiner
founder, ReThink

MERGING FAITH AND ACTION

I am hopeful about the future of Christian engagement because I think Christians are merging faith and action more than ever. I've been reading a book called *What Have You Done for Me Lately?* that documents the history of Christian contribution to culture. Anyone who is a serious student of history would have to say that Christianity and its underpinnings have been, in most cases, the fuel in the engine of social revolution.

Even though Christians have historically been at the forefront of these kinds of movements, I believe in these days it is being embraced as much as ever—it's all about faith plus works. You will show me your faith by your works . . . it is the merging of these two things together that brings amazing power.

Our organization, Passion, recently hosted a global gathering in Atlanta of over 23,000 college students who consider themselves Christians. Instead of the typical Christian conference with a consumerist appetite for great speakers and music, we made the centerpiece of these four days the "Do Something Now!" campaign. We put eight global opportunities on the table and said to students, "We think you have the money in your pockets to change the world."

And sure enough, they responded.

Those poor college students pledged or gave over one million dollars to build fifty-two wells in Africa, to provide New Testament translations for six people groups of Indonesia, and to combat the human sex trafficking industry.

It is clear to me that something significant has absolutely shifted with this generation. I think it is God's great kindness stirring our hearts to show his great kindness to the world. With this behind us, the students at Passion aren't the ones who look good, and this generation doesn't look like a hands-on, get-involved, do-something generation. God looks good. And God looks like a hands-on, get-involved, do-something God. I think that is what this generation wants—an action-based worship. There is nothing wrong with jumping to a David Crowder tune and telling God he is great—that is worship. But worship is also doing the right thing and sharing with others in need. Those are the things that make God happy, and this is a generation that wants to make God happy. They demonstrate this by moving in action to touch the last and least of these in the world.

Louie Giglio
founder, Passion

REDISCOVERING THE KINGDOM

It really bothers me that Christians are perceived as boring. Other perceptions may pass, but the idea that Christianity is boring will not, unless we work hard to recover the true robust nature of the gospel. We have succeeded in making Christianity tepid. We are lukewarm, and God says that he will spit us out. Current forms of Christian practice have become a poor substitute for the real thing. That is why this perception exists.

The excitement of Christianity won't come back because of "happy music"; it will come back when we begin to understand the vibrance and vitality of the biblical story of what the kingdom of God is all about. The kingdom is about helping the suffering and the poor. This is Jesus's message in Luke 4:18, where he picks up the Scripture and goes into the temple and reads about setting the prisoners free. At the time, this was an incredible message for which people tried to kill him.

Christianity is the most exciting story ever told. It needs to be told, not the way we typically dumb it down, but the way it is.

Unfortunately, I believe young people have a legitimate gripe when they say it is boring—that's the watered-down version of Christianity that they have experienced. This is something we must overcome.

Chuck Colson
founder, Prison Fellowship Ministries

BUILDING A COFFEEHOUSE INSTEAD OF A CHURCH

I went into church planting with the traditional mindset: meet in rented facilities until you can buy or build a church building. Then God strategically positioned National Community Church in the middle of the marketplace. NCC started meeting in the movie theaters at Union Station. Not only is Union Station the most visited destination in the nation's capital—approximately twenty-five million people pass through the Station every year—it also has 125 retail shops, a food court, a train station, a metro stop, and a movie theater.

In our early days, well-meaning pastor friends would ask me when NCC was going to get a "church," as if a church without a church building isn't a legitimate church. Part of me wanted to say, "Have you seen our church?" After all, not too many churches have their own subway system or food court. Why build a church building when you can meet in Union Station?

As NCC began to reach unchurched and dechurched twenty-somethings in DC, there was a moment when I realized that even if we could buy or build a church building, there was no way we could vacate such a strategic spiritual beachhead. And doing church in the middle of the marketplace became part of our spiritual DNA. Our vision is to meet in movie theaters at metro stops throughout the DC area. NCC also owns and operates the largest coffeehouse on Capitol Hill. Ebenezers opened for business on National Coffee Day—March 15, 2006. In 2007, it was voted the #2 coffeehouse in the metro DC area by *AOL CityGuide.*

So why did we build a coffeehouse instead of a church building? Because Jesus didn't hang out in synagogues. He hung out at wells. Wells weren't just places to draw water. Wells were natural gathering places in ancient culture. Coffeehouses are postmodern wells. To borrow the sociological term, our coffeehouse is a *third place* where the church and community can cross paths.

Along with serving coffee day in and day out, the performance space at Ebenezers doubles as a sanctuary for two Saturday night services. And most of the attendees are neighbors and customers.

Too many churches expect unchurched people to come to them, but the church is called to go to unchurched people. The church is called to compete for the kingdom in the middle of the marketplace.

Mark Batterson
pastor, National Community Church

A HEART OF COMPASSION

I grew up in a nice suburb of Sacramento, California, that was utterly sheltered from much of the pain and brutality of the world. My heart goes out to Christians who are sheltered in a bubble of unreality because I lived there too, and occasionally, I run back to that bubble. But what I have found is that the true power and joy and goodness and truth of God is not found in the bubble.

When outsiders consider Christians to be "sheltered," they are basically saying that Christians are not living in the real world.

The next generation struggles with Christians who talk about the problems facing the world but don't do anything to stop them. If we were authentic, we would actually take our faith into the hard places of the world rather than try to build a safe shelter away from them.

A heart and compassion to get involved in the tough places of the world is not natural or easy. In my life there were incremental events that helped me develop a heart of compassion. Friends showed me what life was like for the homeless and hosted me in South Africa to show me what apartheid was like in the mideighties. Looking back, I realize that these steps were leading up to a bigger moment. I was working for the United States Department of Justice in 1994 and was commissioned to go to Africa to be the director of the Rwanda Genocide Investigation. It was a huge event in my life to be put face-to-face with the true carnage of genocide, the ultimate aggressive evil that tries to decimate a whole people. Without the incremental preparation of my heart, I could not have engaged this kind of suffering—it was a process.

It starts by setting an intention with a compassionate heart that is willing to stand with people who are hurting. The word *compassion* comes from two Latin words, *cum* and *passio*. *Cum* is defined as "with" and *passio* means "to suffer." Thus, *compassion* means "to suffer with." It says in the Bible that when we follow Christ, there will be suffering because we live in a fallen world. As we go forth, tell the truth, and help people in need, we are going to experience a level of suffering . . . and this is where God is found.

I think that is what the world is looking for in Christians. I think outsiders find it inexplicable when they see Christians with the kind of courage to step into places of real brutality and ugliness because fear is so real. Consider Jesus's example. He was not afraid to come to an earth that was full of violence. He left a heavenly place and came to the dirt of earth to experience life with common, average, and hurting people.

So for me, that is what life has been. It has been this incremental journey to get out of the shelter where God couldn't be experienced because he was not needed, and to go to where people are in need and express the tangible love of God.

Take the first step: who in your family, your neighborhood, or your school is hurting? Stand with them and then expand the circle of your compassion to your city, the nation, and then the world. I believe God pours out unbelievable joy and passion on us and those we are standing with as we get closer to the situations outside of the shelter.

Gary Haugen
founder, International Justice Mission

CHRISTIANS AT THE TOP OF THE CLASS

Most Americans assume that smart people are rarely devout and that devout Christians rarely scale the academic heights. While there certainly are reasons for this perception, we have to remember that throughout church history, learning and piety have been closely wedded. Practically every university in the Ivy League was founded to serve the church, and for most of their history, these institutions have been places where faith and knowledge support one another. In truth, Christian anti-intellectualism was an anomaly of the twentieth century. For the majority of the time, it has not been a part of the church's past, and developments today suggest it will not be a part of the church's future.

The Reverend Peter Gomes—who has taught at Harvard for the last forty years—says, "There are probably more evangelicals [on Harvard's campus today] than at any time since the seventeenth century." Indeed, Christian groups are thriving on college campuses around the country, including those at some of the country's top schools. At Princeton alone, close to 10 percent of the student body is regularly involved in one or more of the Christian groups on campus. And the number of students involved with the Harvard chapter of Campus

Crusade for Christ has increased fivefold over the last two decades. Similar developments can be seen at Stanford, Duke, and Yale.

Student enrollment at Christian colleges and universities has grown 60 percent since 1990, while the general college student population has barely changed. The percentage of evangelicals earning at least a college degree has increased by 133 percent, which is much more than any other religious tradition. Indeed, the rise of evangelicals on America's elite campuses is one of the most notable developments in higher education over the last thirty years. As highly selective universities have sought to diversify their student bodies by race, gender, and ethnicity, they have also unintentionally diversified their campuses' religious makeup. As Gomes said, "A lot of Midwestern white-bread Protestant Christian evangelicals at whom Harvard would never have looked in the past, and who would have never looked at Harvard, suddenly became members of the university."

It is not merely students who are bringing their faith to bear on the life of the mind. A growing number of devout professors have been recognized for their academic excellence. Outspoken Christians are tenured faculty members at places like Berkeley, Virginia, Emory, and Dartmouth. Harvard Divinity School now has an endowed profes-sorship in evangelical theological studies. It is funded by the family of Alonzo McDonald, a senior White House staffer under President Carter and the former worldwide managing partner for McKinsey & Company. In many ways, McDonald embodies this upsurge of smart Christianity. A Harvard alumnus himself, McDonald has sponsored several initiatives surrounding the life of the mind, including programs at Emory.

A growing number of graduate students are also engaging their faith in various ways. The Harvey Fellows Program, sponsored by Den-nis and Eileen Bakke, provides significant financial support for gradu-ate students enrolled in top academic programs like Yale Law School, Harvard Business School, and PhD programs around the country. Modeled in part on the White House Fellows Program, the program has supported approximately 250 fellows worldwide in everything from the arts, humanities, and social sciences to law, medicine, business, science, and engineering. Each summer, new fellows participate in a weeklong seminar. From being hosted at the Supreme Court by an associate justice to interacting with the Librarian of Congress, Harvey Fellows are offered educational experiences that rival those held for Rhodes, Marshall, and Gates scholars. Applicants have to sign a statement of faith and discuss the relevance of their spiritual lives for their chosen vocations. They also must demonstrate the top ranking of their academic department, which ensures that only very talented students are selected. Initiatives like these have contributed to what others have called "an expanding beachhead" for people of faith at America's most selective universities.

Throughout history, the church, in both Roman Catholic and Protestant traditions, has supported a range of intellectual activity, from the scientific research of Newton to the literary contributions of Chesterton. Developments in recent years have enabled a growing number of faithful Christ followers to shed the cultural insularity of Christianity's recent past. If events of the last few years continue, outspoken Christians will come to occupy even more important roles within the intellectual mainstream. Indeed, they are already well on their way.

D. Michael Lindsay
professor of sociology, Rice University

A CALL TO RADICAL DISCIPLESHIP

If we belong to Jesus Christ, we have a double calling in relation to the world. On the one hand, we are to live, serve, and witness in the world and not try to escape from it. On the other hand, we are to avoid being contaminated by the world.

So we have no liberty either to preserve our holiness by escaping from the world or to sacrifice our holiness by conforming to the world.

Escapism and conformism are both forbidden to us. This is one of the major themes of the whole Bible, namely that God is calling out a people for himself and is summoning us to be different from everybody else. "Be holy," he says to us, "because I am holy."

This foundational theme recurs in all four main sections of Scripture—the law, the prophets, the teaching of Jesus, and the teaching of the apostles. Let me give you an example from each. Take the law. God said to the people through Moses: "You must not do as they do in the land of Egypt where you used to live, nor as they do in the land of Canaan to which I am bringing you. Do not follow their practices. You must obey my laws and be careful to follow my decrees. I am the Lord your God" (Lev. 18:3–4). Similarly God complains through Ezekiel, "You have not followed my decrees, but have conformed to the standards of the nations around you" (Ezek. 11:12).

It is similar in the New Testament. In the Sermon on the Mount, Jesus spoke of the hypocrites and the pagans and added: "Do not be like them" (Matt. 6:8). Finally, the apostle Paul could write to the Romans: "Do not conform any longer to the pattern of this world, but be transformed" (Rom. 12:2).

Here then is God's call to a radical discipleship, to a radical nonconformism to the surrounding culture. It is a call to develop a Christian counterculture.

The followers of Jesus, for example, are not to give in to pluralism, which denies the uniqueness and lordship of Jesus, nor be sucked into materialism or become led astray into ethical relativism, which says there are no moral absolutes.

This is God's call to his people to be different. We are not to be like reeds shaken by the wind, as Jesus said, but to be like rocks in a mountain stream; not to be like fish floating with the stream, but to swim against the stream—even the cultural mainstream.

We are faced, in fact, with two cultures, two value systems, two standards, and two lifestyles. Which shall we choose? If we are not to be like chameleons, changing color to suit our surroundings, what are we to be like?

The answer is that we are to be like Christ. The eternal and ultimate purpose of God by his Spirit is to make us like Christ.

John Stott
rector emeritus, All Souls Church, London

7

TOO POLITICAL

Twenty years ago, when I was looking at evangelical Christianity from the inside, it seemed like a movement bursting with energy to spread good news to people. Looking at it from the outside today, this message seems to have been lost in exchange for an aggressive political strategy that demonizes segments of society.

Brandon, 32

PERCEPTION **Christians are primarily motivated by a political agenda and promote right-wing politics.**

NEW PERCEPTION **Christians are characterized by respecting people, thinking biblically, and finding solutions to complex issues.**

Have you ever played the word-association game?

Just to refresh your memory, it works like this: someone mentions a word or phrase, and you must name the first thing or person that comes to mind. For instance, if you hear the phrase *Chicago Bulls*, whom or what do you think of? What about *Scientology*? *Islam*?

Now, consider Christianity. In our survey, we asked young people to identify the best-known Christians, encouraging respondents to mention anyone who came to mind. Among sixteen- to twenty-nine-year-olds outside of Christianity, the top five leader associations included the Pope (mentioned by 16 percent of young outsiders), George W. Bush (13 percent), Jesus (9 percent), Billy Graham (7 percent), and Martin Luther King Jr. (6 percent).

Among young churchgoers, the top three included Mr. Graham (29 percent), followed by the Pope (17 percent) and the president (17 percent). Young Christians also mentioned Martin Luther King Jr. (8 percent), Jesus (7 percent), Mother Teresa (7 percent), Mel Gibson (7 percent), and James Dobson (5 percent). There were smaller levels of awareness for other Christian leaders.

What is your impression of these findings? It is ironic, of course, that Jesus is not at the top of these lists of "famous Christians." Given the fact that the survey was focused on "present-day Christianity," perhaps young people did not think to mention the original.

Still, did you notice that George W. Bush is more likely to be thought of as a Christian leader than are clergy or other influential Christians? In another portion of our research, we found that half of young outsiders said they could think of specific Christian leaders in politics, which means outsiders recognize Christians in politics more readily than in any other sector, including music, movies, sports, or business. Even young churchgoers are more likely to recognize famous Christians involved in politics than other arenas, except music.

In some ways, it is not surprising that politicians are so frequently linked to beliefs and to faith. Christians have made a concerted and coordinated effort to engage the political process in recent decades, so their activity in the political realm can be hard to miss. This profile is intensified in part because the faith of candidates becomes a news item during campaigns. Since political decisions affect every citizen's life, the connection between politics and faith—as well as the link between people's perceptions of the political environment and their views of Christians—is inescapable.

And so for these reasons and others I will discuss in this chapter, Christians are now perceived among Mosaics and Busters as too involved in politics. To be more precise, they think of us as motivated primarily by political goals and as promoting a right-wing agenda.

The fact that there is consternation among young people about the role of religion in politics probably does not surprise you. The important questions are why young outsiders believe Christians are motivated by a political agenda, whether any of the concerns are legitimate, and what should be done, if anything at all, about the perception.

A COMPLETE PICTURE

Let me provide a more complete description of how outsiders feel about Christians. But first you should realize that my goal is not to suggest that Christians should neglect or ignore politics. The political arena is a crucial setting for influencing culture and an important domain for expressing a Christian worldview. On the other hand, we must not be defensive or dismissive about this issue. Yes, sometimes the resentment that outsiders feel stems from the fact that Christians embrace a different set of political perspectives that are not popular. It is also easy for outsiders to resent the times when Christians have been effective in winning elections or in securing legislative victories. Over the last few decades, Christian voters have had quite a dramatic influence on elections, and citizens have frequently selected Christian candidates.

But there is more to it than that. Though Christians have won votes and shaped legislation, this does not ultimately define the success of a Christ follower. We are representatives of Jesus to every person in our culture, regardless of whether we agree politically. Our lives should reflect Jesus, which includes not just *how* we vote, but every element of our political engagement—our conversations about politics as well as our attitudes about ideological opponents. This may seem obvious, but based on our research on this subject, we must realize that our political activism, if expressed in an unChristian manner, prevents a new generation from seeing Christ.

At the very least, we must come to grips with the sheer scope of the issue. The number of young people in our culture who now embrace unflattering perspectives about Christians and politics is astounding. Three-quarters of young outsiders and half of young churchgoers describe present-day Christianity as "too involved in politics." Nearly two-thirds of Mosaic and Buster outsiders and nearly half of young born-again Christians said they perceive "the political efforts of conservative Christians" to be a problem facing America. The conclusion is that millions of young people in their twenties and thirties, including many young Christians, are growing impatient with and feeling disconnected from the political activism of many in the church. We have no tracking measures to determine how this perception may differ from that of, say, ten or twenty years ago, yet it is an unmistakable and unavoidable part of our current environment.

In our exploration of this subject, we also discovered that such concerns are not only the domain of young Mosaics and Busters. One-fifth of all American adults (21 percent) believe "the political efforts of conservative Christians" are a major problem facing the country today. Half of the adult population (48 percent) describe the political involvement of Christians as a concern. The number of people who embrace this perception is significant. More than 110 million adult Americans admit they maintain misgivings about the role of "conservative Christians" in politics.

Young Adults Are Concerned about Conservative Christians in Politics

Percent who believe conservative Christians are a "major" or "minor" problem facing America today

Outsiders	Mosaic/Buster	62%
	Boomer/Elder	48%
Born-Again Christians	Mosaic/Buster	47%
	Boomer/Elder	40%

The Barna Group, Ltd./OmniPoll^{SM} 2007

We should also be willing to examine our role in politics because many Christians think this way themselves. Many believers, including faith segments we define as evangelicals and other born-again Christians, admitted that they perceive the politics of conservative Christians as a challenge facing the country. The study showed that one-sixth of born-again Christians (17 percent) firmly embrace this viewpoint, while nearly half have some degree of concern.[1]

Christians need to be aware of their reputation in this arena, not only because it influences their political engagement, but because it affects their ability to connect with new generations who are innately skeptical of people who appear to use political power to protect their interests and viewpoints. This perception may not always be accurate, but it contributes to outsiders' mistrust of Christians.

The stakes are high. Future elections are likely to be shaped by these attitudes, as will the outcomes of the spiritual search of millions of young adults.

What makes the perception of Christians in politics so difficult to address is that Christians themselves have a hard time agreeing. They disagree not only about the issues but also about the very nature of politics and the role that Christians ought to play. This book does not attempt to address those debates. And if it appears to enter such disputes, it is for the purpose of uncovering what Mosaics and Busters really think and experience related to Christianity and politics.

Instead, my goal is to give Christians greater clarity about engaging the political sphere as well as insights into how our efforts create a (largely negative) reputation for Christianity and how this affects friends and neighbors. I am trying to spur our thinking and engagement in appropriate ways and do not want to discourage Christ followers from participating in politics.

Yet as Christians, we have much to learn about engaging in the right ways and for the right reasons. Based on the data we have been collecting for the last three years, I believe we have to reconsider our strategies and approaches related to politics, or we risk losing appropriate forms of political influence and damaging our credibility in representing Jesus to outsiders.

To address the deep challenges that are facing people in our nation and around the world, Gabe and I have come to the conclusion that being politically engaged is more important than ever. As I discussed in chapter 6, Christians should be known as engaged, informed, and on the leading edge, offering a sophisticated response to issues. Being engaged in politics is a way of doing just that.

Of course, politics is not the only area of influence—it may not even be the most important—but politics does have a significant impact on our lives. The research we conduct at Barna consistently demonstrates that laws and legislation play an important role in creating social and moral boundaries, even though Americans may not always adhere to the rules and may gripe about the restrictions. You cannot change an individual's morality through legislation, but the reality is that laws deeply affect our culture and create social expectations for the people living in it. Political involvement, messy and confusing as it can be, is an important avenue of influence within our community, nation, and world. Christians should be motivated by faith in every dimension of life, and politics is no exception.

If only it were that simple.

COMPLEXITY

The arena of politics is difficult and controversial because of the diversity and complexity of the culture and the issues that consume us. Unfortunately, it's not unusual for people to turn intricate realities of the political landscape into simplistic clichés.

After the last few razor-close presidential elections, we have heard much about "red" and "blue" states. Identifying red states and blue states may give a reasonable snapshot of how our nation selects its president, but often the red-blue story masks huge differences in what motivates people to vote, not to mention where Republicans and Democrats actually live. Often in the bluest of states, red voters represent a significant slice of the population and vice versa. For instance, California, the biggest state, is seen as a blue state, and it typically supports Democratic candidates. However, because of its size, there are more red voters living there than in any other state in the nation.

Christian voters are frequent victims of oversimplification. Sometimes journalists, pundits, politicians, or other experts who have little context or understanding of the faith community develop simplistic explanations. However, Christians who do not appreciate the complexities of the nation's population also make sweeping generalizations—usually about those outside of Christianity but sometimes about the Christian community as well. In other words, everyone makes assumptions about the size and motivations of the Christian community.

The reality is that the Christian electorate is incredibly diverse. For instance, one way of analyzing the electorate is to divide it into four faith segments: evangelical Christians; nonevangelical born-again Christians; other self-identified Christians; and outsiders. In the chart below, the circles represent these four groups, shown in proportion to their size.

Four Faith Slices of the Voting Population

Percent of registered voters (N = 5,067):

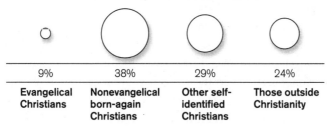

9%	38%	29%	24%
Evangelical Christians	Nonevangelical born-again Christians	Other self-identified Christians	Those outside Christianity

The Barna Group, Ltd. / OmniPoll^{SM}, 2006–7

One of the first things you may notice is that evangelicals represent the smallest portion of the voting population—about one-tenth of registered voters. Many other researchers use self-identification to define the evangelical audience; that is, people who embrace the term *evangelical* to define themselves are assumed to have the beliefs and convictions of an evangelical.[2] This would not be a problem except, when we have used this approach in our research—asking people if they consider themselves to be evangelical—some will say that they are, even though they do not hold to some of the most basic beliefs that ought to define such a believer.

At Barna we classify people as evangelicals based on what an individual believes about a handful of core theological perspectives. First, a person must be a born-again Christian, which means he or she has made a confession of sin and profession of faith in Christ. Second, we define evangelicals as those who also believe that the Bible is accurate in the principles it teaches, who view God as all-powerful and perfect and involved in the world today, who contend that Jesus did not sin, who assert that Satan is a real spiritual being, who reject that heaven can be earned through good works, who believe Christians have a responsibility to share their faith with others, and who say their religious faith is very important in their life.[3] I realize this is a detailed way of defining a group of people. The point of our surveys is not to determine someone's spiritual fate but to try to analyze and understand the nuanced role of faith in our culture.

Still, the beliefs Barna measures as part of our "evangelical" definition are not minor points of theology. And what people believe matters. It affects how they view the world, how they see their place in it, and how they respond to situations and opportunities. In a moment we will examine why these perspectives are so important when it comes to politics.

Back to the slices of the voting population: besides evangelicals, the two largest groups of voters are also Christian-leaning segments— nonevangelical born-again Christians and other self-identified Christians. Nonevangelicals are those who have born-again commitment but do not share other faith perspectives (for example, they reject the reality of Satan or they do not believe the Bible is entirely accurate). Combined, these two groups make up two-thirds of the voting population.

The final group is outsiders, who make up about one-fourth of voters. As I mentioned in chapter 1, outsiders represent a nearly double proportion of young adults, so the growing size and influence of outsiders among young voters should not be overlooked. Their burgeoning ranks will change American politics in the decades to come.

The study of politics and faith is made even more complex because each faith segment votes in diverse and unexpected ways. For instance, among the evangelical segment, only a slight majority are registered Republicans (59 percent). That's a high proportion, but far removed from the monolithic levels one might expect based on media pronouncements or the expectations of Christian leaders. We are projecting, for instance, that in the 2008 election, as many born-again Christians (including both evangelicals and nonevangelicals) will cast a ballot as registered Democrats as will vote as Republicans.[4] Party affiliation does not always translate directly to candidate choice, but it is a reminder that the Christian community is more diverse, less cohesive, and less unified than is typically assumed.

Just as the Christian audience is diverse, we have to understand that a similar reality holds true for the opposite side of the fence. Outsiders have far less political unity, consistency, and commonality than Christians might assume. They are not uniformly antagonistic toward Christians. Their political views are not neat and simple. This has an important implication for Christians: political activism on the part of outsiders is not dead set *against* Christianity.

It is easy to assume that society is divided into "us-versus-them" forces. The reality is much less clear-cut.

WORLDVIEW POLITICS

A person's worldview has significant implications for the political sphere. First, realize that most Christian voters do not embrace foundational evangelical perspectives. Gabe and I contend that these essential beliefs matter because they affect how people perceive society and how they interact with the political environment. For instance, without a conviction that the Bible is accurate in its principles, it is difficult to be motivated or informed by biblical ideals when casting a ballot. Without the belief that Satan is a real spiritual adversary, it is easy to lose sight of the larger spiritual realities and confrontations that exist. As Paul says, believers are not fighting against flesh and blood but against supernatural entities (see Eph. 6:12).

And the list continues: if as a Christian, your faith is not your driving motivation, if you do not believe God is still involved in the world today, if you do not perceive any motivation to influence others spiritually for Christ, your political engagement will ring hollow. Millions of Christian voters—representing a *majority* of the electorate—possess these perspectives on a hit-or-miss basis. But without a consistent and thoughtful biblical worldview, the efforts of Christians to engage politically lack an appropriate foundation.

What does this mean for Christians as we try to understand the skepticism of a new generation? One of the most important implications is this: Christians communicate to many audiences at once. As an evangelical, you are not just speaking to evangelicals but also to other born-again Christians, other self-identified Christians, and outsiders. For instance, when a Christian leader appears on television, he is speaking to all four audiences, some of whom understand and resonate with his or her perspectives and others who have no context for understanding the viewpoint.

Here is an appropriate example that emerged in our research. Usually when a Christian talks about being engaged in a battle, this type of metaphor stems from the scriptural references that describe the spiritual world as an epic struggle (see Eph. 6:10–17). Yet outsiders hear this language and become alarmed by the militaristic talk. And consider what happens when *Christians* are exposed to this warfare verbiage without the benefit of understanding Paul's comments in Ephesians. Without context, these individuals may respond in unChristian ways toward outsiders. And even those with a biblical worldview can internalize this tough talk about spiritual warfare and lose sight of what it means to be full of grace toward skeptics and critics. As James says, "So whatever you say or whatever you do, remember that you will be judged by the law that sets you free. There will be no mercy for those who have not shown mercy to others" (James 2:12–13).

This has special relevance for a number of reasons. First, in an era of mass media, blogs, and viral videos, it is important to remember that your words and actions may endure in the blogosphere, on YouTube, or on some other digital destination. This is particularly important for those Christians who appear in media, because the stakes are high. What you say and how you say it are important issues of stewardship. You are representing Christ to outsiders, even as you articulate a Christian perspective. And in the context of a sound bite or a media interview, this is a tough challenge. We cannot seek popularity, but we also cannot ignore the listeners who may be making spiritual conclusions about whether Christianity rings true or not. Even if we are speaking from the context of a biblical worldview, many will not interpret our comments from that same perspective. So it is incumbent on us to present things clearly, creatively, and without clichés. And particularly among Christians, our calls to action must provoke each other to self-examination, humility, and appropriate engagement. With fellow believers who lack a holistic biblical worldview, we have to be particularly cautious not to create attitudes in them or alarm them in ways that give them an excuse to be unChristian.

This is not a concern only for those with public roles. Every pastor plays a part in shaping Christians' efforts in politics. In your church on any given Sunday, chances are you have all four of the faith slices represented in the audience. How are you communicating so that everyone in the congregation can understand, think about, and respond to social, political, and spiritual issues in appropriate ways? In your sermons as well as in the environments and conversations your church facilitates, are you helping to develop people's capacity to think, act, and pray in terms of a biblical worldview?

And even if you are not in church work, as a Christian, your co-workers and your neighbors are watching and listening to you. How do you represent what it means to be a Christ follower when it comes to your political choices and preferences? If outsiders criticize Christianity for being too politicized, are you part of the problem or part of the solution? Be vigilant that your words and actions don't feed the perception of unChristian faith.

CLIMATE CHANGES

It is more important than ever to think about and respond to political issues in light of a biblical worldview. Mosaics and Busters are placing a new stamp on political engagement that will require thoughtful, Christlike engagement. They criticize us for being unChristian in terms of politics, and if we do not offer them the deep and sophisticated truths of the Christian perspective, we have no chance of connecting with their hearts and minds—politically or otherwise.

To understand the Mosaic and Buster mindset, let's explore some critical shifts that are taking place in the political environment.

☐ *Mosaics and Busters express much less traditional political and social views on many issues than did their parents at the same age.* Their views on matters such as homosexuality, media decency standards, sexuality, and family continue to shift away from traditional perspectives.

☐ *Young people, particularly Mosaics, are driven by pragmatism, a do-what-works mentality.* Young adults are much more likely than are their predecessors to prefer leaders who are willing to compromise to get the job done. This preference stems from their relativistic worldview. For better and for worse, young people embrace decisions that produce greater comfort or the least amount of conflict. The negative reality to this is that they admit to being less principled in their decision making.

☐ *Mosaics are more skeptical than any previous generation of the role of the Bible in public life.* In one study conducted by the Pew Research Center, young Americans were the least likely age group to say that the Bible ought to be the most significant influence on the laws of the country, instead favoring the "will of the people" as the best way to determine legal boundaries.[5] This preference for majority rule stems from not knowing the Bible's content, questioning its truth, and preferring feelings and expediency to absolutes. Of course, just because this is the perception does not mean that we abandon the idea that the Bible should help us determine the laws of the nation. But we must realize this is an increasingly rare sentiment among the nation's younger population.

What Should Determine the Laws of the Country?

Percent of each age group who believe that the Bible, not the will of the people, should drive the laws of the country:

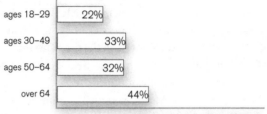

ages 18–29	22%
ages 30–49	33%
ages 50–64	32%
over 64	44%

Pew Research Center

☐ *Young adults are less likely to support a "Christianized" country.* The increasingly secular mentality of young adults carries over into other arenas as well. Mosaics and Busters are less likely than their predecessors to support keeping the motto "In God We Trust" on our currency, the phrase "one nation under God" in the Pledge of Allegiance, or the Ten Commandments posted in government buildings. They are also less likely than Boomers and Elders to support teaching creationism in public schools or to favor a federal marriage amendment defining marriage as possible only between one man and one woman.

Support for a "Christianized" Country

	Mosaics/ Busters	Boomers/ Elders
Strongly oppose removal of "In God We Trust"	61 %	80 %
Strongly oppose removal of "one nation under God"	59	79
Strongly oppose removal of Ten Commandments from government buildings	48	68
Strongly favor federal marriage amendment	29	39
Strongly favor adding the teaching of creationism in public schools	24	32

The Barna Group, Ltd. / OmniPoll[SM]

☐ *Young adults are embracing a worldview at odds with Scripture.* There are subtle yet powerful worldview shifts taking place all around us. For instance, currently just one-third of twentysome-things believe that humans are superior to other living things created by God, which compares to half of those in their thirties and nearly three-fifths of those over the age of forty. As Christians seek to articulate a biblical perspective of creation care and environmental concerns, we have to realize that the worldview of Mosaics and Busters has shifted, which means the deep-seated philosophies that undergird the political issues are changing.

☐ *Young adults are less likely than preceding generations to start their political explorations as Republicans.* As people get older, they usually become more politically conservative. Yet the up-and-coming generation is less likely to rally around Republican and politically conservative banners than were people the same age just twenty years ago. Among young adults under age twenty-six, connection to the Republican Party is at its lowest point in two decades.[6]

You may not know about or welcome all these trends, but they represent not-so-subtle shifts in the thinking of Mosaics and Busters, which will place increasing pressure on social conservatives to find electoral traction in the coming decade.

Whether or not we welcome the changes, we have to be aware of them and what a new generation really thinks about Christians and our politics. If we expect to have influence merely by relying on numerical advantage, we are in for a rude awakening as the weight of our views dwindles and the role of those outside the Christian faith increases.

METHOD AND ATTITUDE

Since every group seems to have a political presence and agenda, why should Christians be subject to special criticism? Are outsiders asking us to stay out of politics? According to our research, not exactly. Many outsiders clarified that they believe Christians have a right (even an obligation) to pursue political involvement, but they disagree with our methods and our attitudes. They say we seem to be pursuing an agenda that benefits only ourselves; they assert that we expect too much out of politics; they question whether we are motivated by our economic status rather than faith perspectives when we support conservative politics; they claim we act and say things in an unChristian manner; they wonder whether Jesus would use political power as we do; and they are concerned that we overpower the voices of other groups.

Let me introduce you to Brandon, one of the young people we interviewed for this project. In relaying his story to us, he described his significant involvement in church as a teenager.

"Sometimes it is a hard for me to reconcile the 'Christian movement' with the people I knew from my own days in the church. Today whenever I experience the activities of American Christians as an organized group—and frequently when I interact with them in politics—it is almost always in terms of them trying to use political force to entice people to behave a certain way. Do I believe a Christian has every right to go and vote as he or she believes? Absolutely.

"But twenty years ago," Brandon continued, "when I was looking at evangelical Christianity from the inside, it seemed like a movement bursting with energy to spread good news to people. Looking at it from the outside today, this message seems to have been lost in exchange for an aggressive political strategy that demonizes segments of society. I believe that American Christians have become tools of the Republican election machine—at the expense of their own image and message."

Brandon is now an avowed agnostic, living in Arizona. He is also an active member of the Republican Party.

An important insight regarding politics and unChristian faith is that it influences people's lives, like Brandon's. *Many issues keep young outsiders from committing to Jesus, but one key barrier is their experience with Christians in politics.*

One outsider we interviewed said he became disillusioned with his church and eventually his faith because he started to question the heavy-handed political involvement that seemed to be a requirement. His comment: "A lot of times the church would take a conservative Republican stance, and anyone who did not fit into that mold was judged as not as good a Christian as everyone else."

This story was driven home by the survey data. Ideological allegiance plays a prominent role in who feels accepted by Christians and who does not. We found that young outsiders who are politically conservative do not feel as much tension with Christianity as do other outsiders. In other words, if a twentysomething shares sociopolitical views with conservative Christians, he or she is much less likely to have negative perceptions of Christianity. On one level, there is nothing inherently wrong if Christians find areas of agreement with other young social conservatives, yet our research also indicates that Christians exhibit more patience with young people with whom they share political views—and less charitable attitudes toward outsiders with divergent perspectives. Is it a mere coincidence that young outsiders who are liberal and moderate are most likely to recall having had a negative experience with a Christian that gave them a negative view of Jesus?

One young Christian, Doug, explained how his efforts to connect his neighbors to the message of Jesus had been undermined because of an unfortunate unChristian interaction. "My neighbor came to me the day after the election. He said, 'Do you know what your Christian friends said to my ten-year-old daughter? They told her she should tell me not to support John Kerry because he supports abortion. Kerry is a baby killer.' I don't even want my daughter thinking about abortion, let alone having them talk to her about who to vote for. What kind of Christian is *that*?"

Doug described his frustration: "I had been carefully nurturing a relationship of trust with my neighbor, and much of it was undone because of careless and offensive words to his young daughter about an election."

The sobering conclusion is that political attitudes and perspectives, when expressed in an unChristian manner, create unintended spiritual barriers between people and Christ.

POLITICS, JESUS STYLE

How do we overcome the perception that Christians are too political? We do not simply change our principles to accommodate people who disagree with us, but we should be willing to look at ourselves in the light of Jesus. We must ask if our political engagement is Christlike. If we are perceived to be *unlike Jesus*, in what ways could our politics reflect his life and priorities more clearly?

Here are five insights about outsiders' perceptions and how these obscure an authentic picture of Jesus. Remember that some outsiders' complaints are brought up by people who have an entirely different take on reality or who have a political ax to grind, but not always. The fact that so many outsiders expressed these perspectives and the fact that they are telling us they get turned off to Christianity because of these issues are powerful signs that we should pay attention to. And besides, with or without criticism, we should always make genuine attempts to think and act in a Christlike manner in every part of our life. Here are some ways to bring balance to our political engagement.

unChristian: *Christians rely too heavily on political influence.*

Christlike: *We are cautious not to place too much emphasis on politics.*

Christians seem to fall on two sides of the path: too political or too apolitical. It is important to find an appropriate balance—neither ignorant and silent nor relying too heavily on political solutions to societal problems. We should make an effort to engage in other culture-shaping activities in addition to politics. As I mentioned at the beginning of this chapter, Christians should not isolate themselves from governmental, legal, or legislative influence. Those arenas, however, should receive only part of our attention. In many ways politics follows culture. As ancient Greek musician Damon of Athens said, "Show me the lyric of a nation and it matters not who writes its laws." Movies, television, books, magazines, the Internet, and music are incredibly significant in shaping the world-views and lifestyles of today's America. And Christians are expressing a growing awareness and response to these avenues of influence. Where is God calling you to serve him—media, arts and entertainment, politics, education, church, business, science?

unChristian: *Christians get enamored with politics.*

Christlike: *There is nothing gained by winning elections if we lose our soul in the process.*

Involvement in politics is seductive. Many aspects of politics feel like the frenzy of a gold rush. Once you start to influence elections, it is tempting to believe that the church is primarily called to shape the electoral process. Remember Jesus's principle when he was cornered about paying taxes? He said, "Give to Caesar what belongs to Caesar, and give to God what belongs to God" (Matt. 22:21). In another episode, Jesus asked this penetrating question: "What do you benefit if you gain the whole world but lose your own soul?" (16:26). It is important that, in trying to achieve political ends, we do not sacrifice our integrity by using unChristian means.

> **unChristian:** *Christians drown out and demonize the voices of others.*
>
> **Christlike:** *Respect our enemies and be aware of our capacity for myopia.*

Guard your attitudes and what you say about outsiders. Our political engagement should not be the only yardstick by which outsiders measure our faith. Our words and actions shape people's experiences and impressions of Jesus. We found that only 9 percent of young outsiders describe Christians as "people they trust a lot." As we probed the reasons for this, the most frequent answer was our involvement in politics. The political process encourages, even thrives on, assumptions about the opposition. Misreading (and sometimes misrepresenting) the motivations of others is part of the "business." What are you doing to facilitate conversations with people you don't agree with? Just asking what they think about certain issues, without having an "agenda" to change their mind, might shift their perceptions of you. Be willing to talk with Christians of different racial and ethnic backgrounds about their political persuasions. Chances are their perspectives will challenge you. Learn how their views of politics and culture are shaping their engagement with the world.

> **unChristian:** *Christians do not respect leaders whose political viewpoint is different from their own.*
>
> **Christlike:** *Respect and listen to our leaders and pray for them.*

In our research we found that many outsiders pointed out our inconsistency by saying that Christians seem ugly and rude toward political opponents. Yet Scripture makes it clear that our responsibility as citizens is to pray for our leaders and makes no allowance for their party affiliation or views (see 1 Tim. 2:1–3). Whom do you trust more—a born-again Christian whose sociopolitical stances are different from yours or someone of a different faith who happens to share your political views? Who is more "right"? It strikes me as unChristian that we often have more charitable attitudes toward ideological allies than we do toward brothers and sisters in Christ with whom we disagree on matters of politics.

> **unChristian:** *Christians are hypocrites when it comes to politics.*

> **Christlike:** *In trying to solve problems in society, be vigilant about our own capacity for hypocrisy.*

Insincerity and duplicity in the political realm are particularly obvious to outsiders. One survey respondent made this intriguing observation: "This always strikes me as ironic—you have a Christian talk about how a majority of Americans support something, like school prayer, or that most Americans do not support homosexual marriage. But then in the same conversation they say politics should not be a matter of majority rule because Americans are morally relativistic. You can't have it both ways, people." This underscores how closely many outsiders pay attention to our words and arguments, and it highlights the fact that hypocrisy related to political issues is a major unChristian barrier. Many outsiders say that their problem with Christians in politics is that lives don't match words. Here are some examples of the comments outsiders made:

- ☐ "Christians don't even follow what the Bible says; why do they try to tell everyone else how to live morally?"

- ☐ "They do not seem to prioritize the poor and needy in their political agenda, as Jesus commands."

- ☐ "Christians do a lot of complaining about the society and how bad things are in politics, but they don't do much more than complain. The point is that you have to offer more than an opinion."

- ☐ "Christians talk about being driven by family values when they vote, but a lot of their families are in bad shape too."

- ☐ "They run the risk of turning people away from the cause they are trying to promote by losing sight of real people. Christians do not show grace toward people. They judge their actions without walking in their shoes."

Outsiders may not always come to the right conclusions about Christians, but many describe us perfectly. Moreover, even if they don't have it all correct, it is a sad fact that we do not give them sufficient evidence to the contrary.

ENGAGING POLITICS

What are the issues and problems that God is leading you to address? It may be the rampant access to and use of pornography, issues of justice in the United States or in developing countries, the plight of the poor in our community, educational policy or curricula in our schools, the moral perspectives exhibited in today's media, the care and nurture of the environment, the need for more Christians to adopt and provide foster care to children in need, exposing more Christians to the international church, increasing awareness of human trafficking around the world. Being involved could range from working for a campaign to serving on the school board.

Rather than being known for criticism, let's learn to step in and work toward a solution for the problems we see. As Michelangelo said, "Critique by creating."

My friend Kimble is getting involved in politics. He's running for public office in our city, despite the costs to his time, money, and energy. His faith has activated his political involvement. Kimble explained, "I think a lot of Christians would really be motivated by the things I am passionate about, and I want to make a positive difference."

After studying the perspectives of outsiders, I cautioned him: "Keep in mind that politics only gets you so far. You change people's lives most deeply by transforming their hearts, by helping them embrace a passionate, thoughtful, personal connection to Jesus."

Kimble and I don't always agree on every topic. But we frequently discuss how a biblical worldview affects his aspiring political career.

CHANGING THE PERCEPTIONS

GAINING THE WORLD, LOSING THE SOUL

From a vantage point further in the future, I think that an honest diagnosis will tell the truth about the pivotal role the Religious Right has played in these depressing statistics. In the aftermath of the Religious Right's ascendancy, it is not an accident that "antihomosexual" is the number one perception of Christians in America these days, followed closely by "judgmental" and "hypocritical" and "insensitive." Young people today could, if we had taken a wiser path for the last few decades, think "antipoverty" or "pro-environment" or "pro-fidelity" or "antiviolence" when they hear "Christian" or "evangelical." But because of the path influential people have taken over the last thirty years or so, what young people think of the Religious Right is what they think about evangelicals and even Christians in general.

That's why some of us believe that leaders in the Religious Right have, in a classic case of gaining the world and losing the soul, successfully gained political clout but helped lose our next generation.

But even so, a diagnosis of the evaporation of Christian commitment in the West and a prescription about how to respond must go deeper than complaining about the mistakes of the Religious Right. There are many factors, and they run deep. As for prescriptions, yes, we need more Bible—but we also need a better, more holistic and profound understanding of the Bible and what it says about justice, compassion, the future, power, poverty, money, war, sex, and the kingdom of God. Yes, we need more maturity—but we also need a better and more holistic maturity, a maturity willing to face the historic and social realities of our so-called Christian past: a past that includes anti-Semitism, racism, chauvinism, holocaust, colonialism, apartheid, slavery, attempted genocide of native peoples, and much else that is ugly and calls not for excuses and minimization but for forthright repentance. Yes, we need more discernment and missional engagement—but we also need better discernment that goes beyond name-calling and making pronouncements on two or three issues.

The data presented here can help us greatly in this regard, prompting us to discern how deep and serious the problems are, so that our missional engagement in the coming years won't be more of the same.

Brian McLaren
founding member, emergentvillage.com

CHRISTIANS AND IDEOLOGY

On the role of Christians in politics, I have done a few unscientific polls myself with young people. It's easy to see that they are turned off by right-winged politics—which is very unfortunate.

Unfortunately, nearly every political issue that Christians are associated with today is from the defensive position. For instance, the abortion issue developed when the Supreme Court ruled that states could no longer decide when life begins, resulting in abortion being legalized. Since then, over twenty established moral conventions have been overturned by state legislatures, and Christians have responded, rightly so. The challenge has been that in defending these, we haven't done a very good job and, at times, we present an ugly picture. We come across even worse than the people attacking us.

The media has also contributed to feeding this perception. Recently there have been over twelve books written about theocracy and several different media appearances by the authors—although I have never met a Christian who believes in theocracy. We don't believe in that; we believe in pluralism. Yet the press has really painted us into a corner.

In my book *Kingdoms in Conflict*, I make the case for why Christians should never have a political party. It is a huge mistake to become married to an ideology, because the greatest enemy of the gospel is ideology. Ideology is a man-made format of how the world ought to work, and Christians instead believe in the revealed truth of Scripture.

Chuck Colson
founder, Prison Fellowship Ministries

AN APOLITICAL CHURCH

I have the privilege of serving a congregation in the heart of democracy. Our flagship location, Union Station, is located four blocks from the Capitol. More than 70 percent of our congregation is made up of twentysomethings. And many of them are congressional staffers who work on Capitol Hill. They live, eat, and breathe politics all day, all week.

From day one, National Community Church has tried to remain absolutely apolitical. That doesn't mean we don't talk about issues. Issues such as the sanctity of life or the sacredness of marriage aren't political issues. They are moral issues. So we talk about them. But we are hyper-careful not to align ourselves with a particular politician or political party. And that apolitical approach has resulted in amazing political diversity. NCC is nearly equally divided between political parties.

I just don't think pastors should turn their pulpits into public policy platforms. It cheapens the gospel. Our congregation doesn't need another political opinion. They need spiritual revelation. They don't need to think about politics on the weekend. They need to be reminded to *seek first the kingdom of God*.

Political diversity is part of our DNA at NCC. And it's most evident in our small groups. We have a free market system of small groups that empowers leaders to get a vision from God and go for it. While we would never endorse a group that goes outside the guardrails of Scripture, we make room for leaders who have varying passions depending on their theological persuasion. In other words, we're not black and white where Scripture is gray. Most semesters we have a variety of social justice groups that revolve around a variety of issues. And not all of those groups see eye to eye. But our primary role as spiritual leaders isn't making people see eye to eye. It's making sure our eyes are focused on Jesus.

Mark Batterson
pastor, National Christian Church

PROMOTE JESUS, NOT POLITICS

The religious leaders of the day attempted to trap Jesus by challenging him on his political stance. They asked him, "Is it right for us to pay taxes to Caesar or not?" Scripture tells us that Jesus saw through their *duplicity*, telling them to give to Caesar what is Caesar's and to God what is God's. Historically the church has struggled with the paradigm of two kingdoms: the kingdom of God and the kingdom of the world. Trying to combine the two is like attempting to mix oil and water. Church history has been consistent on this matter. Every time Christianity has fallen into the trap of using politics to achieve its means, it has lost its power and effectiveness. Relevant Christianity never loses sight of the reality that in the kingdom of God, everything is upside down when contrasted with the world's pursuits. In God's kingdom the greatest is the least; the first is the last; we are to love our enemies; and to be most effective, we are called to servanthood rather than to positions of political power and correctness.

John Wimber, founder of the Vineyard Church movement, once said that if people truly have a relationship with Jesus, they will always vote for the right things ("right" as in ethically and morally correct). He said that our job as followers of Christ was to promote Jesus, not political bias. Getting involved politically can potentially derail our effectiveness, causing us to lose focus on our true vision, thus weakening our cause.

As an involved participant in the Christian environmental movement, I have endeavored to stay nonpolitical. For me, the care of God's creation is purely a biblical matter of obedient stewardship. The world has politically polarized an issue that should be of great concern to every human being. The global environmental condition is an issue that has become a primary cause of human suffering in developing nations. Knowing that Christ has called his people to a ministry of compassion, mercy, and social justice, we cannot allow ourselves to be caught in the duplicity of religion and politics at such a crucial hour. Our effectiveness will come only through authentic biblical conviction and the faith to act on it.

Tri Robinson
pastor, Vineyard Boise, Boise, Idaho

THE NEW POLITICAL FRONTIER

After sixteen years on Capitol Hill as a leading and visible evangelical, the signs are not difficult to read. Young evangelicals born after 1963 are leaving the fold. And they are running as fast as they can.

What are they running from? The perception of an intolerant, unpopular, uncaring, and narrow Religious Right? And if they are running away, what are they running to?

The shift has been subtle and gradual, but I feel like it has accelerated in the past few years. I spent hours on the phone with leading young evangelicals in 2004, convincing them that President Bush would be better for the country, and for those concerned about abortion, than Senator John Kerry. Liberal Democrats, despite opposing a federal marriage amendment and supporting legal abortion rights, appear to be gaining attention and traction among many young and growing evangelical communities.

I cut my teeth on politics in 1984 on a successful Texas challenger race for the US Congress. Groups like the Christian Voice, Freedom Council, and the Moral Majority were created as responses to the Supreme Court ratification of abortion on demand. A political action required a political reaction. If we were going to confront the horror of abortion, there was no other avenue, no greater priority, than political engagement.

Politics was not an option, they said, but an obligation.

Sixteen years later, six of which I spent as the third-highest ranking Republican staffer in the Senate, the sands have shifted, and so has my thinking. It appears that conservative evangelical involvement in politics is being rejected by the under-forty evangelical community, which seems to be pursuing alternative forms of engagement as well as issues not traditionally associated with the Religious Right. I believe that one of the key reasons they are rejecting the Religious Right is not that they fundamentally differ on issues like abortion and marriage (yet), but in part because they are uncomfortable with its perceived narrow and limited agenda and its unpopularity among the cultural elite. It is as much the perception of a sin of omission (the issues not addressed) by the Religious Right that is causing them to disaffiliate as it is a sin of commission (the tactics or positions).

When the Christian Coalition refused to hire an executive director because he wanted global AIDS to be on their agenda, and another director resigned for similar reasons, the fate of the Religious Right was sealed.

This is not entirely a bad thing. The senator I worked for was defeated by a pro-life Democrat, and as much as I believe the country would have been better off if he had been reelected, I pray that this will leaven the Democrat party. The kingdom of God is not captured by either party, and it is a dangerous moment for the church and the gospel when a temporal power is confused with the higher power.

In addition, politics is not everything. We are not going to set aright the sexual revolution on the floor of the Senate. We need new and "saltier" forms of cultural engagement.

My concern, however, is that we could be in danger of losing the next generation of evangelicals over time on "first things" principles, such as life beginning at conception and marriage as one man and one woman, while they look for places to express their concern over issues such as poverty, AIDS, and the environment.

Can evangelicalism navigate these new frontiers? Or will this be a breakup—a civil war within a tradition that has been largely unified by a deep-rooted sense of the moral order? We must avoid an internal struggle that distracts from a common cause and drains precious resources that otherwise should be spent to combat injustice, poverty, and cultural decay?

These are questions largely for the under-forty crowd to answer as the current leadership begins to retire from public life. The ball is in their court. It will take conversation, prayer, humility, fellowship, and grace. But with the Holy Spirit at the helm, we can come out on the other side of the rapids stronger and broader.

Mark Rodgers
former staff director, Senate Republican Conference
president, The Clapham Group

NOT LEFT OR RIGHT—DEEPER

Christians should be involved in politics. The question isn't "should we engage?" but "how?"

The conservative religious movement in America today has been politically corrupted. Evangelicalism has been hijacked and usurped by partisan political forces. Conservative religion is now being driven and dictated by secular, right-wing political forces. So basically, the conservative religious movement—or at least parts of it, the politicized part of it—has sold its soul to partisan politics.

Many young evangelicals see that this is just Republican politics masquerading as conservative religion. When they observe this, they don't like it. And they are concerned it could happen on the Left too—exactly what happened on the Right—the politicizing and corrupting of religion for the sake of political power. That's not what they want.

The young people I meet don't want to go Left or Right. They reject these narrow political orthodoxies. They're not happy with Christianity being either a list of things you shouldn't do, or just about being nice. They want to go deeper.

Instead, young evangelicals really want their faith and lives to count for something. They want their faith to somehow connect with changing the world; they want their love of Jesus to express itself in the world, in relationship to other people, and in the pressing demands and problems of the world. I find this to be true among younger and younger people.

The kind of privatized faith that's just about "me and the Lord" is not enough for young evangelicals. Experience tells us that you can't call something a revival until it has changed society in some way; personal renewal is not enough. There's a new hunger for revival, a hunger to participate in a world-changing faith and movement, which I haven't seen for a long time.

In the end, social movements are what change politics—and the best movements always have spiritual foundations. With his Bible in one hand and the US Constitution in the other, Martin Luther King Jr. changed the wind in our nation, inspiring a whole generation to engage in the struggle for civil rights. The politicians came around last, as they often do.

Jim Wallis
founder and executive director, Sojourners/Call to Renewal

TEACHING KINGDOM PRINCIPLES

In today's church, one reason young people are disillusioned with the role of Christians in politics is because we often teach them only part of God's statutes, not all—and we rarely teach them kingdom principles. We are quick to teach about judgment, self-righteousness, and our perception of holiness, but we often leave out the kingdom principles of love, compassion, justice, and the sovereignty of Christ in shaping our political affairs.

We teach our own political traditions—instead of the ways of Christ—becoming enforcer, judge, and jury toward the sinful lives of others. We seem to forget that we all are sinners saved by grace—a loving, compassionate, merciful Grace who did not try to legislate hell out of us nor give us what we deserved, but who gave his Son as a substitute, a redeemer for our sins.

Make no mistake—there are principalities, powers, rulers of this dark age, against which the church must stand. But we wrestle not against the flesh and blood of our fellow humans who sin.

For each generation, God has a sovereign plan for their role in the political process. We do a disservice to the coming generations if we try to force our political methods and mindset on the issues they face. If we teach our children all the statutes of God and things pertaining to his kingdom—although it may mean putting aside our own ways of doing things—we can trust that God's purposes for the coming generation will be fulfilled.

Rev. Jannah Scott
currently on assignment as policy advisor
Faith & Community Initiatives, Office of the Governor, Arizona

8

JUDGMENTAL

Christians talk about hating sin and loving sinners, but the way they go about things, they might as well call it what it is. They hate the sin *and* the sinner.

Jeff, 25

PERCEPTION **Christians are prideful and quick to find faults in others.**

NEW PERCEPTION **Christians show grace by finding the good in others and seeing their potential to be Christ followers.**

"You know what really bothered me?" the young woman, Lisa, confessed during a recent interview.

I was grateful for the frank thoughts of this twenty-nine-year-old mother of two toddlers.

"Well, you're asking how Christians come across to me. I'll tell you. A few weeks ago I visited a Christian Bible study at a church. Every once in a while I go because I know a few of the women. You know, I am still trying to figure out this Jesus thing. After the speaker talked for a while, we started a conversation at our table—about eight or nine of us women just chatting away. I was probably the youngest one there, but some of them were about my age. We got along pretty well."

"What happened that bothered you?"

"We were talking about sex, intimacy, and pregnancy, stuff like that. I told them about a friend of mine who was considering an abortion. I told them her entire situation, a twenty-year-old, boyfriend left her. She's feeling really alone. I made some comment about really empathizing with my friend, that I could understand that abortion might make sense. I guess that shocked them. I know the women there are pro-life and all—I don't know what I am, pro-life or pro-choice or just myself. But the conversation shifted at that point in a really weird way. Instead of having a dialogue, I was put on the defensive. They were nice enough about it, but the ladies just kept talking *at* me, trying to fix my attitude about abortion."

Lisa paused and softened her tone. "And here is the part that bothered me, something I never told them. What they didn't know is that *I* had an abortion—a long time ago. It was not an experience I would wish on anyone. But I can feel my friend's dilemma because I lived it. I am not sure the Christians I hung out with that morning get that.

"I guess the truth is I was hoping for some empathy myself."

Lisa is describing one of outsiders' most significant concerns about present-day Christianity: Christians are judgmental. Respondents to our surveys believe Christians are trying, consciously or not, to justify feelings of moral and spiritual superiority. One outsider described it like this: "Christians like to hear themselves talk. They are arrogant about their beliefs, *but they never bother figuring out what other people actually think*. They don't seem to be very compassionate, especially when they feel strongly about something."

As you will see later in this chapter, being judgmental is one of those areas of the Christian life in which it is very easy to make mistakes. A definition will help us here. To be judgmental is to point out something that is wrong in someone else's life, making the person feel put down, excluded, and marginalized. Some part of their potential to be Christ followers is snuffed out. Being judgmental is fueled by self-righteousness, the misguided inner motivation to make our own life look better by comparing it to the lives of others.

Unfortunately, Christians in our culture have become identified with this perception. Nearly nine out of ten young outsiders (87 percent) said that the term *judgmental* accurately describes present-day Christianity. This was one of the big three—the three most widely held negative perceptions of Christians (along with being antihomosexual and hypocritical). Just to put this in practical terms, when you introduce yourself to a twentysomething neighbor, and you mention your faith, chances are he or she will think of you as judgmental.

We also discovered that our better-than-thou attitudes are apparent to young churchgoers. Most Christian young people told our interviewers that our faith seems too focused on other people's faults. More than half the young Christians between the ages of sixteen and twenty-nine (53 percent) said they believe that the label *judgmental* accurately fits present-day Christianity.

And judgmental attitudes are particularly difficult for Mosaics and Busters to swallow for two reasons. First, they are insightful about people's motives. They have been the target of endless lectures, sermons, marketing, and advertisement. If you bring up unsolicited advice, they mistrust your motives. They wonder what's in it for you when you offer your opinion.

Second, the new generations are increasingly resistant to simplistic, black-and-white views of the world. We do not have to like this element of their generational coding, but it is a feature of the way they process life—nothing is simple. They esteem context, ambiguity, and tension. Often judgmental attitudes come across as overly simplified, old-fashioned, and out of step with their diverse world. With young people, *how* we communicate is as important as *what* we communicate.

God is wise enough to handle a complex generation, and his people need to be as well.

A CRITICAL DISTINCTION

Like it or not, being judgmental is intricately connected to our image as Christians. Perhaps this gives you a glimmer of satisfaction, because you think this just means believers have stood their ground against sin. Of course Christ followers should feel compelled to reject sinful actions and attitudes. Jesus did. And it is especially tough to stay silent when Americans' hyper-individualism has made us a nation of moral mavericks. You have probably heard people justify their actions by saying things like, "You can't impose your beliefs on me." "That may be right for you, but it's not what's right for me." "Everyone has to find their own path." Our research shows that do-it-yourself morality is gaining momentum, and it is the way most Mosaics and Busters sift through moral decisions.

Given this environment, many Christians get defensive even talking about the perception of being judgmental. Just because others feel judged is not a reason for us to change our beliefs. If Christians do not point out God's standards, who will? This book repeatedly emphasizes this key biblical concept: pointing people to Jesus is not achieved by being popular. The outrage of outsiders does not change or diminish God's expectations. People still have to answer to a holy judge.

Yet an entire generation of those inside and outside the church are questioning our motives as Christians. They believe we are more interested in proving we are right than that God is right. They say Christians are more focused on condemning people than helping people become more like Jesus. Could this be telling us we have lost something in the way we articulate and describe God's expectations? Are we more concerned with the *un*righteousness of others than our own *self*-righteousness?

A critical distinction for Christians is the difference between condemning people (i.e., being judgmental) and helping them become soft-hearted—aware of, and sensitized to God's standards. Protesting a homosexual rally with a "God hates gays" sign is judgmental. It does not help people become receptive to God. Having a meaningful dialogue about homosexuality with someone at your office—if done with the proper motivation—might do so. It is judgmental to feel superior toward a divorced mom in your church; mentoring her son would be much more likely to cultivate God's purposes in that family.

Should Christians talk about the moral appropriateness of things like homosexuality and divorce? Of course. Yet in our efforts to point out sin, we often fail to do anything for the people who are affected by sin. Think of it this way. The perception is that Christians are known more for *talking* about these issues than *doing* anything about them. Based on our survey, a majority of outsiders (57 percent) say Christians are quick to find fault with others.

If we cross the line and judge people to make ourselves feel better, we are just as sinful as those whose actions and attitudes we condemn. Being judgmental pushes people away from God's purposes, and people become repulsed by an image of Jesus that is not at all like the real thing. When Christians are judgmental, when we are arrogant and quick to find fault, we are unChristian.

A LOVING CHURCH?

This raises another important question. Are we perceived to be a loving group of people? In a recent study, we asked outsiders, churchgoers, and pastors to describe whether they perceive Christian churches to be loving environments, places where people are unconditionally loved and accepted regardless of how they look or what they do. Only one out of five outsiders said they perceived churches in this way. Surprisingly, fewer than half of churchgoers, including born-again Christians, felt strongly that their church demonstrates unconditional love.

Of course, what a person *thinks* about the church and what it actually *is* may be two separate things. Pastors certainly have a different view. More than three-quarters of church leaders feel strongly that their church is an unconditionally loving community. Still, even if outsiders are wrong, their perceptions drive their reality. They have difficulty envisioning our churches as loving places.

No matter what we say about ourselves, young people have their doubts. Our research confirmed that perceptions of love and acceptance are less common among Mosaics and Busters than older adults. This was true among churchgoers as well as outsiders. Moreover, only 16 percent of young outsiders say the phrase "consistently shows love for other people" describes us "a lot." Outsiders might think of us as friendly or that we have good principles, but we are not known for our love.

A Loving Church?

Question: Christian churches accept and love people unconditionally, regardless of how people look or what they do.

(pastors, N = 613; adults, N = 1007)

	Percent who agree strongly
pastors	76 %
born-again Christians	47 %
Christian churchgoers	41 %
outsiders (all ages)	20 %

**Mosaics and Busters—More Skeptical
That Churches Are Loving Environments**

Mosaic and Buster outsiders	51
Boomer outsiders	41
Mosaic and Buster churchgoers	38
Boomer churchgoers	23

Percent who disagree

And this raises another question. What if Christians are perceived as judgmental because we are trying to be popular *with the wrong audience*? Scripture makes it clear that we exist only to please God. But what if our judgmental attitudes are just posturing to look good to other believers? Are we trying to please God or polishing our holy credentials in front of fellow insiders? Is it possible that part of the reason that Christians have lost their appeal to outsiders is they have lost passion for people outside the church? Rather than seeing people's potential to be Christ followers, we often set ourselves up as their spiritual judge and jury.

Our research with Christians confirms that often we miss the point of reflecting Jesus to outsiders because we are too busy catering to the expectations of other believers. One church leader explained how a few vocal members of his church prevented him from partnering with another local congregation because the potential partner was "too seeker sensitive." Another believer explained how her efforts to engage people affected by HIV/AIDS have been routinely vilified by some Christians because of the perception that she is being manipulated by homosexual activists. A young Christian leader who developed an inner-city ministry told me how one of his board members questioned whether there were "too many black kids" attending. One influential Christian leader was roundly criticized for engaging in a respectful dialogue with advocates of a different faith.

The common theme in all of these stories is that Christians often err on the side of being quick to judge others, even fellow believers, feeling as though they know the answers, as though they know what God must think. Shifting this perception of judgmentalism is a daunting challenge. But it is possible to do. Our studies also pointed out instances when Christians have been able to articulate and express biblical truths without being judgmental. I will say more about this later. First, though, we need to understand how we judge people inappropriately.

ERRORS IN JUDGMENT

Our investigation of young adults highlighted four forms of judgmental attitudes: wrong verdict, wrong timing, wrong motivation, and playing favorites.

WRONG VERDICT

The first error that Christians make is coming to the wrong conclusion. God's judgments about people are perfect; ours are not. When Christians reach the wrong verdict, it is typically because of our own biases, assumptions, or stereotypes about others. Our superficiality gets the best of us. One Christian I talked to recently said, "Yeah, I know what you mean about stereotypes. When I see a person who is tattooed or pierced up, I try not to judge them based on their outward appearance. I realize that their appearance is probably just a symptom."

I was shocked. Did you notice what he was saying? He may as well have said, "I wouldn't judge based on outward appearance, but there *is* something wrong with these people on the inside." Do you see how subtle judgment can be? It creeps up on us and drips out of our conversations and attitudes.

And consider the lifestyles and self-expressions of today's young people. Fifty-four percent of Americans ages eighteen to twenty-five have significantly altered their appearance at some point in their life, including tattoos, dying their hair an untraditional color, or piercing their body in a place other than an earlobe. In fact, one-third of all young adults have a tattoo.[1] So here is a revealing question: are all of these young adults expressing a symptom of some deep, unresolved spiritual angst? Sure, some of them may be. But is my well-meaning friend, who represents Christ, coming to the wrong conclusion about many people in a generation that expresses itself differently? Absolutely.

We learned that when Christians have the wrong verdict about others, those being judged feel misunderstood—and wronged. *You don't really know me. You have no idea about my life, what I have been through. You are not really interested in me.* Outsiders explained that when they feel judged, they believe the conclusion itself is wrong. It is based on a lack of information about the individual's story, about their background. Outsiders feel stereotyped. Later we will look at how stereotypes affect our ability to connect people to Christ.

WRONG TIMING

A second type of judgmental error we make is having the right verdict, but giving it at the wrong time. We sometimes have the right idea about God's views, but we describe that verdict in the wrong context or at the wrong time. I have a Christian friend who lost his gay brother to AIDS. Can you imagine the response if he reminded his mom that his deceased brother was living in sin?

When to say something and when to stay silent is a tough call for many Christians. Some Christians, though, make virtually no distinction, feeling they should always express themselves in every situation. We must, however, ask ourselves about the person we are seeking to help. Is this person a Christ follower? I was surprised to find in 1 Corinthians that Paul informs the Christian community that they have no responsibility to judge outsiders, but he said, "It certainly is your job to judge those inside the church who are sinning" (1 Cor. 5:12).

WRONG MOTIVATION

We may have the right verdict but give it with the wrong motivation. Scripture makes it clear that we should be motivated by love. When Jesus encounters the woman accused of adultery (an episode of his life described in John 8), we see her accusers driven by the wrong motivation. A crowd of angry religious insiders had gathered to denounce and literally kill this woman for her dark secrets. Her offense was clear, but their approach to punishing her was vindictive and self-righteous.

Jesus turned their anger back at them: "If any one of you is without sin, let him be the first to throw a stone at her" (v. 7). Can you imagine that moment when Jesus, in perfect unison with God's plan, broke ranks with centuries of religious teaching within Jewish law and custom? He challenged the accusers to choose compassion over retribution by considering the impurity in their own lives before passing judgment on someone else. And don't forget the end of the story. Jesus, the perfect judge, tells the woman to abandon her self-destructive behaviors. "Go and sin and no more," he says (v. 11).

This type of error—judging people with the wrong motivation—deeply affects outsiders' perceptions of us. Have you ever heard the Christian mantra, "Hate the sin, but love the sinner"? It is not a direct quote from the Bible, but it reflects the ideal most Christ followers embrace. They would like to extend grace and love toward others (the sinner), while firmly rejecting those attitudes and behaviors that contradict God's standards (the sin). The problem is outsiders don't think we are honest with ourselves. One of our interviews was with Jeff, a twenty-five-year-old agnostic from Oklahoma. He actually mentioned the catchphrase in the conversation: "Christians talk about hating sin and loving sinners, but the way they go about things, they might as well call it what it is. They hate the sin *and* the sinner." If our primary fixation is on the sin, it is virtually impossible to demonstrate love to an individual. Think of it: many outsiders, the broken people who need Jesus most, picture Christians as *haters*.

PLAYING FAVORITES

A final error in judgment is really the problem in reverse: favoritism. It is human nature to show partiality, but favoritism affects the relationships of Christians in unfortunate ways. One young person in our interviews said he overheard his youth pastor make plans to put special priority on the teenagers with the most potential. The young man commented: "I wasn't really what you call a popular person in high school, so when he [the youth pastor] said that he wanted to spend most of his time with popular kids, it just really made me question his motives. I could see how all the time and attention of the church's leaders were given to the same guys and girls who were popular in school. I didn't really want to be a part of that."

This type of partiality has the same outcome as judgmental attitudes. We pigeonhole people and determine who has the greatest spiritual value and the highest potential to be Christ followers, and we focus our efforts on these people. In the Bible, James specifically warns believers against favoritism: "My dear brothers and sisters, how can you claim that you have faith in our glorious Lord Jesus Christ if you favor some people more than others?" (James 2:1).

STEREOTYPES KILL RELATIONSHIPS

As mentioned earlier, one of the errors in judgment involves stereotypes. Christians express their stereotypes of outsiders in diverse ways. Some are overt, others subtle. Sometimes these presumptions relate to other people's morality or spirituality, based simply on their connection to a church. Other times it's an assumption about the way a person looks or dresses. Unfortunately, stemming from our common sin nature, Christians continue to harbor prejudices regarding race, age, gender, and intelligence.

One respondent offered this brusque description of being judged and what it has done to his faith: "Modern-day Christians sicken me to no end. When I was growing up, all they ever did was harass me and say I was poor because I had angered God. I look forward to the day when the religion crumbles and is forgotten."

Regardless of the misperceptions you have, the impact of these attitudes is the same: stereotypes kill relationships; they can undermine other people's trust in you and in God. This is the hard truth when we are perceived as being judgmental. When Christians render wrong judgments, when we are quick to find fault, when we have the wrong motivations, or when we show favoritism, it undermines our efforts to connect outsiders with Jesus.

In a restaurant in San Jose, I was describing this aspect of the research to my friend Steve, a speaker and musician who has ministered to teenagers for many years. Suddenly Steve interrupted me. "David, you won't believe this story," he said.

"Yeah, what you got?" I said, glad to have another chance to dig into my meal.

"A few years ago, a church here in California brought me in to do a youth event. It was supposed to be a free concert, and afterward I was going to present the gospel. Well, before it started, I noticed some teens were not being allowed in. At the time, I thought maybe the church was charging for the event; sometimes churches do that to help offset the cost. So, anyway, I went to the pastor and said that I would be happy to use my honorarium for anyone who wants to come in." Steve shifted a bit in his seat. "David, do you know what he said?"

"What?" I asked, lifting my glass of iced tea.

Steve leaned his imposing frame forward and pointed his fork in my direction. "He told me, 'Steve, no, we're not charging for the event. We just don't want a certain type of kid infecting our youth group.'"

"Infecting?"

"Yes. I was so shocked that I'll never forget it. That's the word he used—*infecting!*" He jabbed his fork in the air for emphasis.

We just sat there. I was amazed that a Christian leader would turn away the open hearts of teenagers and verbalize his resentment of these teens, particularly at a special event designed to reach outsiders! If teens can't find respect and acceptance in the church, especially when looking different is the "new" normal, where can they find it? Imagine the reactions of those teenagers as they walked away from the church that night. Even if they were rough around the edges, or even rowdy, I know Steve, and he wouldn't have been bothered. Instead, they left with less hope and diminished interest in Jesus.

Maybe you would never use the word *infecting*, but our judgmentalism has kept all of us from helping certain people connect to Christ.

UnChristian, isn't it?

THE BLINDING FORCE

Let's face it. Outsiders have a legitimate beef. We are, more than we realize, too anxious to judge others. We deserve the label *judgmental*.

But why is that? Jesus gives a clear example of pursuing people, of accepting people at face value. Often he scandalized others by hanging out with the least desirable people in the culture, and his teaching is unambiguous: do not judge others or you'll face the same yardstick; remove the log from your eye before pulling a splinter from your friend's eye; and you do not have the right to condemn others, unless you are sinless (see Matt. 7:1–5). How have Christians gotten so far from this?

Some people explain it simply—even Christians make mistakes. Believers do not always express Christ perfectly because they are imperfect. This is accurate, but it also misses the point.

Pride fuels judgmental attitudes. Arrogance is perhaps the most socially acceptable form of sin in the church today. In this culture of abundance, one of the only ways Satan can keep Christians neutralized is to wrap us up in pride. Conceit slips in like drafts of cold air in the winter. We don't see it, but outsiders can sense it. One outsider made this observation: "Christians talk about love, but it doesn't feel like love. I get the sense they believe they are better than me, even though their life seems about the same as mine."

A concept like pride is tough to define, and people do not willingly reveal their arrogance, so in our surveys we have to ask about it in indirect ways. Though only God knows each person's true condition, our research provides a helpful snapshot of how people feel about themselves. For instance, we found that a majority of born-again Christians said they are "very convinced they are right about things in life." Also, believers are more likely than others to say they often try to persuade people to change their views. And, compared to outsiders, born-agains admit to being less open to other people's perspectives about life.

Some of these characteristics are not inherently negative or prideful. They might even be indicators of an active faith. But taken in one lump, would you like hanging out with people like this? Would you be eager to hear the input of a person who thinks he or she is always (or mostly) right, who often gives you an earful of unsolicited advice, and who does not seem particularly interested in your opinions? Americans in their teens and twenties, both inside and outside the church, told us they have better ways of spending their time.

THE BIBLE ON JUDGMENT

After having talked to and researched thousands of outsiders, I reread major portions of the Bible to get a clear sense of God's attitude toward outsiders. Judgment is central to the Bible's message, but I was surprised at how relentlessly Scripture warns believers *against being judgmental.*[2] In addition to Jesus's cautionary words, the Bible makes it clear that God, not humans, should judge. It is God's job, and he does it impartially while exposing the true motives of people's hearts. And consider Paul's writing to the Christians in Rome. You've probably encountered believers who justify their own judgmental attitudes by reading you the first chapter of the book of Romans. This is the part of the Bible that describes God's anger "against all sinful, wicked people who push the truth away from themselves" (Rom. 1:18).

It is clear from this that God's laws are inviolable and transcendent. Yet Paul moves from his sharp discussion of sin to this wake-up call for Christians:

> You may be saying, "What terrible people you have been talking about!" But you are just as bad, and you have no excuse! When you say they are wicked and should be punished, you are condemning yourself, for you do these very same things. . . . Don't you realize how kind, tolerant, and patient God is with you? Or don't you care? Can't you see how kind he has been in giving you time to turn from your sin?
>
> *Romans 2:1, 4*

Another translation of the Bible puts it this way: "God's kindness leads you toward repentance" (NIV). Does this describe Christians and their heart for leading others to repentance?

Through my research among outsiders, God has been slowly revealing my own biases. His kindness to me in this process has been overwhelming. I encourage you to consider the same response to the research. What wrong ideas do you harbor about people? If you feel a growing sense of self-justification—*I have the right to be judgmental about sin; that's what God calls me to do*—you may have already missed the chance to have God reveal your blind spots. If people have used the term *arrogant* to describe you, your church, or your ministry, how do you respond? Maybe those critics are right. Are you softhearted enough to see a clear picture of your motivations? Just because you feel as though you are doing the right thing does not mean that you have the right attitudes or motivations toward outsiders.

Instead, arrogance within the Christian community is too frequently accepted or at least excused. The research shows that we tolerate our own pride; we do not feel God's anger at arrogance. God says he "opposes the proud but gives grace to the humble" (James 4:6 NIV). We have to start seeing ourselves and those around us for the people we really are—needy and hurting but with great potential as God's sons and daughters. Maybe then we would reject arrogance as adamantly as we do any other sin, because it is especially corrosive to the faith of Christ followers.

RESPECT EQUALS ACCESS

In the midst of these tough realities of being prideful and judgmental, let me describe one of the most encouraging findings of our research. With the disenchantment so often expressed by outsiders, we were glad to find exceptions to the image of judgmentalism. We found instances in which Christians were able to articulate perspectives about God that did not come across as judgmental. Outsiders are often receptive to the input that Christ followers have to give. They don't always accept everything that is said, but at least they don't dismiss it as unChristian.

For believers, this is significant. It underscores that friendship with outsiders is not a choice between two impossible extremes—being brutally honest with them or blindly accepting their lifestyles. Outsiders understand the nuances of different situations, and we discovered that, when their Christian peers gave them input within the context of relationship and with respect, in general they appreciated it. Human beings are attracted to acceptance and genuine respect; they are repelled by rejection and an air of superiority.

So what does that type of respect look like? Outsiders suggested the following guidelines for facilitating mutual esteem:

1. *Listen to me.* Talk less. Learn to listen better. That way you can understand the needs and backgrounds of people.
2. *Don't label me.* Using terms that put people into boxes is generally offensive to people. Words like "lost," "pagans," and "nonbelievers" are not particularly endearing. Young people often say, "We're all just people. Let's stop making neat little categories for each other."
3. *Don't be so smart.* Don't pretend to have all the answers. If you are not sure, just say so. Besides, outsiders told us they are not always looking for an answer from Christians—usually they are not.
4. *Put yourself in my place.* Christians seem to be concerned only about what people do or don't do—such as whether they go to church and have acceptable behaviors. But outsiders want you to understand some of the things they have suffered and gone through. They believe that Christians should learn to appreciate them and better understand their choices.

5. *Be genuine.* One thing that undermines outsiders' trust is when Christians try to wedge a little spirituality into every opportunity. They feel that it disrespects their intelligence. *Don't you think I am smart enough to notice what you're trying to do? I can see your "Christian" agenda.* Many of them have no problem with the fact that faith is so important to us, and they don't mind hearing about it occasionally. Yet they can usually tell the difference between topics that come up naturally in conversation and the times when we inject some spiritual angle or idea that doesn't fit.

6. *Be my friend with no other motives.* Outsiders say they sometimes get the feeling that Christians have befriended them with the ulterior motive of getting them into church. They like having Christian friends, but not with those who have a not-so-hidden agenda. Outsiders said, for instance, they generally don't mind being prayed for or being served in some way, but they get uneasy when they sense that these efforts are part of a scheme to "warm them up" to go to church someday. Friendship ought to be real, based on genuine interest in one another.

VIRTUE OR GRACE?

If we want to change the perception of outsiders that Christians are judgmental, we have to see them as God does. This is easy to say but tough to do. It affects so many areas of our lives. How do you perceive single parents, gays and lesbians, people with tattoos, your neighbors, your pastor's family? You do not need my research to know how easily self-righteousness and moral superiority come to us. But we are not the judge; God is.

The writer Philip Yancey offers a great insight about judgmental attitudes, pointing out that the opposite of sin is not virtue; it is grace.[3] We need to move beyond expecting people to behave according to our expectations, and instead try to help connect them to God's purposes. Three recent episodes made this vivid to me.

EXPERIENCE 1

At Starbucks last week a pastor friend of mine, Doug, told me about a seventeen-year-old he had been helping. This young woman,

Claire, was struggling. Her older sister, who is not a Christian, is living with her boyfriend.

"David, she asked a bunch of other people, other Christians, what to do," Doug explained. "And all of them, every one of them, said that without a doubt she should confront her older sister and tell her that what she is doing is wrong and that it's against God's plan.

"I told her I agreed that the behavior is wrong, but then I asked her something: 'Claire, do you think it's the right time to say something to your sister? I mean, you know the situation; you know your relationship with her. A loving confrontation might be appropriate. God uses us to speak to others. But are you asking the Holy Spirit to help you know what to say or when to say something? God is concerned with her soul, not just her behavior.'"

EXPERIENCE 2

Shelby, a talented young musician who attends my church, went to Thailand to help organizations ministering to people trapped in the rampant sex industry of that country. I emailed her afterward to catch up. Here is part of her reply: "You have to remember that my father was an LAPD sergeant. He worked all over LA and arrested prostitutes all the time. He would tell me how most of the women were drug addicts and this was a way to 'fund' their habit. I felt sorry for them, but I also felt that they had brought it on themselves. If they hadn't gotten addicted to drugs, then maybe they wouldn't have made this decision to start 'selling themselves.'

"After going to Thailand, I saw a different side of prostitution. Every prostitute I talked to said their reason for doing this was to support their family. Their family?!? Many of the women had been married at one time, but their husbands had left them. Now these women were left to take care of their children. We judge because we don't understand. I didn't understand but now I'm starting to. It's hard to describe what's on my heart . . . but I guess I can just say that after living with these 'prostitutes' I no longer saw them as that. I saw them as mothers, daughters, wives, friends, and most of all as women who are loved by God. And God showed me that I am a work in progress. Some sin is more visible than others, but we all do it. I have no right to judge anyone, because I am just like them! I need to keep an open mind and an open heart."

EXPERIENCE 3

I got an email from Catherine Rohr a few months ago. I will explain the details of the email in a moment. But first, here is some background. In 2004 Gabe introduced Catherine to me. That was the year she and her husband, Steve, were helping a former inmate expand the business plan for an already thriving handyman business. Catherine and her husband realized, as she says, "that inmates and executives have much more in common than one might think—they are creative, passionate, ambitious, courageous, and intelligent individuals with a strong entrepreneurial drive; inmates' energy has just been applied in the wrong direction."

So the husband-and-wife team started an organization called Prison Entrepreneurship Program, a ministry that offers in-depth, in-prison business training to inmates. One of the unique aspects of her program is this: she asks business leaders to come to prison for a day and help evaluate the business plans that prisoners develop.

Back to the recent email I got from her. It described Catherine's speaking at the campuses of Stanford and Berkeley. "Who are you speaking to—and why?" I wrote back. Her reply: "To the MBA students. We recruit MBA business plan advisors for our inmates. Also to get people to think about grace and redemption."

Think about it. Through her willingness to reach people whom others overlook, Catherine is helping to transform the lives of prisoners, businesspeople, *and* MBA students. She helps to shift the perceptions of what Christ followers are all about. And—what a powerful concept—by serving the lowest individuals of the culture, she has access to its leaders.

Catherine sees the potential of inmates to be active members of the business community and to be Christ followers. She celebrates and esteems the possibilities that still exist in their lives, despite their incarceration and despite their reputation as convicts. As she puts aside her prejudices, God is able to use her.

There are many Christians doing sacrificial things like Catherine Rohr, but there are not enough of us serving in enough places to shift the perception that Christians are judgmental.

Not yet, at least.

CHANGING THE PERCEPTIONS

GRACE CITY

I used to cringe when I'd hear the cliché "love the sinner, but hate the sin." I thought it was impossible. I mean, come on, everybody who says that seems to bash both in short order. This is particularly complicated for me because I live in Sin City—Las Vegas, a town built on its exhibitionism and excess. Then I read a paragraph by C. S. Lewis that blew my mind. He notes that there is someone I love, even though I don't approve of what he does. There is someone I accept, though some of his thoughts and actions revolt me. There is someone I forgive, though he hurts the people I love the most. That person is *me*. There are plenty of things I do that I don't like, but if I can love myself without approving of all I do, I can also love others without approving of all they do. As that truth has been absorbed into my life, it has changed the way I view others.

I can love the high rollers and hell raisers that populate Vegas. I can love the gamblers, rebels, strippers, students, and soccer moms no matter what they are currently caught up in. It is not my job to change them or judge them. That's God's job. It is my job to love them and point them to the love of Jesus. He is the one who brings change. And it is a process that takes time. When people perceive they are accepted for who they are, irrespective of what they have done or will do, then they are open to friendship and influence.

This understanding motivated me to place a huge picture on my office wall. It is taken from atop the Stratosphere just as the sun set. The four-mile strip of casinos and hotels is clearly visible along with the high-rises, strip clubs, and suburbs. Across the horizon are the words "GRACE CITY." It reminds me that no matter what a person has done, God's uncensored grace is available. No matter what they are going through, there is hope. So I don't think of Vegas as Sin City anymore—I think of it as Grace City.

What about your city? The people aren't that different after all. They are the ones who populate the planes and cars that make Vegas the most traveled-to destination in the world, rivaled only by Mecca. What could happen if we viewed them with the same grace we extend to ourselves?

Jud Wilhite
pastor, Central Community Church, Las Vegas

FRIENDSHIP OVERCOMES

Anyone who calls anyone judgmental, well, er, is inherently judgmental. That icky substance—judgmentalism—lives inside of all of us. As followers of Jesus we are called to be the least judgmental, but often we find ourselves the most judgmental. Why?

I can offer a laundry list of reasons, but one of the biggest is that we take God's laws, as well as the hedges we build around them, and then place them on people who don't even believe in God. Worse, we become more concerned with behavior modification than real transformation. The result is that judgmentalism springs up in our hearts, shading our every attitude and interaction. So if a sixteen- to twenty-nine-year-old thinks we're judgmental, I'd love to fire back, but sadly, I have to agree. I don't want to agree. I want Christians to be known as the most loving people—the kind of people who love you until it hurts. But so far it seems like we're bringing more hurt than healing to many.

You see, love is the opposite of judgmentalism; it tempers our views, attitudes, and interactions. In our cultural climate, love is foundational. Now some say that love has no agenda, but I believe that love *is* the agenda (see John 13:35). Whether in our communities, workplaces, or government, we must be committed to love those we work with and serve.

One of our weaknesses is that we're far more concerned with being right than being righteous. We become like the Pharisees whenever we focus on issues rather than people. Judgmentalism creeps in whenever we deal with issues as if they were black and white, rather than flesh-and-blood humans in need of redemption. Do you want to remove the unhealthy judgmentalism you have in regard to the poor? Make sure you have poor people who you love and welcome in your life. Do want to remove the unhealthy judgmentalism you have in regard to homosexuals? Make sure you have gay and lesbians whom you love and welcome in your life. Do you want to remove the unhealthy judgmentalism you have in regard to our government? Make sure you have people involved in politics (even if it's just on the local level) whom you love and welcome in your life.

Then, when we talk about issues, we won't just be talking about those *things* we care about but *people* we care about. And the judgmentalism, well, it will naturally begin to fade away like it did for the woman at the well, the woman caught in adultery, and so many others.

Margaret Feinberg
author and speaker

HUMILITY

Everything boils down to how we understand the gospel. The problem with religion is that it makes people believe that "somehow because I go to this church, I am better than other people." The obvious flaw in this is that the gospel says the bloodstained cross means no one is better than any one else—we are all provided equal grace in the eyes of God. We all share the same fallen DNA. The fact that Christians have accepted this grace and are redeemed should create *humility* in us.

I'm perplexed at how anyone can hear the story of Jesus dying in our place and rescuing us out of our helplessness and have it produce arrogance in their life. There should be points of distinction, but those should be not only behavior/morality based, but rather God's love for the world exhibited in his followers who are overflowing with his mercy and compassion.

Rick McKinley
pastor, Imago Dei, Portland

EMBRACE, DON'T ABANDON

I've been meeting every other week at Starbucks with a pastor who had an affair with an employee at his megachurch. A few months ago his actions were found out; he left the ministry disgraced and is now going through a vicious divorce. It's not an unusual story and one that I sadly deal with in my line of work. And though this story is heartbreaking, I'm afraid there is something even more tragic that has occurred in this man's life. You see, this incredibly popular and well-loved pastor now finds himself abandoned by those in the Christian community. When the ugly news got out about his indiscretions, people stopped calling, the invitations to lunch dried up, and he was asked not to be involved in his small group any longer.

I'm not sure how it happened exactly, but it seems that grace, which is Christianity's most core issue, is struggling to survive. It also appears from the findings of people surveyed, that the church has seriously lost its way on this issue. Our culture doesn't look at us as a faith of second chances but rather as a religion of judgment. I had a friend tell me recently that in his opinion, it seems like the teachings of Jesus haven't really rubbed off on his followers. I'm afraid at some level he is right.

Out of all the current negative perceptions of Christians, this one in particular demands our highest priority. Grace is our central issue, and for us to simply ignore this finding will certainly be our unhinging. We will slide down the slippery slope toward irrelevance, and our message of the gospel will no longer be credible in our culture. Why? Because it appears at some level that the secular world is capable of "doing grace" better than we are. Christianity's main export has been co-opted by nonbelievers. Forgiveness, compassion, and second chances are common occurrences as demonstrated by several recent high-profile cases. Whether it is a movie star's addictions, a beauty queen's indiscretions, or a run-in with the law, grace seems to be flourishing in the secular arena. A quick trip to rehab or a heartfelt apology is payment enough in secular society. When Donald Trump becomes the poster boy for second chances and the church is viewed as a place of judgment . . . we have a serious problem.

So how do we become people who are known for grace? First, we must admit that we have a problem. We can't continue to pretend that the church is a place of grace if fundamentally we kick to the curb those within our very own community who screw up. If we can't forgive our pastors, leaders, and friends, then how could we possibly begin to forgive others? My "Starbucks pastor" needs to be embraced, not abandoned. We must begin by loving each other, forgiving each other, and carrying each other's burdens, especially when we fail. When a brother or sister is steamrolled by life, we don't run from them, we rally around them.

Secondly, we must engage with the people whom we have been taught to stay away from for too long. We must boldly enter into the environments where grace flourishes and does its best work. Christian insulation and a safe life are not what you and I signed up for when we said we would follow Jesus. He was never insulated from people's pain, and he sure didn't keep to safe places. He engaged with those who were being crushed by their mistakes and bad choices.

Jesus wiped away the tears of the prostitutes, held the hands of the outcasts, and touched the wounds of the sick and the crazy. He hung with the not-so-perfect people of the world and showed them what Christianity was all about. He was never concerned about a person's title, society's name tag, or the sign on their place of work. Porn stars or preachers, gay or straight, Republican or Democrat, it doesn't mean a rip to God. We are all his children, and we are all in need of this stunningly beautiful thing called grace. We know what we need to do, now let's go do it.

Mike Foster
president, Ethur
founder, XXXchurch.com

THE STATE OF MY SOUL

I struggle with condemning. I have since I can remember.

When my husband and I were engaged, we planned our wedding in three months. One afternoon we were sorting out the next twenty tasks to complete. He hadn't called the bakery about the cake, and he still hadn't finished his guest list. With annoyance dripping out of every pore, I cut into him with all the shame and blame I could conjure up. How dare he drop the ball and ruin my afternoon. Now I would have to pick up after his incompetence!

After my verbal assault, he sat quietly with disbelief and pain in his eyes. I expected he would scold me for my tirade, but he didn't. All he said was, "Jonalyn, is that how you talk to yourself?" I was silent, stunned.

Then, slowly, I nodded and began to weep long and hard, realizing that this wasn't the good life, it wasn't the abundant life Jesus offered. But it was the only way I knew to be a model Christian woman planning a model wedding.

It was the first time someone took time to notice the person behind my judgmental words. He saw the state of my soul. He swallowed his own pain long enough to see that there was something self-destructive eating me. To get anything done right, to be holy, to stay pure, to walk the straight and narrow, I condemned myself into obedience. These were my inner demons:

> "If you don't finish that, who do you think will?"
> "That wouldn't have happened if you had only worked harder."
> "That's what you get when you don't do it right the first time."
> "You deserve what you get."

I was an expert at emotional self-flagellation.

I think many of the judgmental people we know are trembling, guilty, sick. I was. I couldn't extend grace because my own reserve was so low. What did I know of grace? Sure, it was my middle name, but I didn't really need it. It was for those other people who slip up all the time. Dale taught me that we cannot give out something we've never received.

> Christ didn't, and doesn't, wait for us to get ready. . . . God put his love on the line for us by offering his Son in sacrificial death while we were of no use whatever to him.
>
> Romans 5:6–8 Message

Dale was the first person who saw my mess and refused to demand an instant cleanup party. He saw where I was. And he still married me, not to rescue me, but to join me in this journey into abundant life.

Jonalyn Fincher
author, *Ruby Slippers*

9

FROM *UNCHRISTIAN* TO CHRISTIAN

There are no ordinary people. You have never talked to a mere mortal.

C. S. Lewis

This book is just the beginning. Now it's your turn.

A young generation of outsiders is raising significant criticisms of the Christian faith and its people. Knowing the problem and diagnosing the hostility are just the start. How will we respond? What will we do to address the unChristian perception of our faith?

Gabe and I hope this book generates ample conversation about the nature of and solutions for the slipping reputation of Christianity in our culture. Like it or not, there are complex and increasingly hostile factors at work, some that are obvious and others that bubble beneath the surface. My goal has been to engage your heart and mind about these issues. I encourage you to think carefully about and pray hard for Mosaics and Busters, skeptical age groups who are learning to ignore us.

And so it comes back to those critical questions: What will we do? How will we respond to what young generations think of us? If Mosaics and Busters say we no longer look like the people Jesus intended, what do we do about that? How do we move from unChristian to Christian?

In this final chapter I'd like to discuss a straightforward but challenging idea: *to shift our reputation, Christ followers must learn to respond to people in the way Jesus did.* In other words, to reverse the problem of unChristian faith, we have to see people, addressing their needs and their criticism, just as Jesus did. We have to be defined by our service and sacrifice, by lives that exude humility and grace. If young outsiders say they can't see Jesus in our lives, we have to solve our "hidden Jesus" problem.

This may be the hardest thing in the world to get right. We have difficulty just admitting that we have a problem. The truth is we all have much to learn, and the more mature we are in our faith, the more we are able to see our need to grow. In our surveys of people's spiritual perspectives, it is no surprise that mature believers are more likely to identify their weaknesses, because they are able to see themselves more clearly in light of God's standards. They don't fool themselves.

CHANGING THE PERCEPTION

If we are willing to examine our lives, I would like to suggest four insights that can help us move from being unChristian to being known as true Christ followers, enabling us to more accurately represent Jesus to skeptical outsiders. These insights emerged from my research adventure of the last three years. These perspectives stem from the way Jesus lived.

RESPOND WITH THE RIGHT PERSPECTIVE

The first insight is that Jesus had the right perspective when facing criticism. He did not seem to be bothered by critics the way we are. Scripture emphasizes that believers will not be popular and that the message of the cross doesn't make sense to outsiders. Jesus even taught that we would feel "blessed" when we face persecution for following Christ. Paul writes that if we suffer because we are Christians, we should praise God because we are connected to the name of Christ.

Still, fixing the problem is not a matter of *trying* harder. It is not an issue of carefully spin-doctoring our message or managing the "Christian brand" in the public square. Christians should not seek recognition for their efforts, other than to honor God.

When Jesus faced criticism, he did not merely dismiss it as unwarranted persecution. Sometimes he talked; other times he responded with silence. Occasionally he told a story (or a parable) to answer a question; in other instances he quoted Old Testament Scripture. Sometimes he told his listeners what to think; in other settings he would retort with blunt questions, deflecting blame or forcing inquirers to "discover" the truth themselves.

This unpredictability leads to a second insight about how Jesus responded to criticism. He was not willing to be defined by his enemies. When his detractors wanted him to make a clear statement *against* something, he always seemed to redefine the boundaries of the debate. He kept opponents off-balance, leaving them flustered. If his inquisitors tried to corner Jesus about religious laws, customs, and restrictions, his response was often to raise another question or to tell a story that changed the parameters of the argument. Should the Sabbath be kept holy? *Of course, but for what reason?* Should he associate with sinners? *Who needs real help, anyway?* Should the woman "waste" money perfuming Jesus's feet? *If she is baring her soul and honoring God, what's your problem exactly?*[1]

A third insight is that when Jesus responded to critics, he seemed to consider the below-the-surface motives. He could distinguish between hostility and hurt. And he always addressed the core of people's spiritual condition. When the woman at the well said she was not married, Jesus reminded her of her disobedience but did so in a way that seemed to ignite her pursuit of God. The rich young ruler sought kudos from the Messiah, yet Jesus said people who trust in their possessions create their own barriers to serving God. On the cross, Jesus refused to respond with anger toward outsiders, even those who killed him. "Forgive them," he prayed for his killers.

Most people, including Christians, do not know what to do when people find fault with them. They blow it off, minimize it, point to other people who caused the problem, some other way to bury the blame. I have seen leaders, churches, businesses, and other ministries miss the chance to have a spiritual impact because they failed to respond properly to valid criticism. God allowed them to see something about themselves, but they did not have "ears to hear or eyes to see" what was revealed to them.

How do you respond to criticism? Do you get angry and defensive? Do you see what people say in light of their spiritual needs? Do you examine whether the Holy Spirit might be trying to teach you something about yourself? One of my father's teachings that has stuck with me is this: be more concerned with what happens *in* you than what happens *to* you.[2] When I have encountered criticism and challenges in my life, this phrase has been a healthy reminder that God is concerned about *my* response, about teaching *me*, about helping shape *me* into the kind of person he can use. The fact that the odds were stacked against me should be irrelevant.

Like Jesus we have to learn to respond to criticism appropriately and with the proper motivation. Negative responses should not debilitate us; nor should we shy away from tough decisions or unpopular positions. But we should consider whether our response to cynics and opponents is motivated to defend God's fame or our own image.

CONNECT WITH PEOPLE

Another way of moving from unChristian to Christian is to take a sober assessment of how Jesus influenced his disciples. It was primarily through relationships and friendships.

People have observed that Jesus ministered to people on different levels during his time on earth, such as through his teaching, performing miracles, and extensive travels. Yet the devotion of the first Christians was powered primarily by their close association with him. He had lived and walked among them. They were willing to die for Christ because their loyalty had been forged in their interactions with him. There may be no more powerful testimony to the resurrection of Jesus than the fact that so many of his original followers were willing to be martyred for their conviction that he was the Son of God who rose from the dead.

We have no record of anything Jesus wrote. He created no organizations. He eschewed political power, even though people expected him to embrace this form of influence. Instead, Jesus laid the foundation for the church through relationships. His influence was (and is) indelible *because he changed people.* His focus was on reconciling human beings to a holy God through his sacrifice. It's interesting that Jesus frequently referred to God in relational terms, emphasizing the Creator of the universe as a heavenly Father. And one of the few "traditions" Jesus left with us is communion, which began in the context of a meal Jesus shared with his closest friends. Relationships mattered to Jesus.

When it comes to our interaction with outsiders, we have to realize that our relationships, our interactions with people, comprise the picture of Jesus that people retain. God has wired human beings so that spiritual influence occurs most commonly through relationships. One of the clear implications of our research is that the negative image of Christians can be overcome, and this almost always happens in the context of meaningful, trusting relationships. The goal of overcoming their negative baggage is not just to make outsiders think pleasant things about us, but to point them to life in Christ. We do not "spin" the Christian message; we live it. We do not need to exaggerate or hype faith; we embrace and describe all the potency, depth, complexity, and realism of following Christ.

It is encouraging that our research uncovered scenarios in which outsiders' experiences with Christians helped to reshape their perspectives about God and about Jesus. Rather than being unChristian, the Christ follower no longer seemed judgmental, offensive, or insincere. Meeting such Christians made outsiders believe that becoming a Christ follower might actually have merit. For a few moments they discovered that Christians think, love, and listen.

The caveat here is that such interactions were rare. It was also uncommon for an outsider to have a complete 180-degree change of heart as a result of a handful of experiences, although we do not know how his or her life will unfold in the years to come. People's reactions to Christians are not like a sitcom on television, where everything is neatly resolved in a thirty-minute episode. But the important thing is that these outsiders admitted their experience with a Christ follower had activated something in them. It left them more open, hungrier, and more willing to dialogue. And they were less hostile toward Christianity as a result. Because they felt as though Christians had listened and cared about them, they were less likely to reject Jesus.

Again, let me point out that it is not up to us to "fix" everyone's ideas about Jesus. Even with the best intentions, even when we live in a Christlike way, it is still possible to be misunderstood. Thousands of years of church history, as much as our own experiences in today's hostile environment, confirm this. Jesus is a divisive character.

Yet, this does not give us an excuse. We are responsible for faithfully representing Christ within the natural network of our relationships. There are about twenty million born-again Christians in this country who describe faith as their top priority and who say their entire purpose in life is summed up by the statement "love God with all your heart, mind, soul, and strength." This is a small slice of the total population, yet it is an enormous group of Americans. What would be the cumulative effect if this group of believers was *being* a picture of Christ to the people who live on their streets or work in their offices? What would their neighbors and co-workers see and hear?

It is also important to remember that Jesus said we would be known by our love for fellow believers. The reality is that if we do not demonstrate loving relationships *within* the church, it does not matter how much we display Jesus to outsiders. Many outsiders specifically articulated that they think Christians "eat their own." They pointed out that they see us critiquing each other, raising money to rally the troops against other believers, and acting in ways they deem unChristian. Our witness will continue to erode if we cannot embrace fellow Christ followers. Relationships within the Christian community should be beacons of grace and acceptance, of biblical accountability within the context of love and relationship, of unity without blind conformity, of transparency, and of mutual support.

As it was for Jesus, our most important influence comes in the midst of our everyday relationships. Spiritual depth develops slowly, one life at a time. Living life together, learning to become the people Christ intended, being real about our faults—and our continual need for Jesus's grace—are powerful antidotes to unChristian faith among a new generation.

BE CREATIVE

Jesus was a master communicator. He attracted people who were unaccustomed to his style, ability, and message and connected with them in creative ways. He made difficult concepts vivid and used the language of common people to help point them toward spiritual depth. Yet it was not just clever oratorical skills or provocative stories that enthralled people. It was his drive to connect people with God's heart.

Mosaics and Busters are practically begging for creative expressions of the gospel. To connect with them, we have to find new stories, new parables, new ways of telling the timeless truths of the Bible's message. Using tired expressions and clichés make us seem not only old-fashioned but simpleminded.

We cannot ignore the importance of breaking through the "been there, learned that" perspective young people have about Christianity. One of the things that surprised me in this research is how much Mosaics and Busters feel they already understand the message of Jesus. Sometimes they are right; usually they are wrong, having much to learn. Still, it is difficult to help Mosaics and Busters grasp something if they feel they already "get it." Some of our research shows that today's pastors are experimenting increasingly with the way they communicate—not tinkering with the nature of the message itself, but trying to express the gospel with a gravity and buoyancy that catches the attention of a skeptical and disinterested audience.[3]

Yet our research among outsiders shows that we have a long way to go in tapping into the creativity Jesus used. Part of our problem is making assumptions about what people know regarding the Bible, which means we often talk *about* Scripture at a level the audience does not understand. But our society no longer has much background in the Bible. For instance, in an interview for a mainstream magazine, a Christian college administrator described his school's debate team as a "salt" ministry, referring to the biblical passage describing Christians as the salt and light of the earth. The journalist had no idea what he was talking about and quoted him as identifying the debate team as an "assault" ministry. The magazine printed a correction and an apology.

Before we find fault with the writer or the editor and bemoan the lack of basic knowledge of great literature such as the Bible, shouldn't we also raise questions regarding our ability to represent scriptural principles to a skeptical and ignorant culture? We have to be engaged, winsome, and intentional about cultivating people's interest in spiritual truth. If you are a pastor or work with the media, or if you are a Christian trying to explain yourself to your neighbor, there is a greater need today than ever before for effective and clear expression of what it means to be a Christ follower. There is so much noise in the culture and so much ignorance, skepticism, and hostility that we have to find fresh ways of connecting with people. Jesus modeled this type of dynamic communication.

We must grapple with an even deeper issue, and that is how to describe the Bible as authoritative to generations who have no interest in hearing "the-Bible-says-so" arguments. Again, we do not have to like this development in our culture, but the truth is that repeating what the Bible teaches is not considered valid or compelling evidence for most members of the Buster and Mosaic generations. This reality represents a significant challenge, but also an opportunity to engage people's minds about the truths of the Christian life in fresh ways.

Last week over dinner, my friend Curtis was describing a friendly discussion he had with a co-worker who is not a Christian. His co-worker could not fathom why Curtis had paid for his three-year-old son to get into Disneyland, when he could have easily gotten him in for free by simply misrepresenting his son's age.

Curtis described the lunchtime conversation: "My co-worker said to me, 'Are you crazy? Disney makes money hand over fist. Why would you give them more?' So I asked him if he would steal from our company since the firm makes plenty of dough. I asked him if he would steal from me. 'That's different,' he said. When I asked him why, he didn't have much of an answer. We had a long discussion about it. Mostly I just asked him questions about his views. My goal was not to hammer him with what the Bible says about stealing. Actually, I never once mentioned the Bible, because it means little or nothing to him. I was trying to make him think."

Curtis is trying to emulate Jesus by challenging his co-worker, in unconventional ways, to consider God's standards.

SERVE PEOPLE

The fourth challenge for Christ followers lies in how we envision our role among outsiders. The research brought me to this conclusion: *to look more like Christ followers, we must cultivate deep concern and sensitivity to outsiders.* This is what Jesus did.

Currently Christianity is known for being *unlike* Jesus; one of the best ways to shift that perception would be to esteem and serve outsiders. This means being compassionate, soft-hearted, and kind to people who are different from us, even hostile toward us. In this book's afterword, many leaders describe this element, saying that our future reputation as Christians is intricately connected to our passion for justice, service, and sacrifice.

As I wrote at the beginning of this book, I believe the negative perceptions that now exist are partly a symptom of a church that has lost its heart for outsiders. Our posture as Christians toward outsiders ought to reflect the breadth and depth of what Scripture teaches. Consider the many ways that the Bible encourages us to cultivate concern for outsiders:

- ☐ Genesis 12:2–3—God wants the lives of his people to bless others.

- ☐ Isaiah 58:10—God followers should spend themselves on behalf of the poor.

- ☐ Micah 6:8—We should be known for living humbly and pursuing justice and offering mercy.

- ☐ Matthew 5:44—Love people who seem to be "enemies" and pray for them.

- ☐ Matthew 25:34–40—Whatever people do for the "least of these"—forgotten and overlooked people in society—they do for Jesus.

- ☐ Mark 9:35—The greatest role in life is to serve others.

- ☐ Luke 4:18—Jesus's ministry was first introduced as freeing captives, serving the oppressed, and healing the sick.

- ☐ Luke 15:3–7—God pursues people like a shepherd would search for even one straying sheep.

- ☐ Luke 15:11–32—God is described as a father who patiently waits for the return of his child.

- ☐ John 3:17—Jesus came not to condemn the world but to save it.

- ☐ John 15:13—You cannot love a person more than by giving your life up for him or her.

- ☐ Galatians 5:13—Christians have freedom to love unconditionally, as Christ loved people.

☐ Philippians 2:17; 2 Timothy 4:6; 1 John 3:16–19—Our lives are to be "poured out" and spent to serve God's purposes.

☐ Philippians 2:5–11; Colossians 1:21–22—Our attitude should be like that of Jesus, who loved and accepted humans even though they were "enemies" of God. Then he changes their status from enemies to friends, even sons and daughters of God, when they commit themselves to him.

☐ 1 Timothy 3:1–7—One of the qualifications of Christian leadership is to have "a good reputation with outsiders" (v. 7 NIV).

☐ Titus 3:2—Christians should be peaceable and considerate, showing true humility toward everyone.

☐ 2 Peter 3:9—God wants everyone to repent and turn to him.

Would other people describe your life as a Christian in these terms? Do these principles guide your relationships with outsiders? Are you a Christ follower who seeks to live out this picture of Christianity as you interact with others?

A parent doesn't expect his or her children to be perfect in every way. Human perfection is not possible in a fallen world. Rather, you hope that God will use your children to make other people's lives better. If you are a Christian, you want your child's life to point others to Jesus. Nothing makes you more proud. My research has helped me envision God in the same way. We don't please him by pretending to be perfect or by taking offense at outsiders; we please him by making Jesus real to people, even those who don't like us. This is how we start to shift away from unChristian faith. We halt our vain efforts to preserve self-image and start trying to be agents of restoration through self-sacrifice and in blessing the lives of outsiders. This is what pleases God.

Even on a very practical level, this means we learn to listen. I was stunned by how many young outsiders said Christians are poor listeners. Human beings crave relationships. We want to be known by others; even introverts need connection with a handful of people. It is a major indictment of unChristian behavior that outsiders say we are lousy listeners.

There is another reason that serving the poor, seeking justice, and addressing the needs of outsiders are important: Mosaics and Busters, perhaps as much as any American generation before them, need to experience faith that is expressed toward others. They want to do more than a learn *about* their faith; they want to *live* it. We interview many young people who have fallen away from faith because it was never more than a mere allegiance to life principles, not a deep inner connection to a living God who wants his people to give themselves away in sacrifice and service.

And so, to move from unChristian to Christian, young people need to see Christianity rejecting self-preservation and insularity and embracing true concern and compassion for others. This is important for Christian young people as well as Mosaics and Busters who are on the outside, watching to see if the efforts of "those Christians" are worth joining. The initial research we have done on this subject suggests that igniting passion for outsiders in the lives of Mosaics and Busters is one crucial means of making faith relevant, real, and lasting. Something significant is taking shape among Mosaics and Busters: they are becoming increasingly responsive to the global community and to their role in God's plan outside of the comfort and safety of ordinary life.

Keep in mind that this is not without difficulties. Young people are easily distracted, so they do not always stay enthusiastic about the commitments they make. Their excitement for ministry opportunities is often undone by financial, career, or character-related problems. And of course, while Mosaics and Busters like to talk about global awareness and activism, their responsiveness to sacrificial lifestyles is often undermined by their hyper-individualism. Helping Mosaics and Busters make a lasting connection to Christ requires that we show them how to love and serve others, but this is no magic formula. It's hard, spiritual work.

A LIFESTYLE OF COMPASSION

It is easy to say we need to serve outsiders; it is another thing entirely to make that a reality. In my role at The Barna Group, I often have to share information that is not flattering. I still remember one of my first experiences when I shared unwelcome news. It was a project for a Christian nonprofit organization. Lyle, an insightful, middle-aged man, represented my client. We conducted a comprehensive study of the effectiveness of his team's efforts working with people in recovery—for the most part, drug and alcohol abusers. The study showed many things were going well, but just as many were not. Weak spots needed attention. Rather than being defensive or ignoring the data, Lyle flew out to our offices to hear the painful details so that he could accurately and passionately present the news to his fellow leaders.

As I drove him to the airport that afternoon, Lyle seemed almost relieved to have finally gotten a grip on reality and a direction to pursue. Based on the questions he was asking, I could tell our daylong meeting had activated new thoughts and ideas that, if implemented, would enhance the organization.

We were on our way to a small regional airport, passing by the fertile strawberry fields of Ventura County. While trying to keep my eyes on the road and rambling about the research, I didn't realize Lyle was onto a new topic.

"I wonder if anyone is thinking about connecting those people to Christ," he said.

"What?" I said. "What people?"

"The workers there, in the field," he said pointing out a group of people, hunched over the plants, harvesting the berries. I had to strain to see them in the afternoon glare. "I wonder who is thinking about *their* spiritual needs."

I had no answer. I was embarrassed to think I had never thought about them before. I was not unsympathetic to the migrant workers. My grandfather owned a small citrus ranch near San Diego, and when I was a boy, he had taught me respect and compassion for the men and women who worked for him. Nevertheless, years later, I had driven by these strawberry fields time and again and never once considered the workers' spiritual needs.

Lyle was different. He *couldn't help but see the people*—the individuals behind the sweat—despite the economic and language differences. Lyle's ability to picture their genuine emotional, social, and spiritual needs was not limited to mere professional interest. Obviously, working with drug and alcohol addicts was not just a job for him. It oozed throughout his perspectives and priorities.

Lyle saw people in a way I did not.

UNCHRISTIAN DISTRESS

The idea that our faith can be unChristian is not an easy one to swallow. I realize that some will be distressed by it. Consider an episode from the life of Paul. In 2 Corinthians he wrote about his great trepidation at having to reprimand some of the believers in the city of Corinth. Then, when the Christians responded to his correction in a healthy way, Paul was enthusiastic:

> Isn't it wonderful all the ways in which this distress has goaded you closer to God? You're more alive, more concerned, more sensitive, more reverent, more human, more passionate, more responsible. Looked at from any angle, you've come out of this with purity of heart. . . . My primary concern was not for the one who did the wrong or even the one wronged, but for you—that you would realize and act upon the deep, deep ties between us before God.
>
> *2 Corinthians 7:11–12 Message*

The unChristian faith is distressing. So is our culture. Yet to see spiritual resurgence among Mosaics and Busters, I hope our response to this observation is like that of the recipients of Paul's letter. I hope we put aside casual forms of Christianity, piercing the antagonism of our peers with service and sacrifice. We may think the answer to the perception of our being unChristian is for outsiders to understand our faith. The church is not effective when it calls outsiders to live virtuously, which is never really possible apart from regeneration through Christ anyway. The reprieve from our deep-seated image problem comes when Christ followers become more faithful to a God who has redeemed us and more concerned about a hostile culture in need of the same redemption.[4]

Doesn't it strike you as significant that when John writes to the church of Ephesus in the book of Revelation, he doesn't spend any time patting them on the back for their stance against the moral bankruptcy in their culture? He just says, "You don't love me or each other as you did at first!" (2:4). We have lost sight of being *for* Jesus rather than *against* outsiders. And Scripture puts the burden squarely on believers: "If my people who are called by my name will humble themselves and pray and seek my face and turn from their wicked ways, I will hear from heaven and will forgive their sins and restore their land" (2 Chron. 7:14). Are we up to that challenge?

My friends Tim and Wendy became foster parents several years ago. They are currently parenting seventeen-year-old Beth, who has caused them incredible difficulty. Here is an email Tim wrote to a group of friends: "If you've got a moment please pray for Beth. Yesterday the foster agency came over to give her some new restrictions and, as expected, she ran away last night. She's gone AWOL in the past but always returned the same evening. This choice will not bring good things her way so she is going to need all of the grace and mercy God has for her.

"Be praying for Wendy and me as well. We're tired and stretched thin. We lack our own words to know how to pray about this situation anymore. Recently Wendy and I were struggling with a verse in Isaiah 58 that tells us to spend ourselves on behalf of the poor. We wondered what it really meant to spend ourselves, and I think we are finding out."

Tim's email got me thinking. And it also caused me to read Isaiah 58, which has remarkable relevance to this research.

> Tell my people Israel of their sins! Yet they act so pious! They come to the Temple every day and seem delighted to learn all about me. They act like a righteous nation that would never abandon the laws of its God. They ask me to take action on their behalf, pretending they want to be near me. "We have fasted before you!" they say. "Why aren't you impressed? We have been very hard on ourselves, and you don't even notice it!"
>
> "I will tell you why!" I respond. "It's because you are fasting to please yourselves. . . . What good is fasting when you keep on fighting and quarreling? This kind of fasting will never get you anywhere with me. . . .
>
> "No, this is the kind of fasting I want: Free those who are wrongly imprisoned; lighten the burden of those who work for you. Let the oppressed go free, and remove the chains that bind people. Share your food with the hungry, and give shelter to the homeless. Give clothes to those who need them, and do not hide from relatives who need your help.
>
> "Then your salvation will come like the dawn, and your wounds will quickly heal. Your godliness will lead you forward, and the glory of the LORD will protect you from behind. Then when you call, the LORD will answer. 'Yes, I am here,' he will quickly reply. . . .

"Then your light will shine out from the darkness, and the darkness around you will be as bright as noon. The LORD will guide you continually, giving you water when you are dry and restoring your strength. You will be like a well-watered garden, like an ever-flowing spring. Some of you will rebuild the deserted ruins of your cities. Then you will be known as a rebuilder of walls and a restorer of homes."

Isaiah 58:1–4, 6–12

As Christians, we want to believe our efforts are driven by the right motivations. We assume we are pursuing God and his purposes. Yet what if Isaiah 58 pegs our condition as Christians in America these days? What if millions of us are living for ourselves, even while we are going through the motions of religion? What if we seek comfort for ourselves rather than giving comfort to other people? What if our spiritual efforts are focused on maintaining equilibrium rather than addressing the significant spiritual needs of others? If you were to look at the vast reams of data I analyze every year about the state of faith in America, you would find such conclusions inescapable. But as I analyze the research, I realize that this is not just the nation's problem, it's mine. On close examination, my own spirituality looks self-oriented and threadbare.

The passage in Isaiah describes one simple yet difficult solution: *to rebuild our lives and restore our nation, we have to recover love and concern for others.*

I believe part of the reason Christians are known as unChristian is because the church has lost its ability and willingness to love and accept people who are not part of the "insider" club. This failure is draining the vigor from our faith. We say we love outsiders, but in many cases we show love only if it is on our terms, if they are interested in coming to our church, or if they respect our way of life.

We want young generations to participate in our churches, but we expect them to play by the rules, look the part, embrace the music, and use the right language. We condemn the moral compromises of Mosaics and Busters, but we lack the patience to restore them. We want them to become mature Christ followers, though we are unwilling to submit to the significant task of our own spiritual formation.

All of this is making Mosaics and Busters conclude that the faith is unChristian. And while we argue about who is to blame for the problem, the number and influence of young outsiders in American society continue to grow. Not only is Jesus becoming harder for them to see in the efforts and language of Christians, but they are learning to despise or disregard Christians—largely because the Christians they have known either criticize or ignore them.

When Christ followers do engage in conversations with young outsiders, common ground is hard to find. Often they speak different dialects, and they think in stereotypes, which is far easier than engaging in heartfelt conversations about real issues.

Sometimes young outsiders venture into churches, and often they come with an intense load of difficult experiences and deep hurts. They do not want to be scolded; they require our help and empathy. Not unlike an oncologist who must correctly diagnose and treat cancer, a church leader has to pray, counsel, guide, and love people through their frustrations and doubts. Ignoring their personal history at the time they are open to dealing with it means we have failed them spiritually.

While many outsiders feel emboldened to disparage Christians, a cadre of Christians is becoming even more entrenched, defensive, and strident. They are tense and plowing a wider gap between themselves and outsiders. It's a cold war that is becoming more hostile.

Are you ready to face these outcomes of unChristian faith?

My prayer is that this research will help to confirm things in your mind and soul so that your efforts with and concern for young outsiders will grow.

I believe that the new generations of Mosaics and Busters are waiting for us to provide pathways to Jesus, helping them to serve the significant needs of the world. God wants to bring spiritual resurgence to the young, skeptical generations—through your life and mine. Yet for most Mosaics and Busters the barriers to seeing Jesus are getting wider and higher. What image of Jesus do people get from your life?

The unChristian faith is here in force. We have a choice of whether it is here to stay.

 fermi project

For a summary of the Barna Research presented in this book and discussion questions for each chapter, go to www.unchristian.com

AFTERWORD

BY GABE LYONS

THE NEW PERCEPTIONS

I still remember the day I called David to commission this research project. At that point I had little to go on except my gut-level sense that something was desperately wrong with the way Christianity was perceived in our nation. My experience indicated that the Christian faith had a major image problem, but I didn't know why. I wanted to get to the root cause of what seemed to be a rapid deterioration of our identity. I sensed that if we didn't do something now, the reputation of Christianity would be at stake in future generations.

My conviction on the matter was so strong that I decided to launch a nonprofit organization with the purpose of recapturing Christianity's reputation in our culture. It was ambitious, daunting, and unclear, but I felt a call I could not ignore. Try explaining to your family and friends that you plan to leave a promising career and put all your effort into what most consider an idealistic pursuit. As you might imagine, it didn't go over so well. But I felt an unexplainable urgency, despite the risk, and jumped right in. I quit trying to explain to others what I wanted to do and started to do it.

A national study on the attitudes and perceptions of Christians in our culture seemed the perfect starting point. My sense was that if Christians could read the mind of outsiders, filtered through the objective lens of research, it would provide the motivation we needed to change how we see ourselves and our role in culture. And over time it could significantly alter how we live and interact with our friends, colleagues, and neighbors.

Deep down I hoped my intuition would be wrong about how negative the views of my generation were toward Christians. I was unprepared for how resistant, entrenched, and pessimistic the response would be.

I'll never forget sitting in Starbucks, poring through the research results on my laptop. As I soaked it in, I glanced at the people around me and was overwhelmed with the thought that *this is what they think of me*. It was a sobering thought to know that if I had stood up and announced myself as a "Christian" to the customers assembled in Starbucks that day, they would have associated me with every one of the negative perceptions described in this book. My next reaction, however, shocked me.

I was overwhelmed with a sense of hope. Instead of a burden of depression, I was captivated by the opportunity that lay in front of a new generation of Christians. It seemed the only direction these perceptions could go was a more positive one. As I read page after page of research, immersing myself in the painful descriptions from outsiders, I was aware that my heart was changing. I felt my mind transforming. Having access to what those around me really thought challenged me. I had finally been offered a unique glimpse into the perspective of those I'm called to love and embrace, and I was humbled, embarrassed, and provoked to make a difference.

I felt then, and still feel now, optimistic that with this research as the basis, an entirely new conversation could erupt within the Christian community. The results of this study give us a clear picture of how others see us. We have the opportunity to face the truth and own up to our role in contributing to these perceptions. It is time to reexamine what it means to be "Christian" and begin to live it.

PERCEPTION IS REALITY

To assume that the six major labels that David described are merely misperceptions of Christians would be a huge mistake. These perceptions are based on real experiences that outsiders have had with their Christian friends. They are an accurate reflection of the kind of Christians many of us have become. It's embarrassing and shameful, but it's reality.

One helpful way to reflect on this conclusion is through the lens of a brand. Scott Bedbury, creator of the Starbucks and Nike brands, defines a brand as a collection of perceptions in the consumer's mind. For instance, when you hear the word *Starbucks*, what immediately comes to mind? A round green logo? The aroma of coffee? The taste of a vanilla latte? The greeting of a friendly barista? A warm place for conversation? Or perhaps you have an entirely different, negative set of images that comes to mind. The point is, when presented with a brand name, you immediately summon all of your past experiences and interactions with the product and form an instant opinion.

To outsiders the word *Christian* has more in common with a brand than a faith. This shift of meaning in recent decades has been magnified by an increasing use of the term *Christian* to label music, clothes, schools, political action groups, and more. And sadly, it is a bad brand in the minds of tens of millions of people. In the middle of a culture where Christianity has come to represent hypocrisy, judgmentalism, anti-intellectualism, insensitivity, and bigotry, it's easy to see why the next generation wants nothing to do with it.

A SUBSTANCE PROBLEM NOT AN IMAGE PROBLEM

The way forward became clear to me within the pages of a book. I've heard it said that you don't choose the books you read; great books choose you. In some peculiar way, I believe that is what happened when I consumed Charles Colson and Nancy Pearcey's *How Now Shall We Live?* I hadn't planned to read a six-hundred-page nonfiction book while on vacation, but once I had read the introduction, I couldn't put it down.

They laid out clearly what being Christian was about. It felt simple yet complex, true, and historic. I was convinced that if more Christians could grasp this bigger picture, it could change the face of Christianity throughout our nation, and the perceptions of Christianity would subsequently improve.

Colson and Pearcey's explanation of what it means to be a holistic Christian grabbed my mind and my heart:

> God cares not only about redeeming souls but also about restoring his creation. He calls us to be agents not only of his *saving grace* but also of his *common grace*. Our job is not only to build up the church but also to build a society to the glory of God. As agents of God's common grace, we are called to help sustain and renew his creation, to uphold the created institutions of family and society, to pursue science and scholarship, to create

works of art and beauty, and to heal and help those suffering from the results of the Fall.[1]

This understanding of *common grace* has been at the root of Christianity's growth and influence throughout the world for centuries. It was becoming clear to me that if Christians could recapture and live out this holistic view of their calling in this world, new perceptions would quickly follow.

Many modern-day Christians have lost touch with the all-encompassing gospel that goes beyond personal salvation and reaches every corner of society. When conversion growth is the single measure of success, the hard work of discipleship gets ignored. When Christian faith is relegated to a personal, spiritual decision about where you will spend the afterlife, the here and now matters less. When being a Christian can be determined by whether you "prayed the prayer," the focus shifts easily to who is in and who is out. As a result, Christians can be found primarily on the edges of society, pointing their fingers at outsiders, judging and condemning them. Subsequently, the lifestyle of being Christian shifts from being winsome and engaging to pessimistic and manipulative. Many have separated themselves from the world and unknowingly mimick the actions of the Pharisees for whom Jesus had the most contempt when he walked the earth.

Losing the theology and practice of common grace and focusing on conversion over discipleship have contributed greatly to Christianity's perception problem. When we no longer know what it means (much less care) to be salt and light *among* those in our culture and to be an influence for good, we forfeit our role as agents of Christ's kingdom. As I've observed current culture, examined church history, and wrestled with Scripture, it seems clear to me that the source of these negative perceptions is a poorly understood and lived expression of Christianity.

BECOMING CHRISTIAN

It comes down to this: we must become Christlike again.

This is both the good news and the hard reality of accepting the research in this book. At first glance this may seem like an oversimplified solution, but when you recognize that being Christian demands more than simply saying a prayer, assenting to a statement of belief, and going to heaven when you die, it becomes more personally challenging. Add the concept that being Christian means being God's agent of common grace in the world, and the task becomes even more sobering.

We must commit to doing the hard work of recapturing Christianity's essence in our own lives. It's easy to point out the imperfections of others, but it takes much more humility and grace to confront the faults in ourselves. Being Christian is hard work. Putting the needs of others above your own, loving your neighbor, doing good to those who would do evil to you, exercising humility, suffering with those less fortunate, and doing it all with a pure heart is nearly impossible. But it is Jesus's model and call. And that is what it will take. When an aspiring saint asked Mother Teresa, "How can I be like you?" her simple response was, "Find your own Calcutta." She understood the core of the Christian life—the truest knowing comes in the doing.

How might this play out for an entire generation of Christians currently living out a poor expression of Christianity?

Christians in the older generations will need to work hard at rediscovering what it means to follow Christ in today's culture. It may start with an honest admission that some of what you may have called Christianity has no connection to the faith at all. It may require letting go of the baggage that surrounds ardent denominationalism, or decisively stepping away from the comfortable Christian subculture. It could mean taking the risk of being labeled "worldly" or "liberal" because of a biblically based commitment to advocate for cultural issues, like social justice and caring for God's creation. Maybe it's a willingness to consider how much your faith has become entangled with Western values that are at odds with the heart of Christianity, such as consumerism and materialism. Overall, it requires openness to the idea that you may be living an incomplete or inaccurate version of the faith.

For the youngest generations, the challenge will be to live a life that represents a fuller vision of Christianity than you may have seen modeled for you. Have the courage to follow your God-given talents and callings, and take the risk to express your faith in less conventional ways. Local churches should take seriously their opportunity to disciple and celebrate people who have a fully orbed view of Christian thinking and its relationship to all things throughout culture. While this will be difficult and demanding, we have no choice. The outcome of this pursuit by the youngest generations carries a disproportionate amount of influence in reversing the negative reputation of Christ followers in society as we look to the future.

As Christians of all generations allow Christ to transform their hearts, minds, and actions, their expressions of the Christian faith will change, resulting in an influence on society that we have not experienced in decades.

No strategy, tactics, or clever marketing campaign could ever clear away the smokescreen that surrounds Christianity in today's culture. The perceptions of outsiders will change only when Christians strive to represent the heart of God in every relationship and situation. This kind of Christian will attract instead of repel. He is provoked to engage instead of offended by a decadent culture. She lives with the tension of remaining pure without being isolated from this broken world. When outsiders begin to have fresh experiences and interactions with this new kind of Christian, perceptions will change, one person at a time. When they have cataloged enough experiences with this kind of Christian to outweigh their negative ones, the reputation will change.

In due time, the name *Christian* will come to represent something refreshing and positive. One new friendship, a compassionate hug, a kind word, a positive outlook, or a well-meaning affirmation will go a long way in seeing Christ's reputation revitalized throughout our culture.

A LONG-TERM VIEW

I was twenty-eight years old when I commissioned this research three years ago. Quickly I came to understand that if we are ever going to see progress in how Christianity is perceived in our culture, it will likely take several decades to accomplish. We must approach this with a long-term view.

For too long, Christians have adopted short-term mindsets when it comes to interacting with our culture. The tendency can be to try to solve our perception problem quickly and gloss over the root issues that created it in the first place. If you believe the cause of the problem goes deeper than a surface image and reaches to the core of what it means to be a Christian, then you catch a glimpse of how long this might take.

But we shouldn't be discouraged. Instead, we should be challenged to become the kind of Christ followers, friends, and neighbors who are humble and full of grace, love, and compassion. We must take the love of Christ everywhere we go and exhibit an expression of Christianity that seeks to find the good in all people and point them toward their Creator.

Just after my phone conversation with David, I decided to begin an organization that could move these efforts forward. Fermi Project is one of our initiatives, helping to educate and mobilize Christian leaders throughout the church to become a positive force for good in society. Instead of complaining about the negative perceptions surrounding Christianity, we want to be a part of the solution, a hopeful group of people driving forward a new way of being Christian in our culture.

We set out to discover Christians whose lives and work are changing perceptions. These mentors and models are representative of a new way of being Christ followers who are rooted in the practice of the early church by expressing their faith in word and deed. They are embodying a way of life that reflects the truth of who God is and how he has called his followers to live.

For the concluding pages of this book, I asked a few respected leaders in this arena to share their hopes, thoughts, and admonitions for the future of the church. I've asked them to give us their perspective on what Christians could be known for in thirty years, and I believe you'll be encouraged, as I was, with their hopeful visions. As C. S. Lewis believed, imagination precedes fact. Let's imagine together what *could* happen and then commit to *being* the change we want to create.

THE NEW PERCEPTIONS

GLOBAL

My hope is that, in the future, evangelical leaders will ensure that their social agenda includes such vital but controversial topics as halting climate change, eradicating poverty, abolishing armories of mass destruction, responding adequately to the AIDS pandemic, and asserting the human rights of women and children in all cultures.

John Stott
rector emeritus, All Souls Church, London

LOVE

Simply put, I think Christians ought to be known for loving people outside of their social comfort zones. Today we've become pretty good at loving people like ourselves, but the kind of love I hope Christians are known for in thirty years breaks our social love boundaries.

Of course, love is too difficult a word to define. But let me try listing what I think the future of Christian love ought to involve:

- Loving without putting our acts of kindness on a pedestal. What happened to giving in secret? Glamorous charity is not charity at all.
- Loving without strings, unconditionally, no bait and switches.

- Being unconcerned about being unnamed, rewarded, or repaid.
- Prioritizing the other, even in the midst of personal discomfort.
- Advocating for the undefended.
- Being a voice for the voiceless.
- Being better listeners to those who need to be heard.
- Being a church without walls—simple church, organic church, megachurch—it's all good. We're one church.
- Seeing the church as a home of the fringe, the misfits, and the marginalized, where these same people lead with real authority.
- Being willing to die for others, laying our lives down like the first-century Christians did when pandemics struck their cities. They would *stay* to serve the afflicted while others left.
- Responding immediately to any global crisis.
- Thinking of long-term commitment to radical and sacrificial compassion for the poor.
- Being a gentle conversationalist with the world.
- Showing love for Christ more than love for Christianity as a culture.
- Creating a place where all are truly empowered, led, and seen. A place where the next generation finally reflects the majority, multicultural world. Jesus really didn't have blue eyes! (Or did he?)

Dave Gibbons
pastor, New Song Church

AUTHENTIC

Managing perceptions is a tricky business. At the beginning of Jesus's public ministry, Luke tells us that he "began to teach in their synagogues and was praised by everyone" (Luke 4:15 NRSV). Then, a scant few verses later, Jesus narrowly escapes a mob execution after teaching in a synagogue (4:29–30). Jesus warns his disciples, "Woe to you when all speak well of you, for that is what their ancestors did to the false prophets" (6:26 NRSV). Yet Luke also reports that the first Christians spent their time in the temple "praising God and having the goodwill of all the people" (Acts 2:47 NRSV), a few chapters before the early church is scattered by intense persecution.

As any public figure—politician, rock star, or preacher—knows, you can't control how other people perceive you. That's not to say you can't try. You can hide behind an army of PR specialists and spinmeisters; you can rehearse glib lines until your smile is frozen in place. But then you're no longer *you*; you're the public version of you. And it's never long before some enterprising muckraker gets behind the facade.

So I'm not eager for us to manage perceptions of Christians, Christianity, or Christ. Jesus, thankfully, doesn't need our spin control—he emerges in every age and culture as an admirable and compelling figure. Christianity is and has been—at least from the days of the house churches at Corinth and Galatia—quite a remarkable mess, and *that's* surely not going to change in the next thirty years. As for Christians, well, we really have just one thing going for us. We have publicly declared—in my church, we declare every week, aloud, together—that we are desperately in need of Another to give us his righteousness, to complete us, and to live in us. We have publicly and flagrantly abandoned the project of self-justification that is at the heart of every person's compulsion to manage perceptions.

So what remains, I suppose, is for us to become better known for what, and who, we actually are. This means telling the world—before the world does its own investigative journalism—that we're not as bad as they think sometimes. We're worse. For every judgmental thing some TV preacher has said, I've thought something nastier, more bitter, and more biting about one of my neighbors. For every alleged act of homophobia by my fellow Christians, I've done something stupid to try to demonstrate my masculinity or virility. No matter how boring the church may seem to the hipsters, they don't know the half of it; believe me. I've spent weeks and months in desperate boredom, flipping randomly through blogs, ads, and *Vanity Fair*, because I wasn't willing to take a risk God was calling me to take.

And yet there is Another who lives in me. And he is found in some other unlikely places. So we also need to tell the world how we found him. How we found him in a mud house in the slums, a storefront in the hood, a home for the beaten, a circle for the addicted. How we found him in jails, hospitals, and even morgues. How we found him too among the humble at Harvard, the generous on Wall Street, the principled on K Street. How he found us, actually.

Most of the time, the world will get the story wrong, if only because it has a vested interest in getting it wrong. But if we're being honest about our own beauty and brokenness, the beautiful broken One will make himself known to our neighbors—through the chinks in our armor, and in theirs. "He passed through the midst of them and went on his way"—perceived or misperceived, celebrated or crucified, the One who lives in us has a way of walking through walls.

Andy Crouch
journalist and author, *Culture-Makers*

COURAGE

Thirty years from now, Christians won't be known for what they say or what they hope to be; they will be known for one thing—the way they live. We can't change what we are known for unless we change how we live.

I want my grandkids to have the perception that followers of Christ are very courageous. The great yearning in our world today is for an answer to the many fears that we all share. Even the negative perceptions described throughout this book originate from fear and paint a picture of a community of faith that has lived in fear—fear of people that don't understand them, fear of changes in culture, fear of degradations of society, fear to be exposed to the hard things in this world.

I would love thirty years from now for Christians to have such faith in God that they carry themselves with courage and humility in the world. Both courage and humility are pictures of strength. This doesn't mean that all fears disappear, but rather faith points the way to a strength that allows one to do the right thing even when it's scary. And if you truly know God and are secure in the fact that there is a God, that he really loves us and really loves this world, everything will be okay.

With that confidence and strength, you can not only go into the world, you can live out a gospel that is attractive. In a world where there is much fear, people will gravitate to those who are living with a surprising lack of fear.

My prayer is that followers of Jesus Christ would walk through life demonstrating a surprising lack of fear and great humility and courage. This would give the world a more realistic expression of who Jesus Christ is.

Gary Haugen
founder, International Justice Mission

JESUS

I have great optimism about the reputation of Christianity in the future. Right now, the perceptions raised in this book of what our emerging culture thinks of Christians and the church are pretty embarrassing and sadly true. But the good news is that while people have negative perceptions of the church and Christians, they are open to and respect what they know of Jesus. This led me to write a book about this, where I conclude that people *like Jesus but not the church*.

So if over the next thirty years, Christians, and especially church leaders, escape the subculture that we have created, this could really change the climate of how we are viewed by those outside the church. In theory, it really shouldn't be hard to do. Jesus followers need to simply be friends with those outside the church. It's not too complicated—

going to movies with them, caring for them as any friend would, having them over for dinner, being there for them, not just seeing them as evangelistic targets. So even if they stumble at the gospel, as many, of course, will, at least they won't stumble at all the negative stereotypes and perceptions that have developed.

But it does mean that we do need to take the words of Jesus seriously when he said not to be separate from the world but to be in the world, protected from evil. I absolutely know we need Christian community, but we have swung the pendulum so far into Christian "community" that we now live in more of an isolated world. Our time is filled with Christian activities and busyness in the church, taking us away from building normal and healthy friendships with those in the world.

So the future could be quite positive if people experience that not all Christians are antihomosexual, judgmental, and sheltered. I envision Christians naturally befriending those outside the church, understanding their faith, being deeper thinkers theologically, and truly having answers for those who ask. My prayer and hope for the future is that church leaders will become missional leaders, which in turn will produce missional churches, and then the perceptions will be changed to positive as the Spirit of God uses our lives to be salt and light. So when a similar study is undertaken in thirty years, people will describe Christians as "loving, kind, family centered, caring for the poor, good examples, peaceful," and the other fruits of the Spirit.

Dan Kimball
pastor and author

ADMIRED

I would hope people would look at us and say, "Those Christians are the ones who run in when everyone else is running out. Those Christians are the ones who didn't give up on the crumbling inner cities. Those Christians are the ones who brought peace to Darfur. Those Christians are the ones who put an end to human trafficking. Those Christians are the ones who helped win the war on AIDS around the world. Those Christians are the ones who write those incredible lyrics, pen those unforgettable books, and create artwork that's mesmerizing. Those Christians are the ones who helped my mother when she got Alzheimer's. Those Christians are the ones who were kind to me when I was new to the area. Those Christians are the ones that made me want to believe in God."

Margaret Feinberg
author and speaker

RESTORERS

The kingdom of heaven is like leaven: just a little of it leavens the entire loaf.

What if the church, over the next thirty years, truly lives the life that Jesus has taught us to live? What if we love our enemies, pray for those who hate us, and offer our coat when our hat has been taken? Are we ready to truly sacrifice and watch the world move toward the kingdom of God?

The kingdom of heaven is like a man who loses a pearl in a field and purchases the whole field to find it.

If Jesus is as valuable as we say he is, then what will we give up for him to remain alive in us? Can we, the church, spend the next thirty years valuing Jesus Christ and whatever he asks of us above all else? Can we even imagine what the world would become?

If the church will choose now to live this way, we can confidently look forward to seeing our culture influenced and changed. My hope is that when I am seventy-two, I will have seen the kingdoms of this world become the kingdoms of our God. I imagine a world lacking divorce, sexual promiscuity, and poverty, and overflowing with peace, mercy, and justice.

Isaiah prophesies that the old wasted cities will be restored. He says that we shall be called repairers of the breach, the restorers of the streets.

Leroy Barber
president, Mission Year

JUSTICE

The moral values conversation will be wider and deeper in the future, more able to challenge the politics and selective moralities of both the Left and the Right. The church's mission will expand to include protecting the environment, confronting global and domestic poverty, and addressing the ethics of war and peace.

We won't just focus on abortion and gay marriage, as we're often accused of today. These two issues are important, but they're simply not the only important issues we should focus on—especially in a world where every day thirty thousand children needlessly die of hunger, preventable diseases, and a lack of clean drinking water.

And I think maybe there are two more things we'll see.

People are hungry for moral courage in political leaders. They're hungry for people to call them to something bigger or larger than themselves. They're hungry for genuine political leadership and not just political calculation, focus groups, consultants, and polling. I recently read Joe Klein's book *Politics Lost*. It's all about the alarming trend of population-based political strategy and the lack of real leadership in politics. From what I've seen, this isn't what people out there want. They are ready for something different.

There's going to be a growing sense of how social movements can reform politics. I've observed that the two greatest hungers in the world are for authentic, life-changing faith on the one hand and social justice on the other. The connection between the two is one the world is waiting for. The young people I know are more interested in becoming part of this sort of spiritually inspired social movement than in running for political office. Some of them will run for office, and that's fine—but they're more interested in transforming politics than in joining it.

As this happens, I believe we'll see the reinvigoration of social justice coupled with an authentic revival of faith.

Jim Wallis
founder and executive director, Sojourners/Call to Renewal

DIGNITY

We know that historically the youngest generation is impressionable and idealistic. As they mature, they begin to see the things that they were hypercritical of in a more mature way. I think people are going to get over their negative views of Christians and will begin to see that Jesus is real. I believe that it will happen.

Chesterton's words give me great comfort. He said, "I came to the conclusion that the optimist thought everything good except the pessimist, and that the pessimist thought everything bad except himself." We can learn from this that Christians should be neither optimists nor pessimists, but both. Christians must have the right balance and be pessimistic enough to see the sin of man. But they must be optimistic enough to know that God is sovereign, and he will have his way.

I really believe the church is waking up. I spend half of my waking hours and some of my sleeping hours thinking of things we can do to educate young people about the ideas of worldview and common grace. I believe that when we work together to educate Christians on the ideas of worldview, common grace, and the Christian's responsibility for human rights and human dignity, the world will see an entirely different picture painted.

Chuck Colson
founder, Prison Fellowship

GRACE

I have long been taken by the origin of the name "Christian." In Acts 11 there was a community of people who so lived out the Christ-life that they were called "Christians," which means "little Christs." There is no sense that it was ever a term of derision or ridicule—just an observation. Here were people living a life that reflected the person of Jesus.

What should the perceptions of Christians be in thirty years? That there is something supernatural about our lives, that there is something about us that cannot be explained in anything other than a miraculous way, that there seems to be something about us—something that we have—that the world does not have and seemingly cannot offer.

I think of the scandal of grace in the midst of community, the selflessness of compassion in the face of disdain, the aroma of holiness in the teeth of debauchery, the firmness of orthodoxy while immersed in the illusion of various matrices. But most of all, I suppose, I think of the scandal of grace—freely received into our lives and then freely distributed to others. Jesus himself said this should be the mark of the Christian, and the single dynamic that would arrest the world's attention.

Russian novelist Dostoyevsky once wrote that grace heals our vision, that it lets us love people by seeing them as God intended them to be. Compare that to German philosopher Friedrich Nietzsche, who wrote in his autobiography of the ability to "smell" the inmost parts of every soul, especially the "abundant hidden dirt at the bottom" of a character.

May our future be that of clear vision and an inability to smell.

Jim White
author

TRANSFORMED

If followers of Christianity follow Christ for the next thirty years, Christianity will be comprised of faith-filled believers who are focused on the manifestation of God's power in every aspect of their lives, with the purpose of having dominion on earth until Christ returns. This will come as a result of the church shifting its focus from membership to relationship. Power doesn't come from membership at the right church or in the right denomination. Real power comes from a strong personal relationship with God, with encouragement and accountability coming from the body of believers. Christians in 2037 will care more about their personal relationships than their 11 a.m. Sunday morning reservation.

In following Christ, Christians in 2037 will go to places others won't go and say things others won't say in the name of God, so that people are convicted, not entertained. The perception of Christianity will be that of a bold and transforming faith.

Finally, Christians will be perceived as consistent. It is no myth that today we are event-based worshipers, willing to wear a mask on Sunday and Wednesday (or whenever we have Bible study), then go back to business as usual for the duration of the week. Christians in 2037 will equate relationship with God to a lifestyle, not an event. They will stop today's practice of interpreting divine doctrine through a filter of cultural convenience. These Christians will transform the world by letting God shine through us as much on the job, at the mall, at the club, and on the street as we do in the church. Perception is reality. I hope we do change our reality in 2007, to earn this perception change in 2037.

Jeff Johnson
social activist
BET host and international correspondent

COUNTERCULTURE

No one can predict the future, particularly of something as intangible as the "brand" of Christianity. But we can be sure whatever happens must be plausible so we can outline the borders of plausibility, knowing the future must fall within it. The plausible may not be what we hope for, or what ought to be, but what is likely and possible. What is a plausible future for the perception of Christianity in the next thirty years?

In thirty years the Christian "brand" will be shaped primarily by today's infants as they grow in the church, and secondarily by the ripples of influence launched by this current generation of youth as they dwell in middle age. The opinions, actions, and influence of today's parents will vanish quickly and survive only indirectly via the legacy of their child rearing.

American Christian culture as a distinct mainstream identity is rapidly morphing into something closer to a subculture. If trends continue as they are, we might expect the young to:

- embrace cultural idioms rather than avoid common cultural touchstones
- hold strong aversions and intolerances, which will continue to win black marks in a very tolerant society
- be less at odds with scientific views in general, but still not intellectual
- be centered in healing and self-help ministries
- exhibit a softening toward pluralism in reaction to the hard religious politics of their parents' generation
- adopt a hip countercultural stance
- have more Christian-themed works in the mainstream
- delve into mysticism—depending on the path of future technology
- still be remote from the lives of the poor and suffering

> • organize reactions to outright social persecution

So what words do I expect the teenager in the street thirty years hence to use about the Christian brand?

> Healing
> Countercultural
> Intolerant

I hope I am wrong about one of those.

Kevin Kelly
cofounder, *Wired* magazine

CULTIVATORS

In thirty years Christians will have baptized their picture of Christ. He won't be a nice, banal, meek, and bearded man with softly permed hair. Instead, he will fill our imaginations more solidly, more invasively, more unexpectedly. Christ will become That Man who changes people, someone who jumps off of bumper stickers and mediocre praise songs and into lives, a presence much more like Gandalf the Grey than Mr. Rogers.

This change won't come overnight. It will begin with our humility to embrace the Hebraic history of Jesus as part of our own. We will no longer dismiss as irrelevant the way we were grafted into an old, old story. Our churches, Bible studies, and worldviews will be refreshed with stories of God's unpredictable, relentless pursuit of the Hebrews. This will breathe new life into our celebrations (like the Passover), our worship (we might find that dance and poetry, both found in the Psalms as worship, will have a place in the church), and our attitudes (we will realize that Christ was working before America, before Martin Luther, even before the New Testament).

When this change comes and we see Christ differently, others will notice.

Christians will be known not merely as engagers of culture, but as creators and builders of culture. We will not avoid or fear the marketplace of ideas, the museums of modern art, and the assemblies of diplomacy; we will enter them. Christians will cultivate an understanding of art, science, business, engineering, architecture, and medicine because we know that our work tells the world more of what God is like. When any field wants a well-informed expert, Christians will be consulted, not as token evangelicals, not because we have demanded representation, and not because we are so nice, but because we are concerned with excellence.

Christian women will no longer be known as the quiet, meek, and somewhat pathetic group who doesn't experience twenty-first-century freedom. Instead, we will be something of an admired anomaly, sought after as the most informed believers in the value of femininity. We will define womanhood beyond gentle and quiet submission, curves, baby production, and high heels. We will understand and cogently explain how women are both body and soul and valuable for more than sex appeal. We will be known as "those women" who are not afraid of old age and its mark on our bodies. Our self-possession will make us a challenging group for marketers to target. We will be less concerned with proving our equality with men and more intent on building our souls for the kingdom of God.

As Christian men and women, we will be faithful when we demonstrate longsuffering with discernment, joy without everlasting grins, peace when it costs us personally to keep it, patience when our favorite causes are overlooked, and self-control when others are given the credit for changing the world.

In thirty years our souls will be bigger.

Jonalyn Fincher
author, *Ruby Slippers*

ENGAGED

On many occasions on this journey, I have wanted to turn in my evangelical membership card and call it a day. There have been moments when I still wanted to believe in Jesus, but I didn't want to belong to this crazy family anymore. Maybe you've been there too. So thinking about what Christianity might be known for in thirty years can easily feel like a hopeless exercise, and I might be foolish to even consider it. But with all the sincerity that I can muster, I truly believe this dysfunctional and whacked-out family of ours can be healed and find recovery.

And though at times you and I may have only a frayed, doubt-filled faith about the future, I want us to believe that it can be better. Why should we stay and work on these problems? Why not just blow the whole thing up? Because, first off, no one likes a quitter, and second, lobbing hand grenades on the bride of Christ takes zero talent or effort. I also think this really ticks God off. My five-year-old child complains and whines when things aren't the way she wants them, but courageous men and women roll up their sleeves and get busy. I want to be an active participant in putting back together the broken pieces.

I do see the future Christian faith being something that is good, true, and credible in our culture. I can dream of a day when the followers of Jesus are known not for these current tragic perceptions, but for trying to live like Jesus. We will fumble, stumble, and hit some rough patches along the way, but we must not give up.

I look forward to the day when Christian hangouts won't just be Sunday morning church services or praise-band practices, but instead Tuesday night potlucks at the local homeless shelter. One day the world will ask, "Where are all those Christian freaks at?" I pray our answer will be, "We're over here helping in the ravaged slums of

Africa and happily drilling wells in Haitian villages. And, guys, we're going to be here for a while."

I believe thirty years from now, when societies are failing and a country has been devastated by disease, it won't take an Irish rock star to inform us of this tragedy. It won't be news to us because we will have been there from the beginning. Christians will be the first to sound the cry of injustice and rally the nations that we all must do more. We will have officially burned the Christian "bandwagon" and become a people who from the beginning rallied for the oppressed, forgotten, and overlooked. And when we cry out against wrongs and evils in this world, people will listen and know what we say is true because our words will sound a lot like those of our Savior.

I have faith that in the future we will make better decisions on what issues we think are important. When we stand up for something and draw a line in the sand, we will know that it is clearly for the cause of Christ and not for some political, religious, or self-serving agenda. We will pick the hills we die on more wisely and choose to go to battle a little less often. And when we stand up for something, we will take our two favorite companions: grace and love. They will stand on the left and right of us. And we would never be so foolish or unwise as to ever journey without them.

And most important, I hope that thirty years from now we will have a healthy perspective and be able to look back three decades and say that we were courageous enough to change. We might have screwed it up early on and gone badly off course, but we were brave enough to look in the mirror and see our ugliness. And not only see it but do something about it. And just for that fact alone, things will be better in the future, and the face of Christianity will have changed.

Mike Foster
president of Ethur
founder of XXXChurch.com

BOLD

My prayer is that in thirty years Christians will be known for putting their faith into action in their neighborhoods and around the world. Followers of Christ will be on the cutting edge in taking on the most pressing challenges facing humanity—from AIDS and poverty to global debt relief and human trafficking. We'll be known as "world Christians," concerned with and supportive of our brothers and sisters in Christ who choose to serve others.

Kevin Palau
Palau Ministries

PURPOSE

Thirty years from now, regardless of changes in technology, communication, and culture, people will still have the same basic needs. They will need love, acceptance, meaning, purpose, forgiveness, dignity, and significance. They will struggle with selfishness, fear, guilt, resentment, worry, boredom, loneliness, and other universal problems. These won't go away. Thirty years from now the solution will still be the same: Jesus Christ

Since the church is the body of Christ on earth today, then thirty years from now it still will need to be doing what Jesus did while here in his physical body two thousand years ago. While the church's *methods* must constantly change in a changing world, the church's *mandate* will never change: we are called to know and love God (worship), love each other (fellowship), grow in Christlikeness (discipleship), serve God by serving others (ministry), and share the good news (evangelism). These five eternal purposes are modeled by the first church in Acts 2, mentioned in Jesus's prayer for us in John 17, explained by Paul in

Ephesians 4, but are best summarized in Jesus's great commandment and the Great Commission.

Out of these five purposes, Jesus's ministry planted a church, equipped servant leaders, assisted the poor, cared for the sick, and educated the next generation. I am confident that the church will still be doing these things in thirty years because the church has always done them. I just pray and hope that the next generation of Christ followers will do a better job than we did.

My passion is to help the next generation of church leaders guide their congregations in taking on the world's biggest problems (the "global giants"): spiritual emptiness, egocentric leadership, extreme poverty, pandemic disease, and rampant illiteracy. All governments, businesses, and NGOs combined have failed in solving these. The only group large enough to handle these problems is the network of millions of local churches around the world. We have the widest distribution, the largest group of volunteers, local credibility, the promises of God, the power of the Holy Spirit, and the inevitability of history.

My dream is that thirty years from now, the church will be known more by what it is *for* than what it is *against*. For some time now, the hands and feet of the body of Christ have been amputated, and we've been pretty much reduced to a big mouth. We talk far more than we do. It's time to reattach the limbs and let the church be the church in the twenty-first century.

Dr. Rick Warren

www.pastors.com

CHRISTIANS

In thirty years research could tell us that when people think *Christian*, they think things like this:

- Christians are the ones who love people, whoever they are— gay or straight, Jew or Muslim, religious or atheist, capitalist or not, conservative or liberal.
- Christians are the ones who have done more than anyone in the world to stop the HIV/AIDS crisis.
- Christians are the people who gravitate toward the poor and who show compassion through generous action and seek justice so that the systemic causes of poverty are overcome. They call the rich to generosity, and they call on rich nations to work for the common good.
- Christians are people who believe that art and creativity are important, so they consistently produce the most striking, original, and enriching art.
- Christians are willing to give their lives for the cause of peace. They oppose violence in all its forms. They will lay down their lives to protect the vulnerable from the violent.
- Christians care for the environment. They don't just see it as raw materials for economic gain, but they see it as the precious handiwork of their Creator.
- Christians have personal integrity. They keep their marriage vows and are aware of how destructive misused sexuality can be. Yet they are compassionate toward people who make sexual mistakes, and they never consider themselves superior.
- Christians build harmony among races. You always know that you'll be respected when you're around a Christian.

Perhaps I am a dreamer. But when hard realities jolt you out of denial (as the research presented here can help do), the status quo becomes less acceptable, and one is motivated to dream of better possibilities. I hope that this research will push others toward becoming dreamers too, and that those dreams will inspire the needed creative and faithful action.

Brian McLaren
founding member, emergentvillage.com

ACKNOWLEDGMENTS

Every book is a group effort. The development of this book has taken an especially devoted and capable team. Gabe Lyons and I owe much to Dwight Baker, Jack Kuhatschek, Dave Lewis, Don Stephenson, and the team at Baker Books, who believed in the project and have invested significant time and energy in it. Jack masterfully guided the ship and brought clarity to a difficult project. Thanks also to Twila Bennett, Rachel Geerlings, Mary Suggs, Kim De Wall, and Mary Wenger.

My partner Gabe deserves the lion's share of credit: it was his vision, his determination, and his money that made this project a reality. He and the team at the Fermi Project deserve thanks for pursuing and supporting this conversation about Christianity's reputation in culture. The Fermi team includes Gabe's wife, Rebekah, as well as Joanna DeWolf, Courtney Fahey, Danielle Kirkland, and Jeff Shinabarger.

I am also indebted to my colleagues at The Barna Group, who have helped immensely throughout this process. Nancy Barna, Katie Bayless, Terry Gorka, Cameron Hubiak, Pam Jacob, Jamie McLaughlin, and Celeste Rivera are true professionals and good friends.

Thanks as well to the contributors who gave their time and insights to the project. We are humbled that they would consider participating and sharing their voices in these pages. Other collaborators who have left "silent" marks include Doug Colby, Ken Coleman, Ben Ortlip, Nick Purdy, Larry Reichardt, and Roger Thompson. Thanks also to Jason Locy and Patricio Juarez of FiveStone for the terrific book cover and design.

ACKNOWLEDGMENTS

My research work stands on the shoulders of my mentor and friend, George Barna. He has supported, encouraged, cajoled, and challenged me for twelve years, putting up with me far longer than anyone should. If I've written something that doesn't make sense, it's not George's fault; I am a slow learner. Watching George work and pray and lead has been a clear picture of a man devoted to Jesus and passionate about serving God's people.

My family has been incredibly helpful and supportive as well, especially my father, who was a terrific sounding board for the book's content. He knows I steal ideas from him, and he doesn't seem to mind. My kids, Emily, Annika, and Zack, have sacrificed a lot of time with me for this book. I hope this project will enable me to become a better model for them of what it means to be a Christ follower.

My wife, though, deserves the most credit for this book. Jill has endured more than her fair share to see this project completed. Her prayers, stamina, and encouragement made this project doable. Her love and support made the book worth doing. I pray the Lord will repay her many sacrifices.

THE RESEARCH

Outsiders—those individuals who look at Christianity "from the outside in." This group includes atheists and agnostics; those affiliated with a faith other than Christianity (such as Islam, Hinduism, Judaism, Mormonism, and so on), and other unchurched adults who are not born again Christians. The use of the term *outsider* is not meant to be pejorative; other possible labels for this group of people are less applicable or appropriate. (For further discussion of the term *outsider*, see chapter 1.)

Born-again Christians—people who said they have made a personal commitment to Jesus Christ that is still important in their life today, and who also indicated they believe that when they die they will go to heaven because they have confessed their sins and have accepted Jesus Christ as their Savior. Respondents are not asked to describe themselves as "born again."

Evangelicals—people who meet the born-again criteria (described above) plus seven other conditions. Those include (1) saying their faith is very important in their life today; (2) believing they have a personal responsibility to share their religious beliefs about Christ with non-Christians; (3) believing that Satan exists; (4) believing that eternal salvation is possible only through grace, not works; (5) believing that Jesus Christ lived a sinless life on earth; (6) asserting that the Bible is accurate in all that it teaches; and (7) describing God as the all-knowing, all-powerful, perfect deity who created the universe and still rules it today. Being classified as an evangelical is not dependent on church attendance or the denominational affiliation of the church attended. Respondents were not asked to describe themselves as "evangelical."

Biblical worldview—a life perspective that enables a person to understand and respond to reality in light of what the Bible teaches. In its surveys, the Barna team defines a biblical worldview on the basis of several questions about religious beliefs. The definition requires someone to believe that unchanging moral truth exists; that the source of moral truth is the Bible; that the Bible is accurate in all of the principles it teaches; that eternal spiritual salvation cannot be earned; that Jesus lived a sinless life on earth; that every person has a responsibility to share their religious beliefs with others; that Satan is a living force, not just a symbol of evil; and that God is the all-knowing, all-powerful maker of the universe who still rules that creation today.

METHODOLOGY

The core of this book is the research commissioned by the Fermi Project. That project was supplemented through the book by a number of other quantitative and qualitative research studies conducted by The Barna Group. Those studies cited in the book are listed below.

Survey	Data Collection	Dates Conducted	Sample Size	Sampling Error*
OmniPoll–2-95	telephone	July 1995	1107	+ 3.2 points
Fermi Project– qualitative	telephone	April 2004	27	qualitative
Fermi Project study**	online	September 2004	867	+ 3.5 points
YouthPollSM 2005	online	2005	2409	+ 2.1 points
PastorPollSM 2006	telephone	November 2006	613	+ 4.1 points
YouthPollSM 2006	online	June 2006	618	+ 4.1 points
OmniPollSM 1-06	telephone	January 2006	1020	+ 3.2 points
OmniPollSM S-06	telephone	May 2006	1006	+ 3.2 points
OmniPollSM 2-06	telephone	August 2006	1007	+ 3.2 points
OmniPollSM F-06	telephone	October 2006	1005	+ 3.2 points

Survey	Data Collection	Dates Conducted	Sample Size	Sampling Error*
OmniPollSM 1-07	telephone	January 2007	1006	+ 3.2 points
Fermi Project update	online	January 2007	102	qualitative
The Buster Report	telephone	2002-2007	24399	aggregate study
Faith By Market Report	telephone	1997-2004	24147	aggregate study

* Sampling error cited reflects 95 percent confidence level.
** The outsiders in this study included 440 interviews (± 5.0 points). In addition, there were eight additional samples of outsiders examined for the project; each of the YouthPoll and OmniPoll studies facilitated analysis of the "outsider" segment.

Each of these studies was drawn from random, nationally representative samples of adults, teenagers, and pastors. YouthPoll[SM], OmniPoll[SM], and PastorPoll[SM] are annual tracking studies conducted by The Barna Group to remain abreast of what is happening in relation to the intersection of faith and culture. Slight statistical weighting was used for some of the studies to calibrate the sample to known population percentages in relation to demographic variables.

THE RESEARCHER

David Kinnaman is the president and strategic leader of The Barna Group, a research and resource company located in Ventura, California. Since joining Barna in 1995, David has designed and analyzed nearly five hundred projects for a variety of clients, including the Billy Graham Evangelistic Association, Campus Crusade for Christ, Columbia House, Focus on the Family, InterVarsity, NBC-Universal, Time-Life, World Vision, and many others.

As a spokesperson for the firm's research, he is frequently quoted in major media outlets. He is also in demand as a speaker about ministry trends, today's teenagers, the profile of young leaders, and generational changes. He is the author of the Barna report *Ministry to Mosaics: Teens and the Supernatural.*

 fermi project

For a summary of the Barna Research presented in this book and discussion questions for each chapter, go to www.unchristian.com

NOTES

Chapter 1 The Backstory

1. Please note that any interpretations of the research or statements in this book—by David Kinnaman, Gabe Lyons, or any of the contributors who have graciously agreed to participate in this project—do not necessarily reflect the views of every contributor.

2. In our research, a born-again Christian is defined based on his or her beliefs about life after death, not his or her use of the label. A person is classified as a born-again Christian if he or she has made a personal commitment to Jesus Christ that is still important to the person and if he or she has confessed sins and accepted Jesus Christ as his or her Savior. Of course only God knows a person's heart and his or her true reactions to Jesus. But we realize that the Bible says a person is not a Christian just by going to church, identifying as a Christian, reading the Bible, or doing good things for others. Our research takes into account the only thing that matters in God's eyes: what you decide to do

with Jesus Christ. Note that born-again Christians who are unchurched were not included in our definition of an "outsider." For more insight into the faith practices and perspectives of this group of believers, you can check out George Barna's book *Revolution* (Wheaton: Tyndale, 2005).

3. There are, of course, significant differences between the people we call Mosaics and those we term Busters. However, this book is more concerned with how the two groups are similar in their perceptions of and experiences with the Christian faith.

Chapter 2 Discovering *unChristian* Faith

1. We have a team of people who do the hard work of interviewing. It has been my job to supervise and analyze the interviews with all of these people.

2. In our survey with sixteen- to twenty-nine-year-olds, we used the phrase "present-day Christianity" to assess young people's perceptions of the faith.

3. To assess the breadth of these perceptions, we used quantitative surveys to explore how widely these types of images are embraced by Mosaic and Buster outsiders. The survey asked respondents to rate twenty statements about present-day Christianity, including ten favorable and ten negative images.

4. Being antihomosexual is not inherently negative since the Bible condemns homosexuality. But this perception is much deeper than this. Read about this perception in chapter 5.

5. The idea that believers will face special persecution and hatred as a result of their allegiance to Christ is a well-formed theme: Matthew 5:10–11; 10:22; 13:13; Luke 6:22; 21:17; 1 Corinthians 1:18.

Chapter 3 Hypocritical

1. In our research we asked young people if they felt the phrase "hypocritical—saying one thing, doing another" accurately described present-day Christianity.

2. Pew Research Center, "How Young People View Their Lives, Futures, and Politics: A Portrait of 'Generation Next.'" (Washington DC, January 9, 2007).

3. The results of these studies comparing born-again Christians with other adults were discussed in several publications, including George Barna's *Think Like Jesus* (Integrity, 2003) and *The Second Coming of the Church* (Word, 1998). Also see George Barna, "The American Witness," *The Barna Report* (November/December 1997). Unfortunately, the last two resources are now out of print.

4. See the article "American Lifestyles Mix Compassion and Self-Oriented Behavior" (February 5, 2007) at www.barna .org.

5. Some of our research for Mark Matlock of WisdomWorks Ministries has been particularly helpful in understanding the myopia Christians have about the reasons nonbelievers do not come to Christ.

6. More information on these matters is available in our syndicated study, *The Buster Report: A New Generation Describes Their Life and Spirituality* (Ventura, CA: The Barna Group, 2007). You can also access a free online report: "A New Generation of Adults Bends Moral and Sexual Rules to Their Liking," *The Barna Update* (October 31, 2006) at www.barna.org.

7. You can read more about these trends in the online article "A New Generation Bends Moral and Sexual Rules to their Liking" (October 31, 2007) at www.barna .org.

8. Josh told me his idea was inspired by a story that Donald Miller told in *Blue Like Jazz* (Nashville: Thomas Nelson, 2003).

9. Philip Yancey, *What's So Amazing about Grace?* (Grand Rapids: Zondervan, 1997), 249.

Chapter 4 Get Saved!

1. See Barna, *Revolution*, chap. 3.

2. George Barna, *Think Like Jesus* (Brentwood, TN: Integrity, 2003).

Chapter 5 Antihomosexual

1. About two-fifths of the American population have beliefs that qualify them as born-again Christians, while evangelicals, who are a subset of born-again Christians, represent about one-twelfth of the population. These labels are based on what people believe, not on what they call themselves. See p. 251, "Key Terms" for our survey definition of born-again and evangelical Christians.

2. Data from a survey conducted by the Pew Research Center for the People and the Press and the Pew Forum on Religion and Public Life, 2003.

3. We conducted this poll on behalf of World Vision, Federal Way, Washington, November 2004.

4. This was based on a study we conducted for Compassion, Colorado Springs, Colorado, October 2006.

5. The Scriptures make many references to homosexual behavior, typically portraying it as inappropriate and sinful. The three most direct and explicit biblical references to homosexuality, condemning the behavior, are Leviticus 18:22; Romans 1:26–27; and 1 Corinthians 6:9–10.

6. Bay Area Crusade Press Conference, September 24, 1997. This was the answer Mr. Graham gave in response to a question from one of the media representatives about whether or not Mr. Graham agreed with the homosexual lifestyle.

7. Pew Research, "How Young People View Their Lives," 39.

8. Ibid.

9. "Religious Beliefs Underpin Opposition to Homosexuality," Pew Research Center, released November 18, 2003.

10. From www.cnn.com, accessed February 6, 2007.

11. Quoted in Philip Yancey, "Middle East Morass," *Christianity Today* (November 2006), 128.

Chapter 6 Sheltered

1. Pew Research, "How Young People View Their Lives."

2. Alvin J. Schmidt, *How Christianity Changed the World* (Grand Rapids: Zondervan, 2004). See also Jonathan Hill, *What Has Christianity Ever Done for Us?* (Downers Grove, IL: InterVarsity, 2005).

3. William Bennett, *The Index of Leading Cultural Indicators* (New York: Simon and Schuster, 1994), 18, 22.

4. Center for Disease Control and Prevention, "National Youth Risk Behavior Survey," www.cdc.gov/yrbss, 2005.

5. National Center for Health Statistics, http://www.cdc.gov/nchs/fastats/unmarry .htm. See also Bennett, *Index of Leading Cultural Indicators*, 46, 48.

6. Jean Twenge, *Generation Me* (New York: Free Press, 2006), 163.

7. Ibid, 162.

8. William D. Mosher, PhD, Anjani Chandra, PhD, and Jo Jones, PhD, "Sexual Behavior and Selected Health Measures: Men and Women, 15–44 Years of Age, United States, 2002," National Center for Health Statistics, *Advance Data* 362 (September 15, 2005), 6.

9. US Department of Health and Human Services, "Results from the 2005 National Survey on Drug Use and Health: National Findings."

10. "National Youth Risk Behavior Survey," 2005.

11. Ibid.

12. Mike Metzger, *Fine Tuning Tensions within Culture: The Art of Being Salt and Light* (Suwannee, GA: Relevate, 2007), 4.

13. I think he believed me, but that might be because he's my dad.

14. As defined in our surveys, upscale adults have a college degree and an annual household income of at least $70,000. Downscale individuals have no college experience and earn less than $20,000.

15. See www.twloha.com/home.php.

Chapter 7 Political

1. See note in chapter 2 that describes how we define evangelical Christians in our research. The theological perspectives we measure are based on the statement of faith from the National Association of Evangelicals.

2. We have examined Americans who say they are evangelical Christians. Because terms and labels are often used with little or no context, they can lose their meaning. For instance, if you simply use the self-identified evangelical group, you find that many have never made a commitment to Jesus Christ; many do not believe they will enter heaven because of their faith in him, but instead trust in their good works or God's benevolence; and many do not believe Satan is real. These are not small matters of theological perspective and strongly indicate that self-identification is a poor means of defining evangelicals.

3. There are nine questions we ask in our research that define whether a person is an evangelical. For more, check out "Survey Explorers Who Qualifies as an Evangelical" on www.barna.org. The report was released on January 18, 2007.

4. See the March 5, 2007, article "The God Gap? The Faith of Republicans and Democrats." The faith vote in the 2004 election was described in the November 9, 2004, article "Born Again Christians Were a Significant Factor in President Bush's Re-Election." Both articles are available at www.barna.org.

5. Pew Research Center, "Many Americans Uneasy with Mix of Religion and Politics" (Washington DC, August 24, 2006), 6.

6. Pew Research Center, "How Young People View Their Lives," 28–29.

Chapter 8 Judgmental

1. Pew Research, "How Young People View Their Lives."

2. Scripture never condones judgment and criticism aimed at those outside the church. The Bible clearly warns people about avoiding judgment and criticism: Matthew 7:1–2; Luke 6:37; 7:36–47; Romans 2:1–4; 14:4, 10–13; 1 Corinthians 4:5; 5:12; James 4:11–12.

3. See Philip Yancey, *What's So Amazing about Grace?* (Grand Rapids: Zondervan, 1997).

Chapter 9 From *unChristian* to Christian

1. See Luke 13:14–17; Matthew 12:1–8; Mark 14:3–9.

2. My father got this proverb from John Maxwell.

3. You can read about this in the online article "A New Generation of Pastors Places Its Stamp on Ministry" (February 17, 2004) at www.barna.org.

4. The Old Testament book of 2 Chronicles drives home this idea. God says, "If my people who are called by my name will humble themselves and pray and seek my face and turn from their wicked ways, I will hear from heaven and will forgive their sins and restore their land" (7:14).

Afterword

1. Charles Colson and Nancy Pearcey, *How Now Shall We Live?* (Wheaton, IL: Tyndale, 1999), xii.

JOIN THE FERMI PROJECT

Fermi Project is a broad collective of church and cultural leaders experimenting with ways to positively contribute to culture. The focus of this project is strategically placed on Christians and leaders throughout the church.

Learn more about joining the Fermi Project by visiting www.fermiproject.com

---

DOWNLOAD A FREE RESOURCE
Go online for Gabe Lyons' free essay from Fermi Words:

Influencing Culture
An Opportunity for the Church

www.fermiproject.com/culture